Abraham Lincoln
Vol. I

by

John T. Morse, Jr.

Abraham Lincoln
Vol. I
by John T. Morse, Jr.

Copyright © 2023

All Rights reserved.

ISBN: 978-93-59956-02-2

Published by

DOUBLE 9 BOOKS

2/13-B, Ansari Road
Daryaganj, New Delhi – 110002
info@double9books.com
www.double9books.com
Tel. 011-40042856

This book is under public domain

ABOUT THE AUTHOR

John Torrey Morse Jr. (January 9, 1840 – March 28, 1937) was a historian, attorney, and politician in the United States. John Torrey Morse was born on January 9, 1840, in Boston, Massachusetts, to John Torrey Morse Sr. and Lucy Cabot Jackson. After three years of study, he graduated from Harvard College and read law at the office of John Lowell. In 1862, he was admitted to the bar. In 1874, he was elected to the Massachusetts House of Representatives from Boston's Back Bay's 6th Suffolk district. He was sentenced to one year in prison. Morse served on the Harvard Board of Overseers from 1879 until 1891. Harvard conferred on him the honorary degree of Doctor of Literature in 1911. Morse began his legal career by producing many authoritative legal treatises on banking, arbitration, and award, as well as contributing to journals. His legal writing established him as a renowned specialist on the issues. Morse's most major work, a two-volume biography of Alexander Hamilton, was released in 1876. Soon after, in 1880, he left his law practice to pursue literary endeavors. In 1865, Morse married Fanny P. Hovey of Boston. They had two boys, Cabot Jackson Morse and John Torrey Morse III, as well as a daughter, Charlotte. They lived on Boston's Fairfield Street.

CONTENTS

CHAPTER I
THE RAW MATERIAL

Abraham Lincoln knew little concerning his progenitors, and rested well content with the scantiness of his knowledge. The character and condition of his father, of whom alone upon that side of the house he had personal cognizance, did not encourage him to pry into the obscurity behind that luckless rover. He was sensitive on the subject; and when he was applied to for information, a brief paragraph conveyed all that he knew or desired to know. Without doubt he would have been best pleased to have the world take him solely for himself, with no inquiry as to whence he came,—as if he had dropped upon the planet like a meteorite; as, indeed, many did piously hold that he came a direct gift from heaven. The fullest statement which he ever made was given in December, 1859, to Mr. Fell, who had interrogated him with an eye "to the possibilities of his being an available candidate for the presidency in 1860:" "My parents were both born in Virginia, of undistinguished families,—second families, perhaps I should say. My mother ... was of a family of the name of Hanks, some of whom now remain in Adams, some others in Macon, counties, Illinois. My paternal grandfather, Abraham Lincoln, emigrated from Rockingham County, Virginia, to Kentucky, about 1781 or 1782.... His ancestors, who were Quakers, went to Virginia from Berks County, Pennsylvania. An effort to identify them with the New England family of the same name ended in nothing more definite than a similarity of Christian names in both families, such as Enoch, Levi, Mordecai, Solomon, Abraham, and the like." This effort to connect the President with the Lincolns of Massachusetts was afterward carried forward by others, who felt an interest greater than his own in establishing the fact. Yet if he had expected the quest to result satisfactorily, he would probably have been less indifferent about it; for it is obvious that, in common with all Americans of the old native stock, he had a strenuous desire to come of "respectable people;" and his very reluctance to have his apparently low extraction investigated is evidence that he would have been glad to learn that he belonged to an ancient and historical family of the old Puritan Commonwealth, settlers not far from Plymouth Rock, and immigrants not long after the arrival of the Mayflower. This descent has at last been traced by the patient genealogist.

So early as 1848 the first useful step was taken by Hon. Solomon Lincoln of Hingham, Massachusetts, who was struck by a speech delivered by Abraham Lincoln in the national House of Representatives, and wrote to ask facts as to his parentage. The response [1] stated substantially what was afterward sent to Mr. Fell, above quoted. Mr. Solomon Lincoln, however, pursued the search farther, and printed the results [2] . Later, Mr. Samuel Shackford of Chicago, Illinois, himself a descendant from the same original stock, pushed the investigation more persistently [3] . The chain, as put together by these two gentlemen, is as follows: Hingham, Massachusetts, was settled in 1635. In 1636 house lots were set off to Thomas Lincoln, the miller, Thomas Lincoln, the weaver, and Thomas Lincoln, the cooper. In 1638 other lots were set off to Thomas Lincoln, the husbandman, and to Stephen, his brother. In 1637 Samuel Lincoln, aged eighteen, came from England to Salem, Massachusetts, and three years later went to Hingham; he also was a weaver, and a brother of Thomas, the weaver. In 1644 there was a Daniel Lincoln in the place. All these Lincolns are believed to have come from the County of Norfolk in England [4] , though what kinship existed between them is not known. It is from Samuel that the President appears to have been descended. Samuel's fourth son, Mordecai, a blacksmith, married a daughter of Abraham Jones of Hull; [5] about 1704 he moved to the neighboring town of Scituate, and there set up a furnace for smelting iron ore. This couple had six children, of whom two were named respectively Mordecai and Abraham; and these two are believed to have gone to Monmouth County, New Jersey. There Mordecai seems to have continued in the iron business, and later to have made another move to Chester County, Pennsylvania, still continuing in the same business, until, in 1725, he sold out all his "Mynes & Minerals, Forges, etc." [6] Then, migrating again, he settled in Amity, Philadelphia County, Pennsylvania, where, at last, death caught up with him. By his will, February 22, 1735-36, he bequeathed his land in New Jersey to John, his eldest son; and gave other property to his sons Mordecai and Thomas. He belied the old motto, for in spite of more than three removes he left a fair estate, and in the probate proceedings he is described as "gentleman." [7] In 1748 John sold all he had in New Jersey, and in 1758 moved into Virginia, settling in that part of Augusta County which was afterward set off as Rockingham County. Though his will has not been found, there is "ample proof," says Mr. Shackford, that he had five sons, named Abraham, Isaac, Jacob, Thomas, and John. Of these, Abraham went to North Carolina, there married Mary Shipley, and by her had sons Mordecai, Josiah, and Thomas, who was born in 1778. In 1780 or 1782, as it is variously stated, this family moved to Kentucky. There, one day in 1784, the father, at his labor in the field, was shot by lurking Indians. His oldest son, working hard by, ran to the house for a gun; returning toward the spot where lay his father's body, he saw an Indian in the act of seizing his brother, the little boy named Thomas. He fired, with happy aim; the Indian fell dead, and Thomas escaped to the house. This Thomas it was who afterward became the father of Abraham Lincoln. [8] Of the other sons of Mordecai (great-uncles of the President), Thomas also went to Kentucky, Isaac went to Tennessee, while Jacob and John stayed in Virginia, and begat progeny who became in later times ferocious rebels, and of whom one wrote a very comical blustering letter to his relative the President; [9] and probably another, bearing oddly enough the name of Abraham, was a noted fighter. [10] It is curious to observe of what migratory stock we have here the sketch. Mr. Shackford calls attention to the fact that through six successive generations all save one were "pioneers in the settlement of new countries," thus: 1. Samuel came from England to Hingham, Massachusetts. 2. Mordecai lived and died at Scituate, close by the place of his birth. 3. Mordecai moved, and settled in Pennsylvania, in the neighborhood which afterward became Berks County, while it was still wilderness. 4. John moved into the wilds of Virginia. 5. Abraham went to the backwoods of Kentucky shortly after Boone's settlement. 6. Thomas moved first into the sparsely settled parts of Indiana, and thence went onward to a similar region in Illinois.

Thus in time was corroborated what Abraham Lincoln wrote in 1848 in one of the above-mentioned letters to Hon. Solomon Lincoln: "We have a vague tradition that my great-grandfather went from Pennsylvania to Virginia, and that he was a Quaker." It is of little consequence that this "vague tradition" was stoutly contradicted by the President's father, the ignorant Thomas, who indignantly denied that either a Puritan or a Quaker could be found in the line of his forbears, and who certainly seemed to set heredity at defiance if such were the case. But while thus repudiating others, Thomas himself was in some danger of being repudiated; for so pained have some persons been by the necessity of recognizing Thomas Lincoln as the father of the President, that they have welcomed, as a happy escape from this so miserable paternity, a bit of gratuitous and unsupported gossip, published, though perhaps with more of malice than of faith, by Mr. Herndon, to the effect that Abraham Lincoln was the illegitimate son of some person unknown, presumably some tolerably well-to-do Kentuckian, who induced Thomas to assume the rôle of parent.

Upon the mother's side the ancestral showing is meagre, and fortunately so, since the case seems to be a bad one beyond reasonable hope. Her name was Nancy Hanks. She was born in Virginia, and was the illegitimate child of one Lucy Hanks. [11] Nor was she the only instance of illegitimacy [12] in a family which, by all accounts, seems to have been very low in the social scale. Mr. Herndon calls them by the dread name of "poor whites," and gives an unappetizing sketch of them. [13] Throughout his pages and those of Lamon there is abundant and disagreeable evidence to show the correctness of his estimate. Nancy Hanks herself, who certainly was not to blame for her parentage, and perhaps may have improved matters by an infusion of better blood from her unknown father, is described by some as a very rare flower to have bloomed amid the bed of ugly weeds which surrounded her. These friendly writers make her a gentle, lovely, Christian creature, too delicate long to survive the roughness of frontier life and the fellowship of the shiftless rover to whom she was unfittingly wedded. [14] Whatever she may have been, her picture is exceeding dim, and has been made upon scant and not unquestionable evidence. Mr. Lincoln seems not often to have referred to her; but when he did so it was with expressions of affection for her character and respect for her mental qualities, provided at least that it was really of her, and not of his stepmother, that he was speaking,—a matter not clear from doubt. [15]

On June 10, 1806, Thomas Lincoln gave bond in the "just and full sum of fifty pounds" to marry Nancy Hanks, and two days later, June 12, he did so, in Washington County, Kentucky. [16] She was then twenty-three years old. February 12, 1807, their daughter Sarah was born, who was married and died leaving no issue. February 12, 1809, Abraham Lincoln was born; no other children came save a boy who lived only a few days.

The domestic surroundings amid which the babe came into life were wretched in the extreme. All the trustworthy evidence depicts a condition of what civilized people call misery. It is just as well to acknowledge a fact which cannot now be obscured by any amount of euphemism. Yet very many of Lincoln's biographers have been greatly concerned to color this truth, which he himself, with his honest nature, was never willing to misrepresent, however much he resisted efforts to give it a general publicity. He met curious inquiry with reticence, but with no attempt to mislead. Some of his biographers, however, while shunning direct false statements, have used alleviating adjectives with literary skill, and have drawn fanciful pictures of a pious frugal household, of a gallant frontiersman endowed with a long catalogue of noble qualities, and of a mother like a Madonna in the wilderness. [17] Yet all the evidence that there is goes to show that this romantic coloring is purely illusive. Rough, coarse, low, ignorant, and poverty-stricken surroundings were about the child; and though we may gladly avail ourselves of the possibility of believing his mother to have been superior to all the rest of it, yet she could by no means leaven the mass. The father [18] was by calling a carpenter, but not good at his trade, a shiftless migratory squatter by invincible tendency, and a very ignorant man, for a long while able only to form the letters which made his signature, though later he extended his accomplishments a little. He rested not much above the very bottom of existence in the pioneer settlements, apparently without capacity or desire to do better. The family was imbued with the peculiar, intense, but unenlightened form of Christianity, mingled with curious superstition, prevalent in the backwoods, and begotten by the influence of the vast wilderness upon illiterate men of a rude native force. It interests scholars to trace the evolutions of religious faiths, but it might be not less suggestive to study the retrogression of religion into superstition. Thomas was as restless in matters of creed as of residence, and made various changes in both during his life. These were, however, changes without improvement, and, so far as he was concerned, his son Abraham might have grown up to be what he himself was contented to remain.

It was in the second year after his marriage that Thomas Lincoln made his first removal. Four years later he made another. Two or three years afterwards, in the autumn of 1816, he abandoned Kentucky and went into Indiana. Some writers have given to this migration the interesting character of a flight from a slave-cursed society to a land of freedom, but whatever poetic fitness there might be in such a motive, the suggestion is entirely gratuitous and without the slightest foundation. [19] In making this move, Thomas's outfit consisted of a trifling parcel of tools and cooking utensils, with ever so little bedding, and four hundred gallons of whiskey. At his new quarters he built a "half-faced camp" fourteen feet square, that is to say, a covered shed of three sides, the fourth side being left open to the weather. In this, less snug than the winter's cave of a bear, the family dwelt for a year, and then were translated to the luxury of a "cabin," four-walled indeed, but which for a long while had neither floor, door, nor window. Amid this hardship and wretchedness Nancy Lincoln passed away, October 5, 1818, of that dread and mysterious disease, the scourge of those pioneer communities, known as the "milk-sickness." [20] In a rough coffin, fashioned by her husband "out of green lumber cut with a whip-saw," she was laid away in the forest clearing, and a few months afterward an itinerant preacher performed some funeral rites over the poor woman's humble grave.

For a year Thomas Lincoln was a widower. Then he went back to Kentucky, and found there Mrs. Sally Johnston, a widow, whom, when she was the maiden Sarah Bush, he had loved and courted, and by whom he had been refused. He now asked again, and with better success. The marriage was a little inroad of good luck into his career; for the new wife was thrifty and industrious, with the ambition and the capacity to improve the squalid condition of her husband's household. She had, too, worldly possessions of bedding and furniture, enough to fill a four-horse wagon. She made her husband put a floor, a door, and windows to his cabin. From the day of her advent a new spirit made itself felt amid the belongings of the inefficient Thomas. Her immediate effort was to make her new husband's children "look a little more human," and the youthful Abraham began to get crude notions of the simpler comforts and decencies of life. All agree that she was a stepmother to whose credit it is to be said that she manifested an intelligent kindness towards Abraham.

The opportunities for education were scant enough in that day and place. In his childhood in Kentucky Abraham got a few weeks with one teacher, and then a few weeks with another. Later, in Indiana, he studied a few months, in a scattered way. Probably he had instruction at home, for the sum of all the schooling which he had in his whole life was hardly one year; [21] a singular start upon the road to the presidency of the United States! The books which he saw were few, but a little later he laid hands upon them all and read and re-read them till he must have absorbed all their strong juice into his own nature. Nicolay and Hay give the list: The Bible; "Aesop's Fables;" "Robinson Crusoe;" "The Pilgrim's Progress;" a history of the United States; Weems's "Washington." He was doubtless much older when he devoured the Revised Statutes of Indiana in the office of the town constable. Dr. Holland adds Lives of Henry Clay and of Franklin (probably the famous autobiography), and Ramsay's "Washington;" and Arnold names Shakespeare and Burns. It was a small library, but nourishing. He used to write and to do sums in arithmetic on the wooden shovel by the fireside, and to shave off the surface in order to renew the labor.

As he passed from boyhood to youth his mental development took its characteristics from the popular demand of the neighborhood. He scribbled verses and satirical prose, wherein the coarse wit was adapted to the taste of the comrades whom it was designed to please; and it must be admitted that, after giving due weight to all ameliorating considerations, it is impossible to avoid disappointment at the grossness of the jesting. No thought, no word raised it above the low level of the audience made up of the laborers on the farms and the loungers in the groceries. The biographer who has made public "The First Chronicles of Reuben" deserves to be held in detestation. [22]

A more satisfactory form of intellectual effervescence consisted in writing articles on the American Government, Temperance, etc., and in speech-making to any who were near at the moment of inspiration. There is abundant evidence, also, that already Lincoln was regarded as a witty fellow, a rare mimic, and teller of jokes and stories; and therefore was the champion of the fields and the favorite of all the primitive social gatherings. This sort of life and popularity had its perils, for in that day and region men seldom met without drinking together; but all authorities are agreed that Lincoln, while the greatest talker, was the smallest drinker.

The stories told of his physical strength rival those which decorate the memory of Hercules. Others, which show his kindly and humane nature, are more valuable. Any or all of these may or may not be true, and, though they are not so poetical or marvelous as the myths which lend an antique charm to the heroes of classic and romantic lore, yet they compare fairly well with those which Weems has twined about the figure of the youthful Washington. There is a tale of the rescue of a pig from a quagmire, and another of the saving of a drunken man from freezing. There are many stories of fights; others of the lifting of enormous weights; and even some of the doing of great feats of labor in a day, though for such tasks Lincoln had no love. These are not worth recounting; there is store of such in every village about the popular local hero; and though historians by such folk-lore may throw a glamour about Lincoln's daily life, he himself, at the time, could hardly have seen much that was romantic or poetical in the routine of ill-paid labor and hard living. Until he came of age his "time" belonged to his father, who let him out to the neighbors for any job that offered, making him a man-of-all-work, without-doors and within. In 1825 he was thus earning six dollars a month, presumably besides board and lodging. Sometimes he slaughtered hogs, at thirty-one cents a day; and in this "rough work" he was esteemed especially efficient. Such was the making of a President in the United States in this nineteenth century!

Thomas Lincoln, like most men of his stamp, had the cheerful habit of laying the results of his own worthlessness to the charge of the conditions about him, which, naturally, he constantly sought to change, since it seemed that no change could bring him to a lower level than he had already found. As Abraham approached his "freedom-day," his luckless parent conceived the notion that he might do better in Illinois than he had done in Indiana. So he shuffled off the farm, for which he had never paid, and about the middle of February the family caravan, with their scanty household wares packed in an ox team, began a march which lasted fourteen days and entailed no small measure of hardship. They finally stopped at a bluff on the north bank of the north fork of the Sangamon, a stream which empties into the Ohio. Here Thomas Lincoln renewed the familiar process of "starting in life," and with an axe, a saw, and a knife built a rough cabin of hewed logs, with a smoke-house and "stable." Abraham, aided by John Hanks, cleared ten or fifteen acres of land, split the rails and fenced it, planted it with corn, and made it over to Thomas as a sort of bequest at the close of his term of legal infancy. His subsequent relationship with his parents, especially with his father, seems to have been slight, involving an occasional gift of money, a very rare visit, and finally a commonplace letter of Christian comfort when the old man was on his deathbed. [23]

At first Abraham's coming of age made no especial change in his condition; he continued to find such jobs as he could, as an example of which Is mentioned his bargain with Mrs. Nancy Miller "to split four hundred rails for every yard of brown jeans dyed with white walnut bark that would be necessary to make him a pair of trousers." After many months there arrived in the neighborhood one Denton Offut, one of those scheming, talkative, evanescent busybodies who skim vaguely over new territories. This adventurer had a cargo of hogs, pork, and corn, which he wanted to send to New Orleans, and the engagement fell to Lincoln and two comrades at the wage of fifty cents per day and a bonus of $60 for the three. It has been said that this and a preceding trip down the Mississippi first gave Lincoln a glimpse of slavery in concrete form, and that the spectacle of negroes "in chains, whipped and scourged," and of a slave auction, implanted in his mind an "unconquerable hate" towards the institution, so that he exclaimed: "If ever I get a chance to hit that thing, I'll hit it hard." So the loquacious myth-maker John Hanks asserts; [24] but Lincoln himself refers his first vivid impression to a later trip, made in 1841, when there were "on board ten or a dozen slaves shackled together with irons." Of this subsequent incident he wrote, fourteen years later, to his friend, Joshua Speed: "That sight was a continual torment to me; and I see something like it every time I touch the Ohio or any other slave border. It is not fair for you to assume that I have no interest in a thing which has, and continually exercises, the power of making me miserable." [25]

Of more immediate consequence was the notion which the rattle-brained Offut conceived of Lincoln's general ability. This lively patron now proposed to build a river steamboat, with "runners for ice and rollers for shoals and dams," of which his redoubtable young employee was to be captain. But this strange scheme gave way to another for opening in New Salem a "general store" of all goods. This small town had been born only a few months before this summer of 1831, and was destined to a brief but riotous life of some seven years' duration. Now it had a dozen or fifteen "houses," of which some had cost only ten dollars for the building; yet to the sanguine Offut it presented a fair field for retail commerce. He accordingly equipped his "store," and being himself engaged in other enterprises, he installed Lincoln as manager. Soon he also gave Lincoln a mill to run.

Besides all this patronage, Offut went about the region bragging in his extravagant way that his clerk "knew more than any man in the United States," would some day be President, and could now throw or thrash any man in those parts. Now it so happened that some three miles out from New Salem lay Clary's Grove, the haunt of a gang of frontier ruffians of the familiar type, among whom one Jack Armstrong was champion bully. Offut's boasting soon rendered an encounter between Lincoln and Armstrong inevitable, though Lincoln did his best to avoid it, and declared his aversion to "this woolling and pulling." The wrestling match was arranged, and the settlers flocked to it like Spaniards to a bull-fight. Battle was joined and Lincoln was getting the better of Armstrong, whereupon the "Clary's Grove boys," with fine chivalry, were about to rush in upon Lincoln and maim him, or worse, when the timely intervention of a prominent citizen possibly saved even the life of the future President. [26] Some of the biographers, borrowing the license of poets, have chosen to tell about the "boys" and the wrestling match with such picturesque epithets that the combat bids fair to appear to posterity as romantic as that of Friar Tuck and Robin Hood. Its consequence was that Armstrong and Lincoln were fast friends ever after. Wherever Lincoln was at work, Armstrong used to "do his loafing," and Lincoln made visits to Clary's Grove, and long afterward did a friendly service to "old Hannah," Armstrong's wife, by saving one of her vicious race from the gallows, which upon that especial occasion he did not happen to deserve. Also Armstrong and his gang gave Lincoln hearty political support, and an assistance at the polls which was very effective, for success generally smiled on that candidate who had as his constituency [27] the "butcher-knife boys," the "barefooted boys," the "half-horse, half-alligator men," and the "huge-pawed boys."

An item less susceptible of a poetic coloring is that about this time Lincoln ransacked the neighborhood in search of an English grammar, and getting trace of one six miles out from the settlement, he walked over to borrow or to buy it. He brought it back in triumph, and studied it exhaustively.

There are also some tales of his honesty which may stand without disgrace beside that of Washington and the cherry-tree, and may be better entitled to credit. It is said that, while he was "keeping shop" for Offut, a woman one day accidentally overpaid him by the sum of fourpence, and that he walked several miles that night to restore the sum to her before he slept. On another occasion, discovering that in selling half a pound of tea he had used too small a weight, he started instantly forth to make good the deficiency. Perhaps this integrity does not so much differentiate Lincoln from his fellows as it may seem to do, for it is said that honesty was the one distinguishing virtue of that queer society. None the less these legends are exponents, which the numerous fighting stories are not, of the genuine nature of the man. His chief trait all his life long was honesty of all kinds and in all things; not only commonplace, material honesty in dealings, but honesty in language, in purpose, in thought; *honesty of mind*, so that he could never even practice the most tempting of all deceits, a deceit against himself. This pervasive honesty was the trait of his identity, which stayed with him from beginning to end, when other traits seemed to be changing, appearing or disappearing, and bewildering the observer of his career. All the while the universal honesty was there.

It took less than a year for Offut's shop to come to ruin, for the proprietor to wander off into the unknown void from which he had come, and for Lincoln to find himself again without occupation. He won some local reputation by navigating the steamboat Talisman up the Sangamon River to Springfield; but nothing came of it.

The foregoing narrative ought to have given some idea of the moral and physical surroundings of Lincoln's early days. Americans need to carry their memories hardly fifty years back, in order to have a lively conception of that peculiar body of men which for many years was pushed out in front of civilization in the West. Waifs and strays from highly civilized communities, these wanderers had not civilization to learn, but rather they had shuffled off much that belonged to civilization, and afterwards they had to acquire it afresh. Among them crudity in thought and uncouthness in habits were intertwined in odd, incongruous crossings with the remnants of the more respectable customs with which they had once been familiar. Much they forgot and much they put away as being no longer useful; many of them—not all—became very ignorant without being stupid, very brutal without being barbarous. Finding life hard, they helped each other with a general kindliness which is impracticable among the complexities of elaborate social organizations. Those who were born on the land, among whom Lincoln belonged, were peculiar in having no reminiscences, no antecedent ideas derived from their own past, whereby to modify the influences of the immediate present. What they should think about men and things they gathered from what they saw and heard around them. Even the modification to be got from reading was of the slightest, for very little reading was possible, even if desired. An important trait of these Western communities was the closeness of personal intercourse in them, and the utter lack of any kind of barriers establishing strata of society. Individuals might differ ever so widely; but the wisest and the dullest, the most worthless and the most enterprising, had to rub shoulder to shoulder in daily life. Yet the variety was considerable: hardy and danger-loving pioneers fulfilling the requirements of romance; shiftless vagrants curiously combining utter inefficiency with a sort of bastard contempt for hardship; ruffians who could only offset against every brutal vice an ignoble physical courage; intelligent men whose observant eyes ranged over the whole region in a shrewd search after enterprise and profit; a few educated men, decent in apparel and bearing, useful in legislation and in preventing the ideal from becoming altogether vulgarized and debased; and others whose energy was chiefly of the tongue, the class imbued with a taste for small politics and the public business. All these and many other varieties were like ingredients cast together into a caldron; they could not keep apart, each with his own kind, to the degree which is customary in old established communities; but they all ceaselessly crossed and mingled and met, and talked, and dealt, and helped and hustled each other, and exerted upon each other that subtle inevitable influence resulting from such constant intercourse; and so they inoculated each other with certain characteristics which became common to all and formed the type of the early settler. Thus was made "the new West," "the great West," which was pushed ever onward, and endured along each successive frontier for about a generation. An eternal movement, a tireless coming and going, pervaded these men; they passed hither and thither without pause, phantasmagorically; they seemed to be forever "moving on," some because they were real pioneers and natural rovers, others because they were mere vagrants generally drifting away from creditors, others because the better chance seemed ever in the newer place, and all because they had struck no roots, gathered no associations, no home ties, no local belongings. The shopkeeper "moved on" when his notes became too pressing; the schoolmaster, after a short stay, left his school to some successor whose accomplishments could hardly be less than his own; clergymen ranged vaguely through the country, to preach, to pray, to bury, to marry, as the case might be; farmers heard of a more fruitful soil, and went to seek it. Men certainly had at times to work hard in order to live at all, yet it was perfectly possible for the natural idler to rove, to loaf, and to be shiftless at intervals, and to become as demoralized as the tramp for whom a shirt and trousers are the sum of worldly possessions. Books were scarce; many teachers hardly had as much book-learning as lads of thirteen years now have among ourselves. Men who could neither read nor write abounded, and a deficiency so common could hardly imply much disgrace or a marked inferiority; many learned these difficult arts only in mature years. Fighting was a common pastime, and when these rough fellows fought, they fought like savages; Lincoln's father bit off his adversary's nose in a fight, and a cousin lost the same feature in the same way; the "gouging" of eyes was a legitimate resource. The necessity of fighting might at any moment come to any one; even the combination of a peaceable disposition with formidable strength did not save Lincoln from numerous personal affrays, of which many are remembered, and not improbably many more have been forgotten. In spite of the picturesque adjectives which have been so decoratively used in describing the ruffian of the frontier, he seems to have been about what his class always is; and when these fellows had forced a fight, or "set up" a match, their chivalry never prevented any unfairness or brutality. A tale illustrative of the times is told of a closely contested election in the legislature for the office of state treasurer. The worsted candidate strode into the hall of the Assembly, and gallantly selecting four of the largest and strongest of those who had voted against him, thrashed them soundly. The other legislators ran away. But before the close of the session this pugilist, who so well understood practical politics, was appointed clerk of the Circuit Court and county recorder. [28]

Corn bread was the chief article of diet; potatoes were a luxury, and were often eaten raw like apples. To the people at large whiskey "straight" seemed the natural drink of man, and whiskey toddy was not distasteful to woman. To refuse to drink was to subject one's self to abuse and suspicion; [29] Lincoln's notorious lack of liking for it passed for an eccentricity, or a physical peculiarity. The customary social gatherings were at horse-racings, at corn-shuckings, at political speech-makings, at weddings, whereat the coarse proceedings would not nowadays bear recital; at log-rollings, where the neighbors gathered to collect the logs of a newly cleared lot for burning; and at house-raisings, where they kindly aided to set up the frame of a cabin for a new-comer; at camp-meetings, where the hysterical excitement of a community whose religion was more than half superstition found clamorous and painful vent; [30] or perchance at a hanging, which, if it met public approbation, would be sanctioned by the gathering of the neighbors within a day's journey of the scene. At dancing-parties men and women danced barefoot; indeed, they could hardly do better, since their foot-wear was apt to be either moccasins, or such boots as they themselves could make from the hides which they themselves had cured. In Lincoln's boyhood the hunting-shirt and leggings made of skins were a sufficiently respectable garb; and buckskin breeches dyed green were enough to captivate the heart of any girl who wished a fashionable lover; but by the time that he had become a young man, most self-respecting men had suits of jeans. The ugly butcher's knife and tomahawk, which had been essential as was the rapier to the costume of gentlemen two centuries earlier, began now to be more rarely seen at the belt about the waist. The women wore linsey-woolsey gowns, of home manufacture, and dyed according to the taste or skill of the wearer in stripes and bars with the brown juice of the butternut. In the towns it was not long before calico was seen, and calfskin shoes; and in such populous centres bonnets decorated the heads of the fair sex. Amid these advances in the art of dress Lincoln was a laggard, being usually one of the worst attired men of the neighborhood; not from affectation, but from a natural indifference to such matters. The sketch is likely to become classical in American history of the appearance which he presented with his scant pair of trousers, "hitched" by a single suspender over his shirt, and so short as to expose, at the lower end, half a dozen inches of "shinbone, sharp, blue, and narrow."

In the clearings the dwellings of these men were the "half-faced camp" open upon one side to the weather, or the doorless, floorless, and windowless cabin which, with prosperity, might be made luxurious by greased paper in the windows, and "puncheon" floors. The furniture was in keeping with this exterior. At a corner the bed was constructed by driving into the ground crotched sticks, whence poles extended to the crevices of the walls; upon these poles were laid boards, and upon these boards were tossed leaves and skins and such other alleviating material as could be found. Three-legged stools and a table were hewed from the felled trees with an axe, which was often the settler's only and invaluable tool, and which he would travel long miles to sharpen. If a woman wanted a looking-glass, she scoured a tin pan, but the temptation to inspect one's self must have been feeble. A very few kitchen utensils completed the outfit. Troughs served for washtubs, when wash tubs were used; and wooden ploughs broke up the virgin soil. The whole was little, if at all, more comfortable than the red man's wigwam. In "towns," so called, there was of course somewhat more of civilization than in the clearings. But one must not be misled by a name; a "town" might signify only a score of houses, and the length of its life was wholly problematical; a few days sufficed to build the wooden huts, which in a few years might be abandoned. In the early days there was almost no money among the people; sometimes barter was resorted to; one lover paid for his marriage license with maple sugar, another with wolf-scalps. More often a promise sufficed; credit was a system well understood, and promissory notes constituted an unquestioned and popular method of payment that would have made a millennium for Mr. Micawber. But however scant might be cash and houses, each town had its grocery, and these famous "stores" were by far the chief influence in shaping the ideas of the Westerner. There all congregated, the idlers all day long, the busy men in the evening; and there, stimulated by the whiskey of the proprietor, they gossiped about everybody's affairs, talked about business and the prospects of the neighborhood, and argued about the politics of the county, the State, and even of the nation. Jokes and stories, often most uncouth and gross, whiled away the time. It was in these groceries, and in the rough crucible of such talk, wherein grotesque imagery and extravagant phrases were used to ridicule pretension and to bring every man to his place, sometimes also to escape taking a hard fact too hardly, that what we now call "American humor," with its peculiar native flavor, was born. To this it is matter of tradition that Lincoln contributed liberally. He liked neighborly chat and discussion; and his fondness for political debate, and his gifts in tale and jest, made him the most popular man in every "store" that he entered. It is commonly believed that the effect of this familiarity with coarse talk did not afterward disappear, so that he never became fastidious in language or in story. But apologists of this habit are doubtless correct in saying that vulgarity in itself had no attraction for him; it simply did not repel him, when with it there was a flavor of humor or a useful point. Apparently it simply meant nothing to him; a mental attitude which is not difficult of comprehension in view of its origin. [31]

Some of the most picturesque and amusing pages of Ford's "History of Illinois" describe the condition of the bench and bar of these times. [32] "Boys, come in, our John is going to hold court," proclaimed the sheriff; and the "boys" loitered into the barroom of the tavern, or into a log cabin where the judge sat on the bed and thus, really from the woolsack, administered "law" mixed with equity as best he knew it. Usually these magistrates were prudent in guiding the course of practical justice, and rarely summed up the facts lest they should make dangerous enemies, especially in criminal cases; they often refused to state the law, and generally for a very good reason. They liked best to turn the whole matter over to the jurors, who doubtless "understood the case, and would do justice between the parties." The books of the science were scarce, and lawyers who studied them were perhaps scarcer. But probably substantial fairness in decision did not suffer by reason of lack of sheepskin learning.

Politics for a long while were strictly personal; the elections did not turn upon principles or measures, but upon the popular estimate of the candidates individually. Political discussion meant unstinted praise and unbounded vilification. A man might, if he chose, resent a vote against himself as a personal insult, and hence arose much secrecy and the "keep dark" system. Stump-speaking, whiskey, and fighting were the chief elements of a campaign, and the worst class in society furnished the most efficient backing. [33]

Such was the condition of men and things in the neighborhood where Abraham Lincoln was shaping in the days of his youth. Yet it was a condition which did not last long; Illinois herself changed and grew as rapidly as any youngster within her borders. The rate of advance in all that goes to make up what we now regard as a civilized society was astonishing. Between the time when Lincoln was fifteen and when he was twenty-five, the alteration was so great as to be confusing. One hardly became familiar with a condition before it had vanished. Some towns began to acquire an aspect of permanence; clothes and manners became like those prevalent in older communities; many men were settling down in established residence, identifying themselves with the fortunes of their neighborhood. Young persons were growing up and staying where they had been "raised," as the phrase of a farming community had it. Comfortable and presentable two-story houses lent an air of prosperity and stimulated ambition; law-books began to be collected in small numbers; and debts were occasionally paid in money, and could often be collected by legal process. These improvements were largely due to the swelling tide of immigration which brought men of a better type to push their enterprises in a country presumably emerging from its disagreeable stage. But the chief educational influence was to be found in the Anglo-American passion for an argument and a speech. Hand in hand, as has so long been the custom in our country, law and politics moved among the people, who had an inborn, inherited taste for both; these stimulated and educated the settlers in a way that only Americans can appreciate. When Lincoln, as is soon to be seen, turned to them, he turned to what then and there appeared the highest callings which could tempt intellect and ambition.

The preëminently striking feature in Lincoln's nature—not a trait of character, but a characteristic of the man—which is noteworthy in these early days, and grew more so to the very latest, was the extraordinary degree to which he always appeared to be in close and sympathetic touch with the people, that is to say, the people in the mass wherein he was imbedded, the social body amid which he dwelt, which pressed upon him on all sides, which for him formed "the public." First this group or body was only the population of the frontier settlement; then it widened to include the State of Illinois; then it expanded to the population of the entire North; and such had come to be the popular appreciation of this remarkably developed quality that, at the time of his death, his admirers even dared to believe that it would be able to make itself one with all the heterogeneous, discordant, antagonistic elements which then composed the very disunited United States. It is by reason of this quality that it has seemed necessary to depict so far as possible that peculiar, transitory phase of society which surrounded his early days. This quality in him caused him to be exceptionally susceptible to the peculiar influences of the people among whom his lot was cast. This quality for a while prevented his differentiating himself from them, prevented his accepting standards and purposes unlike theirs either in speech or action, prevented his rising rapidly to a higher moral plane than theirs. This quality kept him essentially one of them, until his "people" and his "public" expanded beyond them. It has been the fashion of his admirers to manifest an extreme distaste for a truthful presentation of his earlier days. Some writers have passed very lightly over them; others, stating plain facts with a formal accuracy, have used their skill to give to the picture an untruthful miscoloring; two or three, instinct with the spirit of Zola, have made their sketch with plain unsparing realism in color as well as in lines, and so have brought upon themselves abuse, and perhaps have deserved much of it, by reason of a lack of skill in doing an unwelcome thing, or rather by reason of overdoing it. The feeling which has led to suppression or to a falsely romantic description seems to me unreasonable and wrong. The very quality which made Lincoln, as a young man, not much superior to his coarse surroundings was precisely the same quality which, ripening and expanding rapidly and grandly with maturing years and a greater circle of humanity, made him what he was in later life. It is through this quality that we get continuity in him; without it, we cannot evade the insoluble problem of two men,—two lives,—one following the other with no visible link of connection between them; without it we have physically one creature, morally and mentally two beings. If we reject this trait, we throw away the only key which unlocks the problem of the most singular life, taken from end to end, which has ever been witnessed among men, a life which many have been content to regard as an unsolved enigma. But if we admit and really perceive and feel the full force of this trait, developed in him in a degree probably unequaled in the annals of men, then, besides the enlightenment which it brings, we have the great satisfaction of eliminating much of the disagreeableness attendant upon his youthful days. Even the commonness and painful coarseness of his foolish written expressions become actually an exponent of his chief and crowning quality, his receptiveness and his expression of humanity,—that is to say, of all the humanity he then knew. At first he expressed what he could discern with the limited, inexperienced vision of the ignorant son of a wretched vagrant pioneer; later he gave expression to the humanity of a people engaged in a purpose physically and morally as vast and as grand as any enterprise which the world has seen. Thus, with perfect fairness, without wrenching or misrepresentation or sophistry, the ugliness of his youth ceases to be his own and becomes only the presentation of a curious social condition. In his youth he expressed a low condition, in later life a noble one; at each period he expressed correctly what he found. His day and generation uttered itself through him. With such thoughts, and from this point of view, it is possible to contemplate Lincoln's early days, amid all their degraded surroundings and influences and unmarked by apparent antagonism or obvious superiority on his part, without serious dismay.

[1]   Two letters, now in the possession of Mr. Francis H. Lincoln of Boston, Mass.

[2]   *New England Hist. and Gen. Register*, October, 1865.

[3]   *Ibid.* April, 1887, vol. xli. p. 153.

[4]   See articles in *N.E.H. and G. Reg.* above cited. Mr. Lincoln's article states that in Norwich, Norfolk County, Eng., there is a "curious chased copper box with the inscription 'Abraham Lincoln, Norwich, 1731;'" also in St. Andrew's Church in the same place a mural tablet: "In memory of Abraham Lincoln, of this parish, who died July 13, 1798, aged 79 years." Similarities of name are also noted.

[5]   A town adjoining Hingham, Mass.

[6]   His brother Abraham also resided in Chester County, and died there, April, 1745.

[7]   N. and H. i. 3.

[8]   A different pedigree, published in the *Lancaster Intelligencer*, September 24, 1879, by David J. Lincoln of Birdsboro, Berks County, Penn., is refuted by George Lincoln of Hingham, Mass., in the *Hingham Journal*, October 10, 1879.

[9]   N. and H. i. 4 note.

[10]   N. and H. i. 4 note.

[11]   Herndon, 3.

[12]   The unpleasant Dennis Hanks was an illegitimate son of an "aunt of the President's mother." Herndon, 13; and see Lamon, 12.

[13]   Herndon, 14.

[14]   Holland, 23; Lamon, 11; N. and H. i. 24; Herndon, 13, 28; Raymond, 20; but Raymond is no authority as to Lincoln's youth, and Holland is little more valuable for the same period.

[15]   Lamon, 32. But see Herndon, 13.

[16]   N. and H. 23; Herndon, 5; but see Lamon, 10.

[17] For instance, see the pages of the first chapter of the Life by Arnold, a book which becomes excellent after the author has got free from the fancied necessities of creating an appropriate background for the origin and childhood of the hero. So, more briefly, Raymond, who gives no authority to support the faith which is in him.

[18] For description of him, see Lamon, 8, 9; Herndon, 11.

[19] Herndon, 19; Lamon, 16; Holland, 25.

[20] Herndon, 25-28; Lamon, 26-28.

[21] Herndon, 34-37, 41; Lamon, 34-36; Holland, 28.

[22] Mr. Herndon did this ill deed; 50-54. Lamon prefers to say that most of this literature is "too indecent for publication," 63.

[23] Thomas Lincoln died January 17, 1851.

[24] Herndon, 75, 76; Lamon, 82; Arnold, 30; N. and H. i. 72.

[25] N. and H. i. 74.

[26] Lamon, 92, 93, has the best account of this famous encounter.

[27] Ford, *Hist. of Illinois*, 88.

[28] Ford, *Hist. of Illinois*, 81.

[29] See anecdote in *The Good Old Times in McLean County*, 48.

[30] "The jerks" was the graphic name of an attack not uncommon at these religious meetings.

[31] See Herndon, 104, 118; Holland has some singular remarks on this subject, p. 83; N. and H., i. 121, say that Lincoln was "clean of speech,"—an agreeable statement, for which one would like to have some authority.

[32] Ford, *Hist. of Illinois*, 82-86.

[33] Ford, *Hist. of Illinois*, 55, 86, 88,104; Herndon, 103; N. and H. i. 107; Lamon, 124, 230.

CHAPTER II
THE START IN LIFE

In Illinois during the years of Lincoln's boyhood the red man was retiring sullenly before the fatal advance of the white man's frontier. Shooting, scalping, and plundering forays still occurred, and in the self-complaisant reminiscences of the old settlers of that day the merciless and mysterious savage is apt to lend to the narrative the lively coloring of mortal danger. [34] In the spring of 1832 a noted chief of the Sacs led a campaign of such importance that it lives in history under the dignified title of "the Black Hawk war." The Indians gathered in numbers so formidable that Governor Reynolds issued a call for volunteers to aid the national forces. Lincoln, left unemployed by the failure of Offut, at once enlisted. The custom then was, so soon as there were enough recruits for a company, to elect a captain by vote. The method was simple: each candidate stood at some point in the field and the men went over to one or another according to their several preferences. Three fourths of the company to which Lincoln belonged ranged themselves with him, and long afterward he used to say that no other success in life had given him such pleasure as did this one.

The company was attached to the Fourth Illinois Regiment, commanded by Colonel Samuel Thompson, in the brigade of General Samuel Whiteside. On April 27 they started for the scene of conflict, and for many days endured much hardship of hunger and rough marching. But thereby they escaped serious danger, for they were too fatigued to go forward on May 12, when the cavalry battalions rode out gallantly, recklessly, perhaps a little stupidly, into ambush and death. It so happened that Lincoln never came nearer to any engagement than he did to this one of "Stillman's Run;" so that in place of military glory he had to be content with the reputation of being the best comrade and story-teller at the camp fire. He had, however, an opportunity to do one honorable act: the brief term of service of the volunteers expired on May 27, and most of them eagerly hastened away from an irksome task, without regard to the fact that their services were still much needed, whereas Lincoln and some other officers reënlisted as privates. They were made the "Independent Spy Battalion" of mounted volunteers, were given many special privileges, but were concerned in no engagement, and erelong were mustered out of service. Lincoln's certificate of discharge was signed by Robert Anderson, who afterward was in command at Fort Sumter at the outbreak of the rebellion. Thus, late in June, Lincoln was again a civilian in New Salem, and was passing from war to politics.

Nomination by caucus had not yet been introduced into Illinois, [35] and any person who wished to be a candidate for an elective office simply made public announcement of the fact and then conducted his campaign as best he could. [36] On March 9, 1832, shortly before his enlistment, Lincoln issued a manifesto "To the People of Sangamon County," in which he informed them that he should run as a candidate for the state legislature at the autumn elections, and told them his political principles. [37] He was in favor of internal improvements, such as opening roads, clearing streams, building a railroad across Sangamon County, and making the Sangamon River straight and navigable. He advocated a usury law, and hazarded the extraordinary argument that "in cases of extreme necessity there could always be means found to cheat the law; while in all other cases it would have its intended effect." A law ameliorated by infractions is no uncommon thing, but this is perhaps the only instance in which a law has been befriended on the ground that it can be circumvented. He believed that every man should "receive at least a moderate education." He deprecated changes in existing laws; for, he said, "considering the great probability that the framers of those laws were wiser than myself, I should prefer not meddling with them." The clumsy phraseology of his closing paragraph coupled not badly a frank avowal of ambition with an ingenuous expression of personal modesty. The principles thus set forth were those of Clay and the Whigs, and at this time the "best people" in Sangamon County belonged to this party. The Democrats, on the other hand, did not much concern themselves with principles, but accepted General Jackson in place thereof, as constituting in himself a party platform. In the rough-and-tumble pioneer community they could not do better, and for many years they had controlled the State; indeed, Lincoln himself had felt no small loyalty towards a President who admirably expressed Western civilization. Now, however, he considered himself "an avowed Clay man," [38] and besides the internal improvement system he spoke also for a national bank and a high protective tariff; probably he knew very little about either, but his partisanship was perfect, for if there was any distinguishing badge of an anti-Jackson Whig, it certainly was advocacy of a national bank.

After his return from the "war," Lincoln set about electioneering with a good show of energy. He hardly anticipated success, but at least upon this trial trip he expected to make himself known to the people and to gain useful experience. He "stumped" his own county thoroughly, and is said to have made speeches which were blunt, crude, and inartificial, but not displeasing to his audiences. A story goes that once "a general fight" broke out among his hearers, and one of his friends was getting roughly handled, whereupon Lincoln, descending from the rostrum, took a hand in the affray, tossed one of the assailants "ten or twelve feet easily," and then continued his harangue. Yet not even thus could he win, and another was chosen over his head. He had, however, more reason to be gratified than disappointed with the result; for, though in plain fact he was a raw and unknown youngster, he stood third upon a list of eight candidates, receiving 657 votes; and out of 208 votes cast in his own county he scored 205. [39] In this there was ample encouragement for the future.

The political campaign being over, and legislative functions postponed, Lincoln was brought face to face with the pecuniary problem. He contemplated, not without approbation, the calling of the blacksmith; but the chance to obtain a part interest in a grocery "store" tempted him into an occupation for which he was little fitted. He became junior partner in the firm of Berry & Lincoln, which, by executing and delivering sundry notes of hand, absorbed the whole grocery business of the town. But Lincoln was hopelessly inefficient behind the counter, and Berry was a tippler. So in a year's time the store "winked out," leaving as its only important trace those ill-starred scraps of paper by which it had been founded. Berry "moved on" from the inconvenient neighborhood, and soon afterward died, contributing nothing to reduce the indebtedness. Lincoln patiently continued to make payments during several years to come, until he had discharged the whole amount. It was only a few hundred dollars, but to him it seemed so enormous that betwixt jest and earnest he called it "the national debt." So late as in 1848, when he was a member of the House of Representatives at Washington, he applied part of his salary to this old indebtedness.

During this "store"-keeping episode he had begun to study law, and while "keeping shop" he was with greater diligence reading Blackstone and such other elementary classics of the profession as he could borrow. He studied with zeal and became absorbed in his books. Perched upon a woodpile, or lying under a tree with his feet thrust upwards against the trunk and "grinding around with the shade," he caused some neighbors to laugh uproariously, and others to say that he was daft. In fact, he was in grim earnest, and held on his way with much persistence.

May 7, 1833, Lincoln was commissioned as postmaster at New Salem. His method of distributing the scanty mail was to put all the letters in his hat, and to hand them out as he happened to meet the persons to whom they were addressed. The emoluments could hardly have gone far towards the discharge of "the national debt." His incumbency in this office led to a story worth telling. When New Salem, and by necessity also the post-office, like the grocery shop, "winked out," in 1836, there was a trifling balance of sixteen or eighteen dollars due from Lincoln to the government. Several years afterward, when he was practicing law in Springfield, the government agent at last appeared to demand a settlement. Lincoln went to his trunk and drew forth "an old blue sock with a quantity of silver and copper coin tied up in it," the identical bits of money which he had gathered from the people at New Salem, and which, through many days of need in the long intervening period, he had not once touched.

Fortunately an occupation now offered itself which was more lucrative, and possessed also the valuable quality of leaving niches of leisure for the study of the law. The mania for speculation in land had begun in Illinois; great tracts were being cut up into "town lots," and there was as lively a market for real estate as the world has ever seen. The official surveyor of the county, John Calhoun, had more work than he could do, and offered to appoint Lincoln as a deputy. A little study made him competent for the work, which he performed for some time with admirable accuracy, if the stories are to be believed. But he had not long enjoyed the mild prosperity of this new career ere an untoward interruption came from a creditor of the extinct grocery firm. This man held one of the notes representing "the national debt," and now levied execution upon Lincoln's horse and surveying instruments. Two friends, however, were at hand in this hour of need, and Bolin Greene and James Short are gratefully remembered as the men who generously furnished, in that actual cash which was so scarce in Illinois, the sums of one hundred and twenty-five dollars and one hundred and twenty dollars respectively, to redeem these essential implements of Lincoln's business.

The summer of 1834 found Lincoln again a candidate for the legislature. He ran as a Whig, but he received and accepted offers of aid from the Democrats, and their votes swelled the flattering measure of his success. It has usually been stated that he led the four successful candidates, the poll standing: Lincoln, 1,376; Dawson, 1,370; Carpenter, 1,170; Stuart, 1,164. But Mr. Herndon adduces evidence that Dawson's number was 1,390, whereby Lincoln is relegated to the second place. Holland tells us that he "shouldered his pack and on foot trudged to Vandalia, then the capital of the State, about a hundred miles, to make his entrance into public life." But the correcting pen of the later biographer interferes with this dramatic incident also. For it seems that, after the result of the election was known, Lincoln visited a friend, Coleman Smoot, and said: "Did you vote for me?" "I did," replied Smoot. "Then," said Lincoln, "you must lend me two hundred dollars!" This seemed a peculiar *sequitur*, for ordinary political logic would have made any money that was to pass between voter and candidate move the other way. Yet Smoot accepted the consequence entailed in part by his own act, and furnished the money, whereby Lincoln was able to purchase a new suit of clothes and to ride in the stage to Vandalia.

The records of this legislature show nothing noteworthy. Lincoln was very inappropriately placed on the Committee on Public Accounts and Expenditures; also it is recorded that he introduced a resolution to obtain for the State a part of the proceeds of the public lands sold within it. What has chiefly interested the chroniclers is, that at this session he first saw Stephen A. Douglas, then a lobbyist, and said of him: "He is the least man I ever saw." Lincoln's part seems to have been rather that of an observer than of an actor. The account given is that he was watching, learning, making acquaintances, prudently preparing for future success, rather than endeavoring to seize it too greedily. In fact, there is reason to believe that his thoughts were intent on far other matter than the shaping of laws and statutes. For to this period belongs the episode of Ann Rutledge. The two biographers whose personal knowledge is the best regard this as the one real romance of Lincoln's life. Heretofore he had held himself shyly aloof from women's society, but this maiden won his heart. She comes before posterity amid a glamour of rhetorical description, which attributes to her every grace of form and feature, every charm of character and intellect. She was but a schoolgirl of seventeen years when two men became her lovers; a year or more afterward she became engaged to one of them, but before they could be married he made a somewhat singular excuse for going to New York on family affairs. His absence was prolonged and his letters became few. People said that the girl had been deceived, and Lincoln began to hope that the way was clearing for him. But under the prolonged strain Miss Rutledge's health broke down, and on August 25, 1835, she died of brain fever. Lincoln was allowed to see her as she lay near her end. The effect upon him was grievous. Many declared him crazy, and his friends feared that he might go so far as to take his own life; they watched him closely, and one of them at last kindly took him away from the scene of his sufferings for a while, and bore him constant and cheering company. In time the cloud passed, but it seems certain that on only one or two other occasions in his life did that deep melancholy, which formed a permanent background to his temperament, take such overmastering, such alarming and merciless possession of him. He was afflicted sorely with a constitutional tendency to gloom, and the evil haunted him all his life long. Like a dark fog-bank it hung, always dull and threatening, on the verge of his horizon, sometimes rolling heavily down upon him, sometimes drawing off into a more or less remote distance, but never wholly disappearing. Every one saw it in his face and often felt it in his manner, and few pictures of him have been made so bad as not in some degree to present it. The access of it which was brought on by this unhappy love affair was somewhat odd and uncouth in its manifestations, but was so genuine and sincere that one feels that he was truly undergoing the baptism of a great sorrow.

At no other point is there more occasion to note this trait of character, which presents a curious and interesting subject for study. Probably no exhaustive solution is possible. One wanders off into the mystery of human nature, loses his way in the dimness of that which can be felt but cannot be expressed, and becomes aware of even dimmer regions beyond in which it is vain to grope. It is well known that the coarse and rough side of life among the pioneers had its reaction in a reserved and at times morose habit, nearly akin to sadness, at least in those who frequented the wilderness; it was the expression of the influence of the vast, desolate, and lonely nature amid which they passed their lives. It is true that Lincoln was never a backwoodsman, and never roved alone for long periods among the shadowy forests and the limit-less prairies, so that their powerful and weird influences, though not altogether remote, never bore upon him in full force; yet their effect was everywhere around him, and through others he imbibed it, for his disposition was sensitive and sympathetic for such purposes. That there was also a simple prosaic physical inducement cannot be denied. Hardship and daily discomfort in all the arrangements of life counted for something, and especially so the bad food, greasy, unwholesome, horribly cooked, enough to afflict an ostrich with the blue devils of dyspepsia. The denizen of the town devoured messes vastly worse than the simple meal of the hunter and trapper, and did not counteract the ill effect by hard exercise in the free, inspiring air. Such facts must be considered, though they diminish the poetry which rhetoricians and sentimentalists have cast over the melancholy of Lincoln's temperament. Yet they fall far short of wholly accounting for a gloom which many have loved to attribute to the mysticism of a great destiny, as though the awful weight of his immense task was making itself felt in his strange, brooding nature long years before any human prophet could have forecast any part of that which was to come. In this apparent vague consciousness of the oppression of a great burden of toil, duty, and responsibility, casting its shadow so far before, there is something so fascinating to the imagination of man that we cannot quite forego it, or accept any explanation which would compel us altogether to part with it. The shuddering awe and terrible sense of fate, which the grandeur of the Greek tragedies so powerfully expresses, come to us when we contemplate this strange cloud which never left Lincoln in any year after his earliest youth, although some traits in his character seemed often incomprehensibly to violate it, and like rebellious spirits to do outrage to it, while, in fact, they only made it the more striking, picturesque, and mysterious. But, after all explanations have been made, the conclusion must be that there is no one and only thread to guide us through the labyrinth to the heart of this singular trait, and each of us must follow that which his own nature renders intelligible or congenial for him. To us, who know the awful closing acts of his life-drama, it seems so appropriate that there should be an impressive unity, and so an inevitable backward influence working from the end towards the beginning, that we cannot avoid, nor would avoid, an instinctive belief that an occult moral and mental condition already existed in the years of Lincoln's life which we are now observing, although the profound cause of that condition lay wholly in the future, in the years which were still far away. There is a charm in the very unreason and mysticism of such a faith, and mankind will never quite fail to fancy, if not actually to believe, that the life which Lincoln had to live in the future wrought in some inexplicable way upon the life which he was living in the present. The explanation is not more strange than the enigma.

Returning now to the narrative, an unpleasant necessity is encountered. It must be confessed that the atmosphere of romance which lingers around this love-tale of the fair and sweet Ann Rutledge, so untimely taken away, is somewhat attenuated by the fact that only some fifteen months rolled by after she was laid in the ground before Lincoln was again intent upon matrimony. In the autumn of 1836 Miss Mary Owens, of Kentucky, appeared in New Salem,—a comely lass, with "large blue eyes," "fine trimmings," and a long and varied list of attractions. Lincoln immediately began to pay court to her, but in an ungainly and morbid fashion. It is impossible to avoid feeling that his mind was not yet in a natural and healthy condition. While offering to marry her, he advised her not to have him. Upon her part she found him "deficient in those little links which make up the chain of woman's happiness." So she would none of him, but wedded another and became the mother of some Confederate soldiers. Lincoln did not suffer on this second occasion as he had done on the first; and in the spring of 1838 he wrote upon the subject one of the most unfortunate epistles ever penned, in which he turned the whole affair into coarse and almost ribald ridicule. In fact he seems as much out of place in dealing with women and with love as he was in place in dealing with politicians and with politics, and it is pleasant to return from the former to the latter topics. [40]

The spring of 1836 found Lincoln again nominating himself before the citizens of Sangamon County, but for the last time. His party denounced the caucus system as a "Yankee contrivance, intended to abridge the liberties of the people;" but they soon found that it would be as sensible to do battle with pikes and bows, after the invention of muskets and cannon, as to continue to oppose free self-nomination to the Jacksonian method of nomination by convention. In enjoying this last opportunity, not only of presenting himself, but also of constructing his own "platform," Lincoln published the following card:—

NEW SALEM, June 13, 1836.

TO THE EDITOR OF THE JOURNAL:—

In your paper of last Saturday I see a communication over the signature of "Many Voters" in which the candidates who are announced in the "Journal" are called upon to "show their hands." Agreed. Here's mine.

I go for all sharing the privileges of the government who assist in bearing its burdens. Consequently, I go for admitting all whites to the right of suffrage who pay taxes or bear arms (by no means excluding females).

If elected, I shall consider the whole people of Sangamon my constituents, as well those that oppose as those that support me.

While acting as their representative, I shall be governed by their will on all subjects upon which I have the means of knowing what their will is; and upon all others I shall do what my own judgment teaches me will best advance their interests. Whether elected or not, I go for distributing the proceeds of the sales of public lands to the several States to enable our State, in common with others, to dig canals and construct railroads without borrowing money and paying the interest on it.

If alive on the first Monday in November, I shall vote for Hugh L. White for President.

Very respectfully,

A. LINCOLN.

The canvass was conducted after the usual fashion, with stump-speaking, fighting, and drinking. Western voters especially fancied the joint debate between rivals, and on such exciting occasions were apt to come to the arbitrament of fists and knives. But it is pleasant to hear that Lincoln calmed rather than excited such affrays, and that once, when Ninian W. Edwards climbed upon a table and screamed at his opponent the lie direct, Lincoln replied by "so fair a speech" that it quelled the discord. Henceforward he practiced a calm, carefully-weighed, dispassionate style in presenting facts and arguments. Even if he cultivated it from appreciation of its efficiency, at least his skill in it was due to the fact that it was congenial to his nature, and that his mind worked instinctively along these lines. His mental constitution, his way of thinking, were so honest that he always seemed to be a man sincerely engaged in seeking the truth, and who, when he believed that he had found it, would tell it precisely as he saw it, and tell it all. This was the distinguishing trait or habit which differentiates Lincoln from too many other political speakers and writers in the country. Yet with it he combined the character of a practical politician and a stanch party man. No party has a monopoly of truth and is always in the right; but Lincoln, with the advantage of being naturally fair-minded to a rare degree, understood that the best ingenuity is fairness, and that the second best ingenuity is the appearance of fairness.

A pleasant touch of his humor illumined this campaign. George Forquer, once a Whig but now a Democrat and an office-holder, had lately built for himself the finest house in Springfield, and had decorated it with the first lightning-rod ever seen in the neighborhood. One day, after Forquer had been berating Lincoln as a young man who must "be taken down," Lincoln turned to the audience with a few words: "It is for you, not for me, to say whether I am up or down. The gentleman has alluded to my being a young man; [41] I am older in years than I am in the tricks and trades of politicians. I desire to live, and I desire place and distinction as a politician; but I would rather die now than, like the gentleman, live to see the day when I should have to erect a lightning-rod to protect a guilty conscience from an offended God."

There are other stories of this campaign, amusing and characteristic of the region and the times, but which there is not room to repeat. The result of it was that Sangamon County, hitherto Democratic, was now won by the Whigs, and that Lincoln had the personal satisfaction of leading the poll. The county had in the legislature nine representatives, tall fellows all, not one of them standing less than six feet, so that they were nicknamed "the Long Nine." Such was their authority that one of them afterward said: "All the bad or objectionable laws passed at that session of the legislature, and for many years afterward, were chargeable to the management and influence of 'the Long Nine.'" This was a damning confession, for the "bad and objectionable" laws of that session were numerous. A mania possessed the people. The whole State was being cut up into towns and cities and house-lots, so that town-lots were said to be the only article of export. [42] A system of internal improvements at the public expense was pushed forward with incredible recklessness. The State was to be "gridironed" with thirteen hundred miles of railroad; the courses of the rivers were to be straightened; and where nature had neglected to supply rivers, canals were to be dug. A loan of twelve millions of dollars was authorized, and the counties not benefited thereby received gifts of cash. The bonds were issued and sent to the bankers of New York and of Europe, and work was vigorously begun. The terrible financial panic of 1837 ought to have administered an early check to this madness. But it did not. Resolutions of popular conventions instructed legislators to institute "a general system of internal improvements," which should be "commensurate with the wants of the people;" and the lawgivers obeyed as implicitly as if each delegate was lighting his steps by an Aladdin's lamp.

With this mad current Lincoln swam as wildly and as ignorantly as did any of his comrades. He was absurdly misplaced as a member of the Committee on Finance. Never in his life did he show the slightest measure of "money sense." He had, however, declared his purpose to be governed by the will of his constituents in all matters in which he knew that will, and at this time he apparently held the American theory that the multitude probably possesses the highest wisdom, and that at any rate the majority is entitled to have its way. Therefore, in this ambitious enterprise of putting Illinois at the very forefront of the civilized world by an outburst of fine American energy, his ardor was as warm as that of the warmest, and his intelligence was as utterly misled as that of the most ignorant. He declared his ambition to be "the DeWitt Clinton of Illinois." After the inevitable crash had come, amid the perplexity of general ruin and distress, he honestly acknowledged that he had blundered very badly. Nevertheless, no vengeance was exacted of him by the people; which led Governor Ford to say that it is safer for a politician to be wrong with his constituents than to be right against them, and to illustrate this profound truth by naming Lincoln among the "spared monuments of popular wrath."

"The Long Nine" had in this legislature a task peculiarly their own: to divide Sangamon County, and to make Springfield instead of Vandalia the state capital. Amid all the whirl of the legislation concerning improvements Lincoln kept this especial purpose always in view. It is said that his skill was infinite, and that he never lost heart. He gained the reputation of being the best "log-roller" in the legislature, and no measure got the support of the "Long Nine" without a contract for votes to be given in return for the removal of the state capital. It is unfortunate that such methods should enjoy the prestige of having been conspicuously practiced by Abraham Lincoln, but the evidence seems to establish the fact. That there was anything objectionable in the skillful performance of such common transactions as the trading of votes probably never occurred to him, being a professional politician, any more than it did to his constituents, who triumphed noisily in this success, and welcomed their candidates home with great popular demonstrations of approval. [43]

A more agreeable occurrence at this session is the position taken by Lincoln concerning slavery, a position which was looked upon with extreme disfavor in those days in that State, and which he voluntarily assumed when he was not called upon to act or commit himself in any way concerning the matter. During the session sundry resolutions were passed, disapproving abolition societies and doctrines, asserting the sacredness of the right of property in slaves in the slave States, and alleging that it would be against good faith to abolish slavery in the District of Columbia without the consent of the citizens of the District. Two days before the end of the session, March 3, 1837, Lincoln introduced a strenuous protest. It bore only one signature besides his own, and doubtless this fact was fortunate for Lincoln, since it probably prevented the document from attracting the attention and resentment of a community which, at the time, by no means held the opinion that there was either "injustice" or "bad policy" in the great "institution" of the South. It was within a few months after this very time that the atrocious persecution and murder of Lovejoy took place in the neighboring town of Alton.

In such hours as he could snatch from politics and bread-winning Lincoln had continued to study law, and in March, 1837, he was admitted to the bar. He decided to establish himself in Springfield, where certainly he deserved a kindly welcome in return for what he had done towards making it the capital. It was a little town of only between one and two thousand inhabitants; but to Lincoln it seemed a metropolis. "There is a great deal of flourishing about in carriages here," he wrote; there were also social distinctions, and real aristocrats, who wore ruffled shirts, and even adventured "fair top-boots" in the "unfathomable" mud of streets which knew neither sidewalks nor pavements.

Lincoln came into the place bringing all his worldly belongings in a pair of saddle-bags. He found there John T. Stuart, his comrade in the Black Hawk campaign, engaged in the practice of the law. The two promptly arranged a partnership. But Stuart was immersed in that too common mixture of law and politics in which the former jealous mistress is apt to take the traditional revenge upon her half-hearted suitor. Such happened in this case; and these two partners, both making the same blunder of yielding imperfect allegiance to their profession, paid the inevitable penalty; they got perhaps work enough in mere point of quantity, but it was neither interesting nor lucrative. Such business, during the four years which he passed with Stuart, did not wean Lincoln from his natural fondness for matters political. At the same time he was a member of sundry literary gatherings and debating societies. Such of his work as has been preserved does not transcend the ordinary productions of a young man trying his wings in clumsy flights of oratory; but he had the excuse that the thunderous declamatory style was then regarded in the West as the only true eloquence. He learned better, in course of time, and so did the West; and it was really good fortune that he passed through the hobbledehoy period in the presence of audiences whose taste was no better than his own.

Occasionally amid the tedium of these high-flown commonplaces there opens a fissure through which the inner spirit of the man looks out for an instant. It is well known that Lincoln was politically ambitious; his friends knew it, his biographers have said it, he himself avowed it. Now and again, in these early days, when his horizon could hardly have ranged beyond the state legislature and the lower house of Congress, he uttered some sentences which betrayed longings of a high moral grade, and indicated that office and power were already regarded by him as the opportunities for great actions. Strenuous as ought to be the objection to that tone in speaking of Lincoln which seems to proceed from beneath the sounding-board of the pulpit, and which uses him as a Sunday-school figure to edify a piously admiring world, yet it certainly seems a plain fact that his day-dreams at this period foreshadowed the acts of his later years, and that what he pleased himself with imagining was not the acquirement of official position but the achievement of some great benefit for mankind. He did not, of course, expect to do this as a philanthropist; for he understood himself sufficiently to know that his road lay in the public service. Accordingly he talks not as Clarkson or Wilberforce, but as a public man, of "emancipating slaves," of eliminating slavery and drunkenness from the land; at the same time he speaks thus not as a politician shrewdly anticipating the coming popular impulse, but as one desiring to stir that impulse. When he said, in his manifesto in 1832, that he had "no other ambition so great as that of being truly esteemed by his fellow-men," he uttered words which in the mouths of most politicians have the irritating effect of the dreariest and cheapest of platitudes; but he obviously uttered them with the sincerity of a deep inward ambition, that kind of an ambition which is often kept sacred from one's nearest intimates. Many side glimpses show him in this light, and it seems to be the genuine and uncolored one.

In 1838 Lincoln was again elected a member of the lower house of the legislature, and many are the amusing stories told of the canvass. It was in this year that he made sudden onslaught on the demagogue Dick Taylor, and opening with a sudden jerk the artful colonel's waistcoat, displayed a glittering wealth of jewelry hidden temporarily beneath it. There is also the tale of his friend Baker haranguing a crowd in the store beneath Lincoln's office. The audience differed with Baker, and was about to punish him severely for the difference, when Lincoln dangled down through a trap-door in the ceiling, intimated his intention to share in the fight if there was to be one, and brought the audience to a more pacific frame of mind. Such amenities of political debate at least tested some of the qualities of the individual. The Whig party made him their candidate for the speakership and he came within one vote of being elected. [44] He was again a member of the Finance Committee; but financiering by those wise lawgivers was no longer so lightsome and exuberant a task as it had been. The hour of reckoning had come; and the business proved to be chiefly a series of humiliating and futile efforts to undo the follies of the preceding two and a half years. Lincoln shared in this disagreeable labor, as he had shared in the mania which had made it necessary. He admitted that he was "no financier," and gave evidence of the fact by submitting a bill which did not deserve to be passed, and was not. It can, however, be said for him that he never favored repudiation, as some of his comrades did.

In 1840 [45] Lincoln was again elected, again was the nominee of the Whig party for the speakership, and again was beaten by Ewing, the Democratic candidate, who mustered 46 votes against 36 for Lincoln. This legislature held only one session, and apparently Holland's statement, that "no important business of general interest was transacted," is a fair summary. Lincoln did only one memorable thing, and that unfortunately was discreditable. In a close and exciting contest, he, with two other Whigs, jumped out of the window in order to break a quorum. It is gratifying to hear from the chronicler of the event, who was one of the parties concerned, that "Mr. Lincoln always regretted that he entered into that arrangement, as he deprecated everything that savored of the revolutionary." [46]

The year 1840 was made lively throughout the country by the spirited and rollicking campaign which the Whigs made on behalf of General Harrison. In that famous struggle for "Tippecanoe and Tyler too," the log cabin, hard cider, and the 'coon skin were the popular emblems which seemed to lend picturesqueness and enthusiasm and a kind of Western spirit to the electioneering everywhere in the land. In Illinois Lincoln was a candidate on the Whig electoral ticket, and threw himself with great zeal into the congenial task of "stumping" the State. Douglas was doing the same duty on the other side, and the two had many encounters. Of Lincoln's speeches only one has been preserved, [47] and it leads to the conclusion that nothing of value was lost when the others perished. The effusion was in the worst style of the effervescent and exuberant school of that region and generation. Nevertheless, it may have had the greatest merit which oratory can possess, in being perfectly adapted to the audience to which it was addressed. But rhetoric could not carry Illinois for the Whigs; the Democrats cast the vote of the State.

[34] *The Good Old Times in McLean County*, passim.

[35] It was first advocated in 1835-36, and was adopted by slow degrees thereafter. Ford, *Hist. of Illinois*, 204.

[36] *Ibid.* 201.

[37] Lamon, 129, where is given the text of the manifesto; Herndon, 101; N. and H. i. 101, 105; Holland, 53, says that *after* his return from the Black Hawk campaign, Lincoln "was applied to" to become a candidate, and that the "application was a great surprise to him." This seems an obvious error, in view of the manifesto; yet see Lamon, 122.

[38] N. and H. i. 102. Lamon regards him as "a nominal Jackson man" in contradistinction to a "whole-hog Jackson man;" as "Whiggish" rather than actually a Whig. Lamon, 123, 126.

[39] Herndon, 105. But see N. and H. i. 109.

[40] The whole story of these two love affairs is given at great length by Herndon and by Lamon. Other biographers deal lightly with these episodes. Nicolay and Hay scantly refer to them, and, in their admiration for Mr. Lincoln, even permit themselves to speak of that most abominable letter to Mrs. Browning as "grotesquely comic." (Vol. i. p. 192.) It is certainly true that the revelations of Messrs. Herndon and Lamon are painful, and in part even humiliating; and it would be most satisfactory to give these things the go-by. But this seems impossible; if one wishes to study and comprehend the character of Mr. Lincoln, the strange and morbid condition in which he was for some years at this time cannot possibly be passed over. It may even be said that it would be unfair to him to do so; and a truthful idea of him, on the whole, redounds more to his credit than a maimed and mutilated one, even though the mutilation seems to consist in lopping off and casting out of sight a deformity. Psychologically, perhaps physiologically, these episodes are interesting, and as aiding a comprehension of Mr. Lincoln's nature they are indispensable; but historically they are of no consequence, and I am glad that the historical character of this work gives me the right to dwell upon them lightly.

[41] It is amusing-to compare this Western oratory with the famous outburst of the younger Pitt which he opened with those familiar words: "The atrocious crime of being a young man which the honorable gentleman has with such spirit and decency charged upon me," etc., etc.

[42] For the whole history of the rise, progress, and downfall of this mania, see Ford, *Hist. of Illinois*, ch. vi.

[43] Ford, *Hist. of Illinois*, 186; Lamon, 198-201; Herndon, 176, 180. N. and H., i. 137-139, endeavor to give a different color to this transaction, but they make out no case as against the statements of writers who had such opportunities to know the truth as had Governor Ford, Lamon, and Herndon.

[44] N. and H. i. 160; Holland, 74; Lamon, 212; but see Herndon, 193.

[45] For the story of *The Skinning of Thomas*, belonging to this campaign, see Herndon, 197; Lamon, 231; and for the Radford story, see N. and H. i. 172; Lamon, 230.

[46] Lamon, 216, 217. Nicolay and Hay, i. 162, speak of "a number" of the members, among whom Lincoln was "prominent," making this exit; but there seem to have been only two besides him.

[47] N. and H. i. 173-177.

CHAPTER III
LOVE; A DUEL; LAW, AND CONGRESS

Collaterally with law and politics, Lincoln was at this time engaged with that almost grotesque courtship which led to his marriage. The story is a long and strange one; in its best gloss it is not agreeable, and in its worst version it is exceedingly disagreeable. In any form it is inexplicable, save so far as the apparent fact that his mind was somewhat disordered can be taken as an explanation. In 1839 Miss Mary Todd, who had been born in Lexington, Kentucky, December 13, 1818, came to Springfield to stay with her sister, Mrs. Ninian W. Edwards. The Western biographers describe her as "gifted with rare talents," as "high-bred, proud, brilliant, witty," as "aristocratic" and "accomplished," and as coming from a "long and distinguished ancestral line." Later in her career critics with more exacting standards gave other descriptions. There is, however, no doubt that in point of social position and acquirements she stood at this time much above Lincoln.

Upon Lincoln's part it was a peculiar wooing, a series of morbid misgivings as to the force of his affection, of alternate ardor and coldness, advances and withdrawals, and every variety of strange language and freakish behavior. In the course of it, oddly enough, his omnipresent competitor, Douglas, crossed his path, his rival in love as well as in politics, and ultimately outstripped by him in each alike. After many months of this queer, uncertain zigzag progress, it was arranged that the marriage should take place on January 1, 1841. At the appointed hour the company gathered, the supper was set out, and the bride, "bedecked in veil and silken gown, and nervously toying with the flowers in her hair," according to the graphic description of Mr. Herndon, sat in her sister's house awaiting the coming of her lover. She waited, but he came not, and soon his friends were searching the town for him. Towards morning they found him. Some said that he was insane; if he was not, he was at least suffering from such a terrible access of his constitutional gloom that for some time to come it was considered necessary to watch him closely. His friend Speed took him away upon a long visit to Kentucky, from which he returned in a much improved mental condition, but soon again came under the influence of Miss Todd's attractions.

The memory of the absurd result of the recent effort at marriage naturally led to the avoidance of publicity concerning the second undertaking. So nothing was said till the last moment; then the license was procured, a few friends were hastily notified, and the ceremony was performed, all within a few hours, on November 4, 1842. A courtship marked by so many singularities was inevitably prolific of gossip; and by all this tittle-tattle, in which it is absolutely impossible to separate probably a little truth from much fiction, the bride suffered more than the groom. Among other things it was asserted that Lincoln at last came to the altar most reluctantly. One says that he was "pale and trembling, as if being driven to slaughter;" another relates that the little son of a friend, noticing that his toilet had been more carefully made than usual, asked him where he was going, and that he gloomily responded: "To hell, I suppose." Probably enough, however, these anecdotes are apocryphal; for why the proud and high-tempered Miss Todd should have held so fast to an unwilling lover, who had behaved so strangely and seemed to offer her so little, is a conundrum which has been answered by no better explanation than the very lame one, that she foresaw his future distinction. It was her misfortune that she failed to make herself popular, so that no one has cared in how disagreeable or foolish a position any story places her. She was charged with having a sharp tongue, a sarcastic wit, and a shrewish temper, over which perilous traits she had no control. It is related that her sister, Mrs. Edwards, opposed the match, from a belief that the two were utterly uncongenial, and later on this came to be the accepted belief of the people at large. That Mrs. Lincoln often severely harassed her husband always has been and always will be believed. One would gladly leave the whole topic veiled in that privacy which ought always to be accorded to domestic relations which are supposed to be only imperfectly happy; but his countrymen have not shown any such respect to Mr. Lincoln, and it no longer is possible wholly to omit mention of a matter about which so much has been said and written. Moreover, it has usually been supposed that the influence of Mrs. Lincoln upon her husband was unceasing and powerful, and that her moods and her words constituted a very important element in his life. [48]

Another disagreeable incident of this period was the quarrel with James A. Shields. In the summer of 1842 sundry coarse assaults upon Shields, attributed in great part, or wholly, to the so-called trenchant and witty pen of Miss Todd, appeared in the Springfield "Journal." Lincoln accepted the responsibility for them, received and reluctantly accepted a challenge, and selected broadswords as the weapons! "Friends," however, brought about an "explanation," and the conflict was avoided. But ink flowed in place of blood, and the newspapers were filled with a mass of silly, grandiloquent, blustering, insolent, and altogether pitiable stuff. All the parties concerned were placed in a most humiliating light, and it is gratifying to hear that Lincoln had at least the good feeling to be heartily ashamed of the affair, so that he "always seemed willing to forget" it. But every veil which he ever sought to throw over anything concerning himself has had the effect of an irresistible provocation to drag the subject into the strongest glare of publicity. [49]

All the while, amid so many distractions, Lincoln was seeking a livelihood at the bar. On April 14, 1841, a good step was taken by dissolving the partnership with Stuart and the establishment of a new partnership with Stephen T. Logan, lately judge of the Circuit Court of the United States, and whom Arnold calls "the head of the bar at the capital." This gentleman, though not averse to politics, was a close student, assiduous in his attention to business, and very accurate and methodical in his ways. Thus he furnished a shining example of precisely the qualities which Lincoln had most need to cultivate, and his influence upon Lincoln was marked and beneficial. They continued together until September 20, 1843, when they separated, and on the same day Lincoln, heretofore a junior, became the senior in a new partnership with William H. Herndon. This firm was never formally dissolved up to the day of Lincoln's death.

When Lincoln was admitted to the bar the practice of the law was in a very crude condition in Illinois. General principles gathered from a few text-books formed the simple basis upon which lawyers tried cases and framed arguments in improvised court-rooms. But the advance was rapid and carried Lincoln forward with it. The raw material, if the phrase may be pardoned, was excellent; there were many men in the State who united a natural aptitude for the profession with high ability, ambition, and a progressive spirit. Lincoln was brought in contact with them all, whether they rode his circuit or not, because the federal courts were held only in Springfield. Among them were Stephen A. Douglas, Lyman Trumbull, afterward for a long while chairman of the Judiciary Committee of the national Senate, David Davis, afterward a senator, and an associate justice of the Supreme Court of the United States; O.H. Browning, Ninian W. Edwards, Edward D. Baker, Justin Butterfield, Judge Logan, and more. Precisely what position Lincoln occupied among these men it is difficult to say with accuracy, because it is impossible to know just how much of the praise which has been bestowed upon him is the language of eulogy or of the brotherly courtesy of the bar, and how much is a discriminating valuation of his qualities. That in the foregoing list there were better and greater lawyers than he is unquestionable; that he was primarily a politician and only secondarily a lawyer is equally beyond denial. He has been described also as "a case lawyer," that is to say, a lawyer who studies each case as it comes to him simply by and for itself, a method which makes the practitioner rather than the jurist. That Lincoln was ever learned in the science is hardly pretended. In fact it was not possible that the divided allegiance which he gave to his profession for a score of years could have achieved such a result. [50] But it is said, and the well-known manner of his mental operations makes it easy to believe, that his arguments had a marvelous simplicity and clearness, alike in thought and in expression. To these traits they owed their great force; and a legal argument can have no higher traits; fine-drawn subtlety is undeniably an inferior quality. Noteworthy above all else was his extraordinary capacity for statement; all agree that his statement of his case and his presentation of the facts and the evidence were so plain and fair as to be far more convincing than the argument which was built upon them. Again it may be said that the power to state in this manner is as high in the order of intellectual achievement as anything within forensic possibilities.

As an advocate Lincoln seems to have ranked better than he did in the discussion of pure points of law. When he warmed to his work his power over the emotions of a jury was very great. A less dignified but not less valuable capacity lay in his humor and his store of illustrative anecdotes. But the one trait, which all agree in attributing to him and which above all others will redound to his honor, at least in the mind of the layman, is that he was only efficient when his client was in the right, and that he made but indifferent work in a wrong cause. He was preëminently the honest lawyer, the counsel fitted to serve the litigant who was justly entitled to win. His power of lucid statement was of little service when the real facts were against him; and his eloquence seemed paralyzed when he did not believe thoroughly that his client had a just cause. He generally refused to take cases unless he could see that as matter of genuine right he ought to win them. People who consulted him were at times bluntly advised to withdraw from an unjust or a hard-hearted contention, or were bidden to seek other counsel. He could even go the length of leaving a case, while actually conducting it, if he became satisfied of unfairness on the part of his client; and when a coadjutor won a case from which he had withdrawn *in transitu*, so to speak, he refused to accept any portion of the fee. Such habits may not meet with the same measure of commendation from professional men [51] which they will command on the part of others; but those who are not members of this ingenious profession, contemning the fine logic which they fail to overcome, stubbornly insist upon admiring the lawyer who refuses to subordinate right to law. In this respect Lincoln accepted the ideals of laymen rather than the doctrines of his profession. [52]

In the presidential campaign of 1844, in which Henry Clay was the candidate of the Whig party, Lincoln was nominated upon the Whig electoral ticket. He was an ardent admirer of Clay and he threw himself into this contest with great zeal. Oblivious of courts and clients, he devoted himself to "stumping" Illinois and a part of Indiana. When Illinois sent nine Democratic electors to vote for James K. Polk, his disappointment was bitter. All the members of the defeated party had a peculiar sense of personal chagrin upon this occasion, and Lincoln felt it even more than others. It is said that two years later a visit to Ashland resulted in a disillusionment, and that his idol then came down from its pedestal, or at least the pedestal was made much lower. [53]

In March, 1843, Lincoln had hopes that the Whigs would nominate him as their candidate for the national House of Representatives. In the canvass he developed some strength, but not quite enough, and the result was somewhat ludicrous, for Sangamon County made him a delegate to the nominating convention with instructions to vote for one of his own competitors, Colonel Edward D. Baker, the gallant gentleman and brilliant orator who fell at Ball's Bluff. The prize was finally carried off by Colonel John J. Hardin, who afterward died at Buena Vista. By a change of election periods the next convention was held in 1844, and this time Lincoln publicly declined to make a contest for the nomination against Colonel Baker, who accordingly received it and was elected. It has been said that an agreement was made between Hardin, Baker, Lincoln, and Judge Logan, whereby each should be allowed one term in Congress, without competition on the part of any of the others; but the story does not seem altogether trustworthy, nor wholly corroborated by the facts. Possibly there may have been a courteous understanding between them. It has, however, been spoken of as a very reprehensible bargain, and Lincoln has been zealously defended against the reproach of having entered into it. Why, if indeed it ever was made, it had this objectionable complexion is a point in the inscrutable moralities of politics which is not plain to those uninitiated in these ethical mysteries.

In the year 1846 Lincoln again renewed his pursuit of the coveted honor, as Holland very properly puts it. Nothing is more absurd than statements to the purport that he was "induced to accept" the nomination, statements which he himself would have heard with honest laughter. Only three years ago [54] he had frankly written to a friend: "Now, if you should hear any one say that Lincoln don't want to go to Congress, I wish you, as a personal friend of mine, would tell him you have reason to believe he is mistaken. The truth is I would [should] like to go very much." Now, the opportunity being at hand, he spared no pains to compass it. In spite of the alleged agreement Hardin made reconnoissances in the district, which Lincoln met with counter-manifestations so vigorous that on February 26 Hardin withdrew, and on May 1 Lincoln was nominated. Against him the Democrats set Peter Cartwright, the famous itinerant preacher of the Methodists, whose strenuous and popular eloquence had rung in the ears of every Western settler. Stalwart, aggressive, possessing all the qualities adapted to win the good-will of such a constituency, the Apostle of the West was a dangerous antagonist. But Lincoln had political capacity in a rare degree. Foresight and insight, activity and the power to organize and to direct, were his. In this campaign his eye was upon every one; individuals, newspaper editors, political clubs, got their inspiration and their guidance from him. [55] Such thoroughness deserved and achieved an extraordinary success; and at the polls, in August, the district gave him a majority of 1,511. In the latest presidential campaign it had given Clay a majority of 914; and two years later it gave Taylor a majority of 1,501. Sangamon County gave Lincoln a majority of 690, the largest given to any candidate from 1836 to 1850, inclusive. Moreover, Lincoln was the only Whig who secured a place in the Illinois delegation.

Though elected in the summer of 1846, it was not until December 6, 1847, that the Thirtieth Congress began its first session. Robert C. Winthrop was chosen speaker of the House, by 110 votes out of 218. The change in the political condition was marked; in the previous House the Democrats had numbered 142 and the Whigs only 75; in this House the Whigs were 116, the Democrats 108. Among the members were John Quincy Adams, Andrew Johnson, Alexander H. Stephens, Howell Cobb, David Wilmot, Jacob Collamer, Robert Toombs, with many more scarcely less familiar names. The Mexican war was drawing towards its close, [56] and most of the talking in Congress had relation to it. The whole Whig party denounced it at the time, and the nation has been more than half ashamed of it ever since. By adroit manoeuvres Polk had forced the fight upon a weak and reluctant nation, and had made to his own people false statements as to both the facts and the merits of the quarrel. The rebuke which they had now administered, by changing the large Democratic majority into a minority, "deserves," says von Holst, "to be counted among the most meritorious proofs of the sound and honorable feeling of the American nation." [57] But while the administration had thus smirched the inception and the whole character of the war with meanness and dishonor, the generals and the army were winning abundant glory for the national arms. Good strategy achieved a series of brilliant victories, and fortunately for the Whigs General Taylor and General Scott, together with a large proportion of the most distinguished regimental officers, were of their party. This aided them essentially in their policy, which was, to denounce the entering into the war but to vote all necessary supplies for its vigorous prosecution.

Into this scheme of his party Lincoln entered with hearty concurrence. A week after the House met he closed a letter to his partner with the remark: "As you are all so anxious for me to distinguish myself, I have concluded to do so before long," and what he said humorously he probably meant seriously. Accordingly he soon afterward [58] introduced a series of resolutions, which, under the nickname of "The Spot Resolutions," attracted some attention. Quoting in his preamble sundry paragraphs of the President's message of May 11, 1846, to the purport that Mexico had "invaded *our territory*" and had "shed the blood of our citizens on *our own soil*" he then requested the President to state "*the spot*" where these and other alleged occurrences had taken place. His first "little speech" was on "a post-office question of no general interest;" and he found himself "about as badly scared and no worse" than when he spoke in court. So a little later, January 12, 1848, he ventured to call up his resolutions and to make an elaborate speech upon them. [59] It was not a very great or remarkable speech, but it was a good one, and not conceived in the fervid and florid style which defaced his youthful efforts; he spoke sensibly, clearly, and with precision of thought; he sought his strength in the facts, and went in straight pursuit of the truth; his best intellectual qualities were plainly visible. The resolutions were not acted upon, and doubtless their actual passage had never been expected; but they were a good shot well placed; and they were sufficiently noteworthy to save Lincoln from being left among the herd of the nobodies of the House.

In view of his future career, but for no other reason, a brief paragraph is worth quoting. He says:—

"Any people anywhere, being inclined and having the power, have the *right* to rise up and shake off the existing government, and form a new one that suits them better. This is a most valuable, a most sacred right,—a right which, we hope and believe, is to liberate the world. Nor is this right confined to cases in which the whole people of an existing government may choose to exercise it. Any portion of such people, that *can*, may revolutionize, and make their *own* of so much of the territory as they inhabit." This doctrine, so comfortably applied to Texas in 1848, seemed unsuitable for the Confederate States in 1861. But possibly the point lay in the words, "having the power," and "can," for the Texans "had the power" and "could," and the South had it not and could not; and so Lincoln's practical proviso saved his theoretical consistency; though he must still have explained how either Texas or the

South could know whether they "had the power," and "could," except by trial.

Lincoln's course concerning the war and the administration did not please his constituents. With most of the Whigs he voted for Ashmun's amendment, which declared that the war had been "unnecessarily and unconstitutionally commenced by the President." But soon he heard that the people in Springfield were offended at a step which might weaken the administration in time of stress; and even if the President had transcended the Constitution, they preferred to deny rather than to admit the fact. When Douglas afterward charged Lincoln with lack of patriotism, Lincoln replied that he had not chosen to "skulk," and, feeling obliged to vote, he had voted for "the truth" rather than for "a lie." [60] He remarked also that he, with the Whigs generally, always voted for the supply bills. He took and maintained his position with entire manliness and honesty, and stated his principles with perfect clearness, neither shading nor abating nor coloring by any conciliatory or politic phrase. It was a question of conscience, and he met it point-blank. Many of his critics remained dissatisfied, and it is believed that his course cost the next Whig candidate in the district votes which he could not afford to lose. It is true that another paid this penalty, yet Lincoln himself would have liked well to take his chance as the candidate. To those "who desire that I should be reflected," he wrote to Herndon, "I can say, as Mr. Clay said of the annexation of Texas, that *'personally* I would not object.' ... If it should so happen *that nobody else wishes to be elected,* I could not refuse the people the right of sending me again. But to enter myself as a competitor of others, or to authorize any one so to enter me, is what my word and honor forbid." It did so happen that Judge Logan, whose turn it seemed to be, wished the nomination and received it. He was, however, defeated, and probably paid the price of Lincoln's scrupulous honesty.

In the canvassing of the spring of 1848 Lincoln was an ardent advocate for the nomination of General Taylor as the Whig candidate for the presidency; for he appreciated how much greater was the strength of the military hero, with all that could be said against him, than was that of Mr. Clay, whose destiny was so disappointingly non-presidential. When the nomination went according to his wishes, he entered into the campaign with as much zeal as his congressional duties would permit,—indeed, with somewhat an excess of zeal, for he delivered on the floor of the House an harangue in favor of the general which was little else than a stump speech, admirably adapted for a backwoods audience, but grossly out of place where it was spoken. He closed it with an assault on General Cass, as a military man, which was designed to be humorous, and has, therefore, been quoted with unfortunate frequency. So soon as Congress adjourned he was able to seek a more legitimate arena in New England, whither he went at once and delivered many speeches, none of which have been preserved.

Lincoln's position upon the slavery question in this Congress was that of moderate hostility. In the preceding Congress, the Twenty-ninth, the famous Wilmot Proviso, designed to exclude slavery from any territory which the United States should acquire from Mexico, had passed the House and had been killed in the Senate. In the Thirtieth Congress efforts to the same end were renewed in various forms, always with Lincoln's favor. He once said that he had voted for the principle of the Wilmot Proviso "about forty-two times," which, if not an accurate mathematical computation, was a vivid expression of his stanch adherence to the doctrine. At the second session Mr. Lincoln voted against a bill to prohibit the slave trade in the District of Columbia, because he did not approve its form; and then introduced another bill, which he himself had drawn. This prohibited the bringing slaves into the District, except as household servants by government officials who were citizens of slave States; it also prohibited selling them to be taken away from the District; children born of slave mothers after January 1, 1850, were to be subject to temporary apprenticeship and finally to be made free; owners of slaves might collect from the government their full cash value as the price of their freedom; fugitive slaves escaping into Washington and Georgetown were to be returned; finally the measure was to be submitted to popular vote in the District. This was by no means a measure of abolitionist coloring, although Lincoln obtained for it the support of Joshua R. Giddings, who believed it "as good a bill as we could get at this time," and was "willing to pay for slaves in order to save them from the Southern market." It recognized the right of property in slaves, which the Abolitionists denied; also it might conceivably be practicable, a characteristic which rarely marked the measures of the Abolitionists, who professed to be pure moralists rather than practical politicians. From this first move to the latest which he made in this great business, Lincoln never once broke connection with practicability. On this occasion he had actually succeeded in obtaining from Mr. Seaton, editor of the "National Intelligencer" and mayor of Washington, a promise of support, which gave him a little prospect of success. Later, however, the Southern Congressmen drew this influential gentleman to their side, and thereby rendered the passage of the bill impossible; at the close of the session it lay with the other corpses in that grave called "the table."

When his term of service in Congress was over Lincoln sought, but failed to obtain, the position of Commissioner of the General Lands Office. He was offered the governorship of the newly organized Territory of Oregon; but this, controlled by the sensible advice of his wife, he fortunately declined.

[48]   Lamon, pp. 238-252, tells the story of Lincoln's marriage at great length, sparing nothing; he liberally sets forth the gossip and the stories; he quotes the statements of witnesses who knew both parties at the time, and he gives in full much correspondence. The spirit and the letter of his account find substantial corroboration in the narrative of Herndon, pp. 206-231. So much original material and evidence of acquaintances have been gathered by these two writers, and their own opportunities of knowing the truth were so good, that one seems not at liberty to reject the *substantial* correctness of their version. Messrs. Nicolay and Hay, vol. i. ch. 11, give a narrative for the most part in their own language. Their attempt throughout to mitigate all that is disagreeable is so obvious, not only in substance but in the turn of every phrase, that it is impossible to accept their chapter as a picture either free from obscurity or true in color, glad as one might be to do so. Arnold, pp. 68, 72, and Holland, p. 90, simply mention the marriage, and other biographers would have done well to imitate this forbearance; but too much has been said to leave this course now open.

[49]   It is fair to say that my view of this "duel" is not that of other writers. Lamon, p. 260, says that "the scene is one of transcendent interest." Herndon, p. 260, calls it a "serio-comic affair." Holland, pp. 87-89, gives a brief, deprecatory account of what he calls "certainly a boyish affair." Arnold, pp. 69-72, treats it simply enough, but puts the whole load of the ridicule upon Shields. Nicolay and Hay, vol. i. ch. 12, deal with it gravely, and in the same way in which, in the preceding chapter, they deal with the marriage; that is to say, they eschew the production of original documents, and, by their own gloss, make a good story for Lincoln and a very bad one for Shields; they speak lightly of the "ludicrousness" of the affair. To my mind the opinion which Lincoln himself held is far more correct than that expressed by any of his biographers.

[50]   Serious practice only began with him when he formed his partnership with Judge Logan in 1841; in 1860 his practice came to an end; in the interval he was for two years a member of Congress.

[51] A story is told by Lamon, p. 321, which puts Lincoln in a position absolutely indefensible by any sound reasoning.

[52] For accounts of Lincoln at the bar, as also for many illustrative and entertaining anecdotes to which the plan of this volume does not permit space to be given, see Arnold, 55-59, 66, 73, 84-91; Holland, 72, 73, 76-83, 89; Lamon, 223-225, ch. xiii. 311-332; N. and H. i. 167-171, 213-216, ch. xvii. 298-309; Herndon, 182-184, 186, 264-266, 306 n., 307-309, 312-319, 323-331, ch. xi. 332-360.

[53] Holland, 95; but *per contra* see Herndon, 271.

[54] March, 1843.

[55] By way of example of his methods, see letter to Herndon, June 22, 1848, Lamon, 299.

[56] The treaty of peace, subject to some amendments, was ratified by the Senate March 10, 1848, and officially promulgated on July 4.

[57] Von Holst, *Const. Hist. of U.S.* iii. 336. All historians are pretty well agreed upon the relation of the Polk administration to the Mexican war. But the story has never been so clearly and admirably traced by any other as by von Holst in the third volume of his history.

[58] December 22, 1847.

[59] Printed by Lamon, 282. See, also, Herndon, 277.

[60] Herndon, 281; see letters given in full by Lamon, 291, 293, 295 (at 296); N. and H. i. 274

CHAPTER IV
NORTH AND SOUTH

The Ordinance of 1787 established that slavery should never exist in any part of that vast northwestern territory which had then lately been ceded by sundry States to the Confederation. This Ordinance could not be construed otherwise than as an integral part of the transaction of cession, and was forever unalterable, because it represented in a certain way a part of the consideration in a contract, and was also in the nature of a declaration of trust undertaken by the Congress of the Confederation with the granting States. The article "was agreed to without opposition;" but almost contemporaneously, in the sessions of that convention which framed the Constitution, debate waxed hot upon the topic which was then seen to present grave obstacles to union. It was true that many of the wisest Southerners of that generation regarded the institution as a menacing misfortune; they however could not ignore the fact that it was a "misfortune" of that peculiar kind which was endured with much complacency by those afflicted by it; and it was equally certain that the great body of slave-owners would resent any effort to relieve them of their burden. Hence there were placed in the Constitution provisions in behalf of slavery which involved an admission that the institution needed protection, and should receive it. The idea of protection implied the existence of hostility either of men or of circumstances, or of both. Thus by the Ordinance and the Constitution, taken together, there was already indirectly recognized an antagonism between the institutions, interests, and opinions of the South and those of the North.

Slowly this feeling of opposition grew. The first definite mark of the growth was the struggle over the admission of Missouri, in 1820. This was settled by the famous "Compromise," embodied in the Act of March 6, 1820, whereby the people of the Territory of Missouri were allowed to frame a state government with no restriction against slavery; but a clause also enacted that slavery should never be permitted in any part of the remainder of the public territory lying north of the parallel of 36° 30'. By its efficiency during thirty-four years of constantly increasing strain this legislation was proved to be a remarkable political achievement; and as the people saw it perform so long and so well a service so vital they came to regard it as only less sacred than the Constitution itself. Even Douglas, who afterward led in repealing it, declared that it had an "origin akin to the Constitution," and that it was "canonized in the hearts of the American people as a sacred thing." Yet during the long quietude which it brought, each section kept a jealous eye upon the other; and especially was the scrutiny of the South uneasy, for she saw ever more and more plainly the disturbing truth that her institution needed protection. Being in derogation of natural right, it was peculiarly dependent upon artificial sustention; the South would not express the condition in this language, but acted upon the idea none the less. It was true that the North was not aggressive towards slavery, but was observing it with much laxity and indifference; that the crusading spirit was sleeping soundly, and even the proselyting temper was feeble. But this state of Northern feeling could not relieve the South from the harassing consciousness that slavery needed not only toleration, but positive *protection* at the hands of a population whose institutions were naturally antagonistic to the slave idea. This being the case, she must be alarmed at seeing that population steadily outstripping her own in numbers and wealth. [61] Since she could not possibly even hold this disproportion stationary, her best resource seemed to be to endeavor to keep it practically harmless by maintaining a balance of power in the government. Thus it became unwritten law that slave States and free States must be equal in number, so that the South could not be outvoted in the Senate. This system was practicable for a while, yet not a very long while; for the North was filling up that great northwestern region, which was eternally dedicated to freedom, and full-grown communities could not forever be kept outside the pale of statehood. On the other hand, apart from any question of numbers, the South could make no counter-expansion, because she lay against a foreign country. After a time, however, Texas opportunely rebelled against Mexico, and then the opportunity for removing this obstruction was too obvious and too tempting to be lost. A brief period of so-called independence on the part of Texas was followed by the annexation of her territory to the United States, [62] with the proviso that from her great area might in the future be cut off still four other States. Slavery had been abolished in all Mexican territory, and Texas had been properly a "free" country; but in becoming a part of the United States she became also a slave State.

Mexico had declared that annexation of Texas would constitute a *casus belli*, yet she was wisely laggard in beginning vindictive hostilities against a power which could so easily whip her, and she probably never would have done so had the United States rested content with an honest boundary line. But this President Polk would not do, and by theft and falsehood he at last fairly drove the Mexicans into a war, in which they were so excessively beaten that the administration found itself able to gather more plunder than it had expected. By the treaty of peace the United States not only extended unjustly the southwestern boundary of Texas, but also got New Mexico and California. To forward this result, Polk had asked the House to place $2,000,000 at his disposal. Thereupon, as an amendment to the bill granting this sum, Wilmot introduced his famous proviso, prohibiting slavery in any part of the territory to be acquired. Repeatedly and in various shapes was the substance of this proviso voted upon, but always it was voted down. Though New Mexico had come out from under the rule of despised Mexico as "free" country, a contrary destiny was marked out for it in its American character. A plausible suggestion was made to extend the sacred line of the Missouri Compromise westward to the Pacific Ocean; and very little of the new country lay north of that line. By all these transactions the South seemed to be scoring many telling points in its game. They were definite points, which all could see and estimate; yet a price, which was considerable, though less definite, less easy to see and to estimate, had in fact been paid for them; for the antagonism of the rich and teeming North to the Southern institution and to the Southern policy for protecting it had been spread and intensified to a degree which involved a menace fully offsetting the Southern territorial gain. One of the indications of this state of feeling was the organization of the "Free Soil" party.

Almost simultaneously with this important advancement of the Southern policy there occurred an event, operative upon the other side, which certainly no statesman could have foreseen. Gold was discovered in California, and in a few months a torrent of immigrants poured over the land. The establishment of an efficient government became a pressing need. In Congress they debated the matter hotly; the friends of the Wilmot proviso met in bitter conflict the advocates of the westward extension of the line of 36° 30'. Neither side could prevail, and amid intense excitement the Thirtieth Congress expired. For the politicians this was well enough, but for the Californians organization was such an instant necessity that they now had to help themselves to it. So they promptly elected a Constitutional Convention, which assembled on September 1, 1849, and adjourned on October 13. Though this body held fifteen delegates who were immigrants from slave States, yet it was unanimous in presenting a Constitution which prohibited slavery, and which was at once accepted by a popular vote of 12,066 yeas against 811 nays.

Great then was the consternation of the Southern leaders when Californian delegates appeared immediately upon the assembling of the Thirty-first Congress, and asked for admission beneath this unlooked-for "free" charter of statehood. The shock was aggravated by the fact that

New Mexico, actually instigated thereto by the slaveholding President Taylor himself, was likely to follow close in the Californian foot-tracks. The admission of Texas had for a moment disturbed the senatorial equilibrium between North and South, which, however, had quickly been restored by the admission of Wisconsin. But the South had nothing to offer to counterbalance California and New Mexico, which were being suddenly filched from her confident expectation. In this emergency those extremists in the South who offset the Abolitionists at the North fell back upon the appalling threat of disunion, which could hardly be regarded as an idle extravagance of the "hotspurs," since it was substantially certain that the Senate would never admit California with her anti-slavery Constitution; and thus a real crisis seemed at hand. Other questions also were cast into the seething caldron. Texas, whose boundaries were as uncertain as the ethics of politicians, set up a claim which included nearly all New Mexico, and so would have settled the question of slavery for that region at least. Further, the South called for a Fugitive Slave Law sufficiently stringent to be serviceable. Also, in encountering the Wilmot proviso, Southern statesmen had asserted the doctrine, far-reaching and subversive of established ideas and of enacted laws, that Congress could not constitutionally interfere with the property-rights of citizens of the United States in the Territories, and that slaves were property. Amid such a confused and violent hurly-burly the perplexed body of order-loving citizens were, with reason, seriously alarmed.

To the great relief of these people and to the equal disgust of the extremist politicians, Henry Clay, the "great compromiser," was now announced to appear once more in the rôle which all felt that he alone could play. He came with much dramatic effect; an aged and broken man, he emerged from the retirement in which he seemed to have sought a brief rest before death should lay him low, and it was with an impressive air of sadness and of earnestness that he devoted the last remnants of his failing strength to save a country which he had served so long. His friends feared that he might not survive even a few months to reach the end of his patriotic task. On January 29, 1850, he laid before the Senate his "comprehensive scheme of adjustment." But it came not as oil upon the angry waters; every one was offended by one or another part of it, and at once there opened a war of debate which is among the most noteworthy and momentous in American history. Great men who belonged to the past and great men who were to belong to the future shared in the exciting controversies, which were prolonged over a period of more than half a year. Clay was constantly on his feet, doing battle with a voice which gained rather than lost force from its pathetic feebleness. "I am here," he solemnly said, "expecting soon to go hence, and owing no responsibility but to my own conscience and to God." Jefferson Davis spoke for the extension westward of the Missouri Compromise line to the Pacific Ocean, with a proviso positively establishing slavery south of that line. Calhoun, from the edge of the grave, into which only a few weeks later he was to fall, once more faced his old adversaries. On March 4 he sat beside Mason of Virginia, while that gentleman read for him to a hushed audience the speech which he himself was too weak to deliver. Three days later Webster uttered that speech which made the seventh day of March almost as famous in the history of the United States as the Ides of the same month had been in that of Rome. In the eyes of the anti-slavery men of New England the fall of Webster was hardly less momentous than the fall of Caesar had appeared in the Eternal City. Seward also spoke a noteworthy speech, bringing upon himself infinite abuse by his bold phrase, *a higher law than the Constitution*. Salmon P. Chase followed upon the same side, in an exalted and prophetic strain. In that momentous session every man gave out what he felt to be his best, while anxious and excited millions devoured every word which the newspapers reported to them.

Clay had imprudently gathered the several matters of his Compromise into one bill, which was soon sneeringly nicknamed "the Omnibus Bill." It was sorely harassed by amendments, and when at last, on July 31, the Omnibus reached the end of its journey, it contained only one passenger, viz., a territorial government for Utah. Its trip had apparently ended in utter failure. But a careful study of individual proclivities showed that not improbably those measures might be passed one by one which could not be passed in combination. In this hope, five several bills, being all the ejected contents of the Omnibus, were brought forward, and each in turn had the success which had been denied to them together. First: Texas received $10,000,000, and for this price magnanimously relinquished her unfounded claim upon New Mexico. Second: California was admitted as a free State. Third: New Mexico was organized as a Territory, with the proviso that when she should form a state constitution the slavery question should be determined by the people, and that during her territorial existence the question of property in a slave should be left undisturbed by congressional action, to be determined by the Supreme Court of the United States. Fourth: A more efficient Fugitive Slave Law was passed. Fifth: Slave trading in the District of Columbia was abolished. Such were the terms of an arrangement in which every man saw so much which he himself disliked that he felt sure that others must be satisfied. Each plumed himself on his liberality in his concessions nobly made in behalf of public harmony. "The broad basis," says von Holst, "on which the compromise of 1850 rested, was the conviction of the great majority of the people, both North and South, that it was fair, reasonable, and patriotic to come to a friendly understanding."

Thus in the midsummer of 1850 did the nation, with intense relief, see the imminent disaster of civil discord averted,—or was it only postponed? It was ominous that no men who were deeply in earnest in public affairs were sincerely satisfied. The South saw no gain which offset the destruction of the balance of power by the admission of California. Thinking men at the North were alarmed at the recognition of the principle of non-intervention by Congress concerning slavery in the Territories, a principle which soon, under the seductive title of "popular sovereignty" in the Territories, threatened even that partial restriction heretofore given by the Missouri Compromise. Neither party felt sufficiently secure of the strength of its legal position to be altogether pleased at seeing the doctrine of treating the slave in the Territories as "property" cast into the lottery of the Supreme Court. Lincoln recognized the futility of this whole arrangement, and said truly that the slavery question could "never be successfully compromised." Yet he accepted the situation, with the purpose of making of it the best that was possible. The mass of the people, less far-sighted, were highly gratified at the passing of the great danger; refused to recognize that a more temporary compromise was never patched up to serve a turn; and applauded it so zealously that in preparing for the presidential campaign of 1852 each party felt compelled to declare emphatically—what all wise politicians knew to be false—the "finality" of the great Compromise of 1850. Never, never more was there to be a revival of the slavery agitation! Yet, at the same time, it was instinctively felt that the concord would cease at once if the nation should not give to the South a Democratic President! In this campaign Lincoln made a few speeches in Illinois in favor of Scott; but Herndon says that they were not very satisfactory efforts. Franklin Pierce was chosen, and slavery could have had no better man.

This doctrine of non-intervention by Congress with slavery in the Territories lay as the seed of mortal disease imbedded in the vitals of the great Compromise even at the hour of its birth. All the howlings of the political medicine-men in the halls of Congress, and in the wigwams where the party platforms were manufactured, could not defer the inevitable dissolution. The rapid peopling of the Pacific coast already made it imperative to provide some sort of governmental organization for the sparsely inhabited regions lying between these new lands and the fringe of population near the Mississippi. Accordingly bills were introduced to establish as a Territory the region which was afterward divided between Kansas and Nebraska; but at two successive sessions they failed to pass, more, as it seemed, from lack of interest than from any open hostility. In the course of debate it was explained, and not contradicted, that slavery was not mentioned in the bills because the Missouri Compromise controlled that matter. Yet it was well known that the Missouri Compromise was no longer a sure barrier; for one wing of the pro-slavery party asserted that it was unconstitutional on the ground that slaves, being property, could not be touched in the Territories by congressional enactments; while another wing of the party preferred the plausible cry of "popular sovereignty," than which no words could ring truer in American ears; and no one doubted that, in order to give that sovereignty full sway, they would at any convenient moment vote to repeal even the "sacred" Compromise. It could not be denied that this was the better course, if it were practicable; and accordingly, January 16, 1854, Senator Dixon of Kentucky offered an amendment to the pending Nebraska bill, which substantially embodied the repeal. In the Senate Douglas was chairman of the Committee on Territories, and was induced to coöperate. [63] January 23, 1854, he introduced his famous "Kansas-Nebraska bill," establishing the two Territories and declaring the Missouri Compromise "inoperative" therein. A later amendment declared the Compromise to be "inconsistent with the principle of non-intervention by Congress with slavery in the States and Territories, as recognized by the legislation of 1850," and therefore "inoperative and void; it being the true intent and meaning of this Act not to legislate slavery into any Territory or State, nor to exclude it therefrom, but to leave the people thereof perfectly free to form and regulate their domestic institutions in their own way, subject only to the Constitution." After a long and hard fight the bill was passed with this clause in it, which Benton well stigmatized as a "stump speech injected into the belly of the bill." The insertion of the word State was of momentous significance.

This repeal set the anti-slavery party all ablaze. Among the rest Lincoln was fired with strenuous indignation, and roused from the condition of apparent indifference to public affairs in which he had rested since the close of his term in Congress. Douglas, coming home in the autumn, was so disagreeably received by an angry audience in Chicago that he felt it imperative to rehabilitate his stricken popularity. This difficult task he essayed at the great gathering of the State Fair in October. But Lincoln was put forward to answer him, and was brilliantly successful in doing so, if the highly colored account of Mr. Herndon may be trusted. Immediately after Lincoln's close, Owen Lovejoy, the Abolitionist leader, announced "a meeting in the same place that evening of all the friends of freedom." The scheme was to induce Lincoln to address them, and thus publicly to commit him as of their faith. But the astute Herndon, though himself an Abolitionist, felt that for Lincoln personally this was by no means desirable.

So he hastened to Lincoln and strenuously said: "Go home at once! Take Bob with you, and drive somewhere into the country, and stay till this thing is over;" and Lincoln did take Bob and drove away to Tazewell Court House "on business." Herndon congratulates himself upon having "saved Lincoln," since either joining, or refusing to join, the Abolitionists at that time would have been attended with "great danger." Lincoln had upon his own part a wise instinct and a strong purpose to keep hard by Douglas and to close with him as often as opportunity offered. Soon afterward the two encountered again, and on this occasion it is narrated that Lincoln gave Douglas so much trouble that Douglas cried for a truce, proposing that neither of them should make any more speeches that autumn, to which Lincoln good-naturedly assented.

During this winter Lincoln was elected to the state legislature, but contrary to his own wish. For he designed to be a candidate for the United States Senate, and there might be a question as to his eligibility if he remained a member of the electing body. Accordingly he resigned his seat, which, to his surprise and chagrin, was immediately filled by a Democrat; for there was a reaction in Sangamon County. On February 8, 1855, the legislature began voting to elect a senator. The "Douglas Democrats" wished to reelect Shields, the present incumbent. The first ballot stood, Lincoln, 45, Shields, 41, Lyman Trumbull, 5, scattering, 5 (or, according to other authority, 8). After several ballots Shields was thrown over in favor of a more "practicable" candidate, Governor Matteson, a "quasi-independent," who, upon the ninth ballot, showed a strength of 47, while Trumbull had 35, Lincoln had run down to 15, and "scattering" caught 1. Lincoln's weakness lay in the fact that the Abolitionists had too loudly praised him and publicly counted him as one of themselves. For this reason five Democrats, disgusted with Douglas for his attack on the Missouri Compromise, but equally bitter against Abolitionism, stubbornly refused ever to vote for a Whig, above all a Whig smirched by Abolitionist applause. So it seemed that Owen Lovejoy and his friends had incumbered Lincoln with a fatal handicap. The situation was this: Lincoln could count upon his fifteen adherents to the extremity; but the five anti-Douglas Democrats were equally stanch against him, so that his chance was evidently gone. Trumbull was a Democrat, but he was opposed to the policy of Douglas's Kansas-Nebraska bill; his following was not altogether trustworthy, and a trifling defection from it seemed likely to occur and to make out Matteson's majority. Lincoln pondered briefly; then, subjecting all else to the great principle of "anti-Nebraska," he urged his friends to transfer their votes to Trumbull. With grumbling and reluctance they did so, and by this aid, on the tenth ballot, Trumbull was elected. In a letter to Washburne, Lincoln wrote: "I think you would have done the same under the circumstances, though Judge Davis, who came down this morning, declares he never would have consented to the 47 men being controlled by the 5. I regret my defeat moderately, but am not nervous about it." If that was true which was afterwards so frequently reiterated by Douglas during the campaign of 1858, that a bargain had been struck between Lincoln and Trumbull, whereby the former was to succeed Shields and the latter was to succeed Douglas at the election two years later, then Lincoln certainly displayed on this occasion a "generosity" which deserves more than the very moderate praise which has been given it, of being "above the range of the mere politician's vision." [64]

An immediate effect of this repealing legislation of 1854 was to cast Kansas into the arena as booty to be won in fight between anti-slavery and pro-slavery. For this competition the North had the advantage that its population outnumbered that of the South in the ratio of three to two, and emigration was in accord with the habits of the people. Against this the South offset proximity, of which the peculiar usefulness soon became apparent. Then was quickly under way a fair fight, in a certain sense, but most unfairly fought. Each side contended after its fashion; Northern anti-slavery merchants subscribed money to pay the expenses of free-state immigrants. "Border ruffians" and members of "Blue Lodges" and of kindred fraternities came across the border from Missouri to take a hand in every politico-belligerent crisis. The parties were not unequally matched; by temperament the free-state men were inclined to orderly and legitimate ways, yet they were willing and able to fight fire with fire. On the other hand, the slave-state men had a native preference for the bowie-knife and the shot-gun, yet showed a kind of respect for the ballot-box by insisting that it should be stuffed with votes on their side. Thus for a long while was waged a dubious, savage, and peculiar warfare. Imprisonments and rescues, beatings, shootings, plunderings, burnings, sieges, and lootings of towns were interspersed with elections of civil officers, with legislative enactments in ordinary form, with trials, suits at law, legal arguments, and decisions of judges. It is impossible here to sketch in detail this strange phantasmagory of arson, bloodshed, politics, and law.

Meantime other occurrences demand mention. In May, 1854, the seizure in Boston of Anthony Burns, as an escaped slave, caused a riot in which the court-house was attacked by a mob, one of the assailants was killed, and the militia were called out. Other like seizures elsewhere aroused the indignation of people who, whatever were their abstract theories as to the law, revolted at the actual spectacle of a man dragged back from freedom into slavery. May 22, 1856, Preston S. Brooks strode suddenly upon Charles

Sumner, seated and unarmed at his desk in the senate-chamber, and beat him savagely over the head with a cane, inflicting very serious injuries. Had it been a fair fight, or had the South repudiated the act, the North might have made little of it, for Sumner was too advanced in his views to be politically popular. But, although the onslaught was even more offensive for its cowardice than for its brutality, nevertheless the South overwhelmed Brooks with laudation, and by so doing made thousands upon thousands of Republican votes at the North. The deed, the enthusiastic greeting, and the angry resentment marked the alarming height to which the excitement had risen.

The presidential campaign of the following summer, 1856, showed a striking disintegration and re-formation of political groups. Nominally there were four parties in the field: Democrats, Whigs, Native Americans or Know-Nothings, and Republicans. The Know-Nothings had lately won some state elections, but were of little account as a national organization, for they stood upon an issue hopelessly insignificant in comparison with slavery. Already many had gone over to the Republican camp; those who remained nominated as their candidates Millard Fillmore and Andrew J. Donelson. The Whigs were the feeble remnant of a really dead party, held together by affection for the old name; too few to do anything by themselves, they took by adoption the Know-Nothing candidates. The Republican party had been born only in 1854. Its members, differing on other matters, united upon the one doctrine, which they accepted as a test: opposition to the extension of slavery. They nominated John C. Fremont and William L. Dayton, and made a platform whereby they declared it to be "both the right and the duty of Congress to prohibit in the Territories those twin relics of barbarism, polygamy and slavery;" by which vehement and abusive language they excited the bitter resentment of the Southern Democracy. In this convention 110 votes were cast for Lincoln for the second place on the ticket. Lamon tells the little story that when this was told to Lincoln he replied that he could not have been the person designated, who was, doubtless, "the great Lincoln from Massachusetts." [65] In the Democratic party there were two factions. The favorite candidate of the South was Franklin Pierce, for reëlection, with Stephen A. Douglas as a substitute or second choice; the North more generally preferred James Buchanan, who was understood to be displeased with the repeal of the Missouri Compromise. The struggle was sharp, but was won by the friends of Buchanan, with whom John C. Breckenridge was coupled. The campaign was eager, for the Republicans soon developed a strength beyond what had been expected and which put the Democrats to their best exertions. The result was

	Popular vote	Electoral vote
Democrats.	1,838,169	174
Republicans.	1,341,264	114
Know-Nothings and Whigs.	874,534	8

Thus James Buchanan became President of the United States, March 4, 1857,—stigmatized somewhat too severely as "a Northern man with Southern principles;" in fact an honest man and of good abilities, who, in ordinary times, would have left a fair reputation as a statesman of the second rank; but a man hopelessly unfit alike in character and in mind either to comprehend the present emergency or to rise to its demands. [66] Yet, while the Democrats triumphed, the Republicans enjoyed the presage of the future; they had polled a total number of votes which surprised every one; on the other hand, the Democrats had lost ten States [67] which they had carried in 1852 and had gained only two others, [68] showing a net loss of eight States; and their electoral votes had dwindled from 254 to 174.

On the day following Buchanan's inauguration that occurred which had been foreshadowed with ill-advised plainness in his inaugural address. In the famous case of Dred Scott, [69] the Supreme Court of the United States established as law the doctrine lately advanced by the Southern Democrats, that a slave was "property," and that his owner was entitled to be protected in the possession of him, as such, in the Territories. This necessarily demolished the rival theory of "popular sovereignty," which the Douglas Democrats had adopted, not without shrewdness, as being far better suited to the Northern mind. For clearly the people enjoyed no sovereignty where they had no option. Consequently in the Territories there was no longer a slavery question. The indignation of anti-slavery men of all shades of opinion was intense, and was unfortunately justifiable. For wholly apart from the controversy as to whether the law was better expounded by the chief justice or by Judge Curtis in his dissenting opinion, there remained a main fact, undeniable and inexcusable, to wit: that the court, having decided that the lower court had no jurisdiction, and being therefore itself unable to remand the cause for a new trial, had then outstepped its own proper function and outraged legal propriety by determining the questions raised by the rest of the record,—questions which no longer had any real standing before this tribunal. This course was well known to have been pursued with the purpose on the part of the majority of the judges to settle by judicial authority, and by a *dictum* conspicuously *obiter*, that great slavery question with which Congress had grappled in vain. It was a terrible blunder, for the people were only incensed by a volunteered and unauthorized interference. Moreover, the reasoning of Chief Justice Taney was such that the Republicans began anxiously to inquire why it was not as applicable to States as to Territories, and why it must not be extended to States when occasion should arrive; and in this connection it seemed now apparent why "States" had been named in the bill which repealed the Missouri Compromise. [70] In spite of this menace the struggle in Kansas was not slackened. Time had been counting heavily in favor of the North. Her multitudinous population ceaselessly fed the stream of immigrants, and they were stubborn fellows who came to stay, and therefore were sure to wear out the persistence of the boot-and-saddle men from over the Missouri border. Accordingly, in 1857, the free-state men so vastly outnumbered the slavery contingent, that even pro-slavery men had to acknowledge it. Then the slavery party made its last desperate effort. Toward the close of that year the Lecompton Constitution was framed by a convention chosen at an election in which the free-state men, perhaps unwisely, had refused to take part. When this pro-slavery instrument was offered to the people, they were not allowed to vote simply Yea or Nay, but only "for the Constitution with slavery," or "for the Constitution with no slavery." Again the free-state men refrained from voting, and on December 21, 6,143 ballots were declared to have been cast "for the Constitution with slavery," and 589 "for the Constitution with no slavery." Much more than one third of the 6,143 were proved to be fraudulent, but the residue far exceeded the requisite majority. January 4, 1858, state officers were to be chosen, and now the free-state men decided to make an irregular opportunity to vote, in their turn, simply for or against the Lecompton Constitution. This time the pro-slavery men, considering the matter already lawfully settled, refused to vote, and the result was that this polling showed 10,226 against the Constitution, 138 for the Constitution with slavery, 24 for the Constitution without slavery. It is an instance of Lincoln's political foresight that nearly two years and a half before this condition of affairs came about he had written: "If Kansas fairly votes herself a slave State, she must be admitted, or the Union must be dissolved. But how if she votes herself a slave State unfairly?... Must she still be admitted, or the Union be dissolved? That will be the phase of the question when it first becomes a practical one." [71]

The struggle was now transferred to Washington. President Buchanan had solemnly pledged himself to accept the result of the popular vote. Now he was confronted by two popular votes, of which the one made somewhat the better technical and formal showing, and the other undeniably expressed the true will of a large majority of lawful voters. He selected the former, and advised Congress to admit Kansas under the Lecompton Constitution with slavery. But Douglas took the other side. The position of Douglas in the nation and in the Democratic party deserves brief consideration, for in a way it was the cause of Lincoln's nomination as the Republican candidate for the presidency in 1860. From 1852 to 1860 Douglas was the most noteworthy man in public life in the country. Webster, Clay, and Calhoun had passed away. Seward, Chase, and Sumner, still in the earlier stages of their brilliant careers, were organizing the great party of the future. This interval of eight years belonged to Douglas more than to any other one man. He had been a candidate for the Democratic nomination for the presidency in 1852 and again in 1856; and had failed to secure it in part by reason of that unwritten rule whereby the leading statesmen are so often passed over, in order to confer the great prize upon insignificant and therefore presumably submissive men. Douglas was not of this type; he had high spirit, was ambitious, masterful, and self-confident; he was also an aggressive, brilliant, and tireless fighter in a political campaign, an orator combining something of the impressiveness of Webster with the readiness and roughness of the stump speaker. He had a thorough familiarity with all the politics, both the greater and the smaller, of the time; he was shrewd and adroit as a politician, and he had as good a right as any man then prominent in public life to the more dignified title of statesman. He had the art of popularity, and upon sufficient occasion could be supple and accommodating even in the gravest matters of principle. He had always been a Democrat. He now regarded himself as properly the leader of the Democratic party; and of course he still aimed at the high office which he had twice missed. [72] With this object in view, he had gone very far to retain his hold upon the South. He told Southerners that by his happy theory of "popular sovereignty" he had educated the public mind, and accomplished the repeal of the Missouri Compromise. When the Dred Scott decision took the life out of his "popular sovereignty," he showed his wonted readiness in adapting himself to the situation. To the triumphant South he graciously admitted the finality of a decision which sustained the most extreme Southern doctrine. To the perturbed and indignant North he said cheeringly that the decision was of no practical consequence whatsoever! For every one knew that slavery could not exist in any community without the aid of friendly legislation; and if any anti-slavery community should by its anti-slavery legislature withhold this essential friendly legislation, then slavery in that State might be lawful but would be impossible. So, he said, there is still in fact "popular sovereignty." [73] When the pro-slavery Lecompton Constitution came up for consideration Douglas decided not to rest content with the form of popular approval, but to stand out for the substance. He quarreled with Buchanan, and in an angry interview they exchanged threats and defiance. Douglas felt himself the greater man of the two in the party, and audaciously indicated something like contempt for the rival who was not leader but only President. Conscience, if one may be allowed gravely to speak of the conscience of a professional politician, and policy were in comfortable unison in commending this choice to Douglas. For his term as senator was to expire in 1858, and reëlection was not only in itself desirable, but seemed essential to securing the presidency in 1860. Heretofore Illinois had been a Democratic State; the southern part, peopled by immigrants from neighboring slave States, was largely pro-slavery; but the northern part, containing the rapidly growing city of Chicago, had been filled from the East, and was inclined to sympathize with the rest of the North. Such being the situation, an avowal of Democratic principles, coupled with the repudiation of the Lecompton fraud, seemed the shrewd and safe course in view of Douglas's political surroundings, also the consistent, or may we say honest, course in view of his antecedent position. If, in thus retaining his hold on Illinois, he gave to the Southern Democracy an offense which could never be forgotten or forgiven, this misfortune was due to the impracticable situation and not to any lack of skillful straegy t on his part. In spite of him the bill passed the Senate, but in the House twenty-two Northern Democrats went over to the opposition, and carried a substitute measure, which established that the Lecompton Constitution must again be submitted to popular vote. Though this was done by the body of which Douglas was not a member, yet every one felt that it was in fact his triumph over the administration. A Committee of Conference then brought in the "English bill." Under this the Kansans were to vote, August 3, 1858, either to accept the pro-slavery Lecompton Constitution, with the *douceur* of a land grant, or to reject it. If they accepted it, the State was to be admitted at once; if they rejected it, they were not to be admitted until the population should reach the number which was required for electing a member to the House of Representatives. At present the population was far short of this number, and therefore rejection involved a long delay in acquiring statehood. Douglas very justly assailed the unfairness of a proposal by which an anti-slavery vote was thus doubly and very severely handicapped; but the bill was passed by both Houses of Congress and was signed by the President. The Kansans, however, by an enormous majority, [74] rejected the bribes of land and statehood in connection with slavery. For his action concerning the Lecompton Constitution and the "English bill" Douglas afterward took much credit to himself.

Such was the stage of advancement of the slavery conflict in the country, and such the position of Douglas in national and in state politics, when there took place that great campaign in Illinois which made him again senator in 1858, and made Lincoln President in 1860.

[61] For a striking comparison of the condition of the South with that of the North in 1850, see von Holst's *Const. Hist, of U.S.* v. 567-586.

[62] December, 1845.

[63] For a description of Douglas's state of mind, see N. and H. i. 345-351, quoting original authorities.

[64] N. and H. i. 388.

[65] Thus when John Adams first landed in Europe, and was asked whether he was "the great Mr. Adams," he said: No, the great Mr. Adams was his cousin, Samuel Adams of Boston.

[66] For a fair and discriminating estimate of Buchanan, see Blaine, *Twenty Years in Congress*, vol. i. ch. x., especially pp. 239-241.

[67] Maine, New Hampshire, Rhode Island, Connecticut, New York, Ohio, Michigan, Wisconsin, Iowa, all for Fremont; Maryland for Fillmore.

[68] Tennessee and Kentucky.

[69] Dred Scott, plff. in error, *vs.* Sandford, Sup. Ct. of U.S. Dec. Term, 1856, 19 Howard, 393. After the conclusion of this case Scott was given his freedom by his master.

[70] *Ante*, pp. 94, 95.

[71] August 24, 1855; Holland, 145.

[72] For a good sketch of Douglas, see Elaine, *Twenty Years of Congress*, i. 144.

[73] This doctrine was set forth by Douglas in a speech at Springfield, Ill., June 12, 1857. A fortnight later, June 26, at the same place, Lincoln answered this speech. N. and H. ii. 85-89.

[74] By 11,300 against 1,788, August 2, 1858. Kansas was admitted as a State at the close of January, 1861, after many of the Southern States had already seceded.

CHAPTER V
THE LINCOLN-DOUGLAS JOINT DEBATE

About this time Lincoln again became active in the politics of his State, aiding in the formation of the Republican party there. On May 29, 1856, a state convention of "all opponents of anti-Nebraska legislation" was held at Bloomington. After "a platform ringing with strong anti-Nebraska sentiments" had been adopted, Lincoln, "in response to repeated calls, came forward and delivered a speech of such earnestness and power that no one who heard it will ever forget the effect it produced." It was "never written out or printed," which is to be regretted; but it lives in one of those vivid descriptions by Herndon which leave nothing to the imagination. For the moment this triumph was gratifying; but when Lincoln, leaving the hot enthusiasts of Bloomington, came home to his fellow townsmen at Springfield, he passed into a chill atmosphere of indifference and disapproval. An effort was made to gather a mass meeting in order to ratify the action of the state convention. But the "mass" consisted of three persons, viz., Abraham Lincoln, Herndon, and one John Pain. It was trying, but Lincoln was finely equal to the occasion; in a few words, passing from jest to earnest, he said that the meeting was larger than he *knew* it would be; for while he knew that he and his partner would attend, he was not sure of any one else; and yet another man had been found brave enough to come out. But, "while all seems dead, the age itself is not. It liveth as sure as our Maker liveth. Under all this seeming want of life and motion the world does move, nevertheless. Be hopeful, and now let us adjourn and appeal to the people!"

In the presidential campaign of 1856 the Republicans of Illinois put Lincoln on their electoral ticket, and he entered into the campaign promptly and very zealously. Traveling untiringly to and fro, he made about fifty speeches. By the quality of these, even more than by their number, he became the champion of the party, so that pressing demands for him came from the neighboring States. He was even heard of in the East. But there he encountered a lack of appreciation and in some quarters an hostility which he felt to be hurtful to his prospects as well as unjust towards a leading Republican of the Northwest. Horace Greeley, enthusiastic, well meaning, ever blundering, the editor of the New York "Tribune," cast the powerful influence of that sheet against him; and as the senatorial contest of 1858 was approaching, in which Lincoln hoped to be a principal, this ill feeling was very unfortunate. [75] "I fear," he said, "that Greeley's attitude will damage me with Sumner, Seward, Wilson, Phillips, and other friends in the East," —and by the way, it is interesting to note this significant list of political "friends." Thereupon Herndon, as guardian of Lincoln's political prospects, went to pass the opening months of the important year upon a crusade among the great men of the East, designing to extinguish the false lights erroneously hung out by persons ignorant of the truth. Erelong he cheered Lincoln by encouraging accounts of success, and of kind words spoken by many Eastern magnates.

In 1858, ability, courage, activity, ambition, the prestige of success, and a plausible moderation in party politics combined to make Douglas the most conspicuous individual in the public view. There was no other way whereby any other man could so surely attract the close and interested attention of the whole people as by meeting Douglas in direct personal competition. If Douglas had not held the position which he did, or if, holding it, he had lived in another State than Illinois, Lincoln might never have been President of the United States. But the essential facts lay favorably for effecting that presentation before the people which was indispensable for his fortunes. In April, 1858, the Democratic State Convention of Illinois indorsed the position which Douglas had taken in the Kansas business. This involved that the party should present him as its candidate for reëlection to the national Senate by the legislature whose members were to be chosen in the following autumn. "In the very nature of things," says the enthusiastic Herndon, Lincoln was at once selected by the Republicans, and on June 16 their convention resolved that "Hon. Abraham Lincoln is our first and only choice for United States senator to fill the vacancy about to be created by the expiration of Mr. Douglas's term of office." Immediately the popular excitement gave measure of the estimate placed upon the two men by those who most accurately knew their qualities. All Illinoisians looked forward eagerly to the fine spectacle of a battle royal between real leaders.

The general political condition was extremely confused. The great number of worthy citizens, who had been wont to save themselves from the worry of critical thought in political matters by the simple process of uniform allegiance to a party, now found the old familiar organizations rapidly disintegrating. They were dismayed and bewildered at the scene; everywhere there were new cries, new standards, new leaders, while small bodies of recruits, displaying in strange union old comrades beside old foes, were crossing to and fro and changing relationships, to the inextricable confusion of the situation. In such a chaos each man was driven to do his own thinking, to discover his genuine beliefs, and to determine in what company he could stand enduringly in the troublous times ahead. It was one of those periods in which small men are laid aside and great leaders are recognized by popular instinct; when the little band that is in deepest earnest becomes endowed with a force which compels the mass of careless, temporizing human-kind to gravitate towards it. Such bands were now the Abolitionists at the North and the Secessionists at the South. Between them lay the nation, disquieted, contentious, and more than a little angry at the prevalent discomfort and alarm. At the North nine men out of ten cared far less for any principle, moral or political, than they did for the discovery of some course whereby this unwelcome conflict between slavery and freedom could be prevented from disorganizing the course of daily life and business; and since the Abolitionists were generally charged with being in great measure responsible for the present menacing condition, they were regarded with bitter animosity by a large number of their fellow citizens. The Secessionists were not in equal disfavor at the South, yet they were still very much in the minority, even in the Gulf States.

Illinois had been pretty stanchly Democratic in times past, but no one could forecast the complexion which she would put on in the coming campaign. The Whigs were gone. The Republican party, though so lately born, yet had already traversed the period of infancy and perhaps also that of youth; men guessed wildly how many voters would now cast its ballot. On the other hand, the Democrats were suffering from internal quarrels. The friends of Douglas, and all moderate Democrats, declared him to be the leader of the Democracy; but Southern conventions and newspapers were angrily "reading him out" of the party, and the singular spectacle was witnessed of the Democratic administration sending out its orders to all Federal office-holders in Illinois to oppose the Democratic nominee, even to the point of giving the election to the Republicans; for if discipline was to exist, a defection like that of which Douglas had been guilty must be punished with utter and everlasting destruction at any cost. This schism of course made the numerical uncertainties even more uncertain than they rightfully should have been. Yet, in an odd way, the same fact worked also against Lincoln; for Douglas's recent votes against the pro-slavery measures of the administration for the admission of Kansas, together with his own direct statements on recent occasions, had put him in a light which misled many Northern anti-slavery men, whose perception did not penetrate to the core-truth. For example, not only Greeley, but Henry Wilson, Burlingame, Washburne, Colfax, and more, really believed that Douglas was turning his back upon his whole past career, and that this brilliant political strategist was actually bringing into the anti-slavery camp [76] all his accumulations of prestige, popularity, and experience, all his seductive eloquence, his skill, and his grand mastery over men. Blinded by the dazzling prospect, they gave all their influence in favor of this priceless recruit, forgetting that, if he were in fact such an apostate as they believed him to be, he would come to them terribly shrunken in value and trustworthiness. Some even were so infatuated as to insist that the Republicans of Illinois ought to present no candidate against him. Fortunately the Illinoisians knew their fellow citizen better; yet in so strange a jumble no one could deny that it was a doubtful conflict in which these two rivals were joining.

Lincoln had expected to be nominated, and during several weeks he had been thinking over his speech of acceptance. However otherwise he might seem at any time to be engaged, he was ceaselessly turning over this matter in his mind; and frequently he stopped short to jot down an idea or expression upon some scrap of paper, which then he thrust into his hat. Thus, piece by piece, the accumulation grew alike inside and outside of his head, and at last he took all his fragments and with infinite consideration moulded them into unity. So studiously had he wrought that by the time of delivery he had unconsciously committed the whole speech accurately to memory. If so much painstaking seemed to indicate an exaggerated notion of the importance of his words, he was soon vindicated by events; for what he said was subjected to a dissection and a criticism such as have not often pursued the winged words of the orator. When at last the composition was completed, he gathered a small coterie of his friends and admirers, and read it to them. The opening paragraph was as follows:—

"If we could first know where we are, and whither we are tending, we could better judge what to do and how to do it. We are now far into the fifth year since a policy was initiated with the avowed object and confident promise of putting an end to slavery agitation. Under the operation of that policy, that agitation has not only not ceased, but has constantly augmented. In my opinion, it will not cease until a crisis shall have been reached and passed. 'A house divided against itself cannot stand.' I believe this government cannot endure permanently half slave and half free. I do not expect the Union to be dissolved,—I do not expect the house to fall,—but I do expect it will cease to be divided. It will become all one thing or all the other. Either the opponents of slavery will arrest the further spread of it, and place it where the public mind shall rest in the belief that it is in the course of ultimate extinction; or its advocates will push it forward, till it shall become alike lawful in all the States, old as well as new,—North as well as South."

As the reader watched for the effect of this exordium he only saw disapproval and consternation. His assembled advisers and critics, each and all save only the fiery Herndon, protested that language so daring and advanced would work a ruin that might not be mended in years. Lincoln heard their condemnation with gravity rather than surprise. But he had worked his way to a conviction, and he was immovable; all he said was, that the statement was true, right, and just, that it was time it should be made, and that he would make it, even though he might have "to go down with it;" that he would "rather be defeated with this expression in the speech ... than to be victorious without it." Accordingly, on the next day he spoke the paragraph without the change of a word.

It is not without effort that we can now appreciate fully why this utterance was so momentous in the spring of 1858. [77] By it Lincoln came before the people with a plain statement of precisely that which more than nine hundred and ninety-nine persons in every thousand, especially at the North, were striving with all their might to stamp down as an untruth; he said to them what they all were denying with desperation, and with rage against the asserters. Their bitterness was the greater because very many, in the bottom of their hearts, distrusted their own painful and strenuous denial. No words could be more unpopular than that the divided house could not permanently stand, when the whole nation was insisting, with the intensity of despair, that it could stand, would stand, must stand. Consequently occurrences soon showed his friends to be right so far as concerned the near, practical point: that the paragraph would cost more voters in Illinois than Lincoln could lose without losing his election. But beyond that point, a little farther away in time, much deeper down amid enduring results, Lincoln's judgment was ultimately seen to rest upon fundamental wisdom, politically as well as morally. For Lincoln was no idealist, sacrificing realities to abstractions; on the contrary, the right which he saw was always a practical right, a right which could be compassed. In this instance, the story goes that he retorted upon some of those who grumbled about his "mistake," that in time they "would consider it the wisest thing he ever said." In this he foretold truly; that daring and strong utterance was the first link in the chain of which a more distant link lay across the threshold of the White House.

A battle opened by so resounding a shot was sure to be furious. Writers and speakers fell upon the fateful paragraph and tore it savagely. They found in it a stimulus which, in fact, was not needed; for already were present all the elements of the fiercest struggle,—the best man and the best fighter in each party at the front, and not unevenly matched; a canvass most close and doubtful; and a question which stirred the souls of men with the passions of crusading days. Douglas added experience and distinction to gallantry in attack, adroitness in defense, readiness in personalities, and natural aptitude for popular oratory. Lincoln frankly admitted his formidable qualifications. But the Republican managers had a shrewd appreciation of both opponents;

they saw that Lincoln's forte lay in hitting out straight, direct, and hard; and they felt that blows of the kind he delivered should not go out into the air, but should alight upon a concrete object,—upon Douglas. They conceived a wise plan. On July 24, 1858, Lincoln challenged Douglas to a series of joint debates. Douglas accepted, and named seven meetings, which he so arranged that he opened and closed four times and Lincoln opened and closed three times; but Lincoln made no point of the inequality; the arrangement was completed, and this famous duel constituted another link in that White House chain.

The setting of the spectacle had the picturesqueness of the times and the region. The people gathered in vast multitudes, to the number of ten thousand, even of twenty thousand, at the places named for the speech-making; they came in their wagons from all the country round, bringing provisions, and making camps in the groves and fields. There were bonfires and music, parading and drinking. He was a singular man in Illinois who was not present at some one of these encounters.

Into a competition so momentous Lincoln entered with a full appreciation of the burden and responsibility which it put upon him. He had at once to meet a false gloss of his famous sentence; and though he had been very precise and accurate in his phraseology for the express purpose of escaping misinterpretation, yet it would have been a marvel in applied political morals if the paraphrases devised by Douglas had been strictly ingenuous. The favorite distortion was to alter what was strictly a forecast into a declaration of a policy, to make a prediction pass for an avowal of a purpose to wage war against slavery until either the "institution" or "Abolitionism" should be utterly defeated and forever exterminated. It was said to be a "doctrine" which was "revolutionary and destructive of this government," and which "invited a warfare between the North and the South, to be carried on with ruthless vengeance, until the one section or the other shall be driven to the wall and become the victim of the rapacity of the other." Such misrepresentation annoyed Lincoln all the more because it was undeserved. The history of the utterance thus maltreated illustrates the deliberate, cautious, thorough way in which his mind worked. So long ago as August 15, 1855, he had closed a letter with the paragraph: "Our political problem now is: Can we, as a nation, continue together *permanently—forever*, half slave and half free? The problem is too mighty for me. May God in his mercy superintend the solution." [78] This is one among many instances which show how studiously Lincoln pondered until he had got his conclusion into that simple shape in which it was immutable. When he had found a form which satisfied him for the expression of a conviction, he was apt to use it repeatedly rather than to seek new and varied shapes, so that substantially identical sentences often recur at distant intervals of time and place.

When one has been long studying with much earnest intensity of thought a perplexing and moving question, and at last frames a conclusion with painstaking precision in perfectly clear language, it is not pleasant to have that accurate utterance misstated with tireless reiteration, and with infinite art and plausibility. But for this vexation Lincoln could find no remedy, and it was in vain that he again and again called attention to the fact that he had expressed neither a "doctrine," nor an "invitation," nor any "purpose" or policy whatsoever. But as it seemed not altogether courageous to leave his position in doubt, he said: "Now, it is singular enough, if you will carefully read that passage over, that I did not say in it that I was in favor of anything. I only said what I expected would take place.... I did not even say that I desired that slavery should be put in course of ultimate extinction. I do say so now, however, so there need be no longer any difficulty about that." He felt that nothing short of such extinction would surely prevent the revival of a dispute which had so often been settled *"forever."* "We can no more foretell," he said, "where the end of this slavery agitation will be than we can see the end of the world itself.... There is no way of putting an end to the slavery agitation amongst us but to put it back upon the basis where our fathers placed it.... Then the public mind will rest in the belief that it is in the course of ultimate extinction."

There was much of this eloquence about "the fathers," much evocation of the shades of the great departed, who, having reached the eternal silence, could be claimed by both sides. The contention was none the less strenuous because it was entirely irrelevant; since the opinion of "the fathers" could not make slavery right or wrong. Many times therefore did Douglas charge Lincoln with having said "that the Union could not endure divided as our fathers made it, with free and slave States;" as though this were a sort of blasphemy against the national demigods. Lincoln aptly retorted that, as matter of fact, these same distinguished "fathers" — "Washington, Jefferson, Franklin, Madison, Hamilton, Jay, and the great men of that day" — did not *make*, but *found*, the nation half slave and half free; that they set "many clear marks of disapprobation" upon slavery, and left it so situated that the popular mind rested in the belief that it was in the course of ultimate extinction. Unfortunately it had not been allowed to remain as they had left it; but on the contrary, "all the trouble and convulsion has proceeded from the efforts to spread it over more territory."

Pursuing this line, Lincoln alleged the purpose of the pro-slavery men to make slavery "perpetual and universal" and "national." In his great speech of acceptance at Springfield he put this point so well that he never improved upon this first presentation of it. The repeal of the Missouri Compromise in 1854 "opened all the national territory to slavery, and was the first point gained. But so far Congress only had acted, and an indorsement by the people, real or imaginary," was obtained by "the notable argument of 'squatter sovereignty,' otherwise called 'sacred right of self-government,' which latter phrase, though expressive of the only rightful basis of any government, was so perverted in this attempted use of it as to amount to just this: that if any *one* man choose to enslave *another*, no *third* man shall be permitted to object. That argument was incorporated into the Nebraska bill." In May, 1854, this bill was passed. Then the presidential election came. "Mr. Buchanan was elected, and the indorsement was secured. That was the second point gained." Meantime the celebrated case of the negro, Dred Scott, was pending in the Supreme Court, and the "President in his inaugural address fervently exhorted the people to abide by the forthcoming decision, whatever it might be. Then in a few days came the decision," which was at once emphatically indorsed by Douglas, "the reputed author of the Nebraska bill," and by the new President.

"At length a squabble springs up between the President and the author of the Nebraska bill on the mere question of *fact*, whether the Lecompton Constitution was or was not, in any just sense, made by the people of Kansas; and in that quarrel the latter declares that all he wants is a fair vote for the people, and that he cares not whether slavery be voted *down* or voted *up*.

... "The several points of the Dred Scott decision in connection with Senator Douglas's 'care not' policy constitute the piece of machinery in its present state of advancement. This was the third point gained.

... "We cannot absolutely know that all these exact adaptations are the result of preconcert. But when we see a lot of framed timbers, different portions of which we know have been gotten out at different times and places and by different workmen, —Stephen, Franklin, Roger, and James, for instance,—and when we see these timbers joined together, and see they exactly make the frame of a house or a mill, all the tenons and mortices exactly fitting, and all the lengths and proportions of the different pieces exactly adapted to their respective places, and not a piece too many or too few,—not omitting even scaffolding; or, if a single piece be lacking, we see the place in the frame exactly fitted and prepared yet to bring such piece in,—in such a case, we find it impossible not to believe that Stephen and Franklin and Roger and James all understood one another from the beginning, and all worked upon a common plan or draft drawn up before the first blow was struck.

"It should not be overlooked that by the Nebraska bill the people of a *State* as well as a Territory were to be left 'perfectly free,' 'subject only to the Constitution.' Why mention a *State*?... Why is mention of this lugged into this merely territorial law?

... "Put this and that together, and we have another nice little niche, which we may erelong see filled with another Supreme Court decision, declaring that the Constitution of the United States does not permit a *State* to exclude slavery from its limits. And this may especially be expected if the doctrine of 'care not whether slavery be voted down or voted up' shall gain upon the public mind sufficiently to give promise that such a decision can be maintained when made. Such a decision is all that slavery now lacks of being alike lawful in all the States." Following out this idea, Lincoln repeatedly put to Douglas a question to which he could never get a direct answer from his nimble antagonist: "If a decision is made, holding that the people of the *States* cannot exclude slavery, will he support it, or not?"

Even so skillful a dialectician as Douglas found this compact structure of history and argument a serious matter. Its simple solidity was not so susceptible to treatment by the perverting process as had been the figurative and prophetic utterance about the "house divided against itself." Neither could he find a chink between the facts and the inferences. One aspect of the speech, however, could not be passed over. Lincoln said that he had not charged "Stephen and Franklin and Roger and James" with collusion and conspiracy; but he admitted that he had "arrayed the evidence tending to prove," and which he "thought did prove," these things. [79] It was impossible for the four distinguished gentlemen [80] who owned the rest of these names to refuse to plead. Accordingly Douglas sneered vehemently at the idea that two presidents, the chief justice, and he himself had been concerned in that grave crime against the State which was imputed to them; and when, by his lofty indignation, he had brought his auditors into sympathy, he made the only possible reply: that the real meaning, the ultimate logical outcome, of what Lincoln had said was, that a decision of the Supreme Court was to be set aside by the political action of the people at the polls. The Supreme Court had interpreted the Constitution, and Lincoln was inciting the people to annul that interpretation by some political process not known to the law. For himself, he proclaimed with effective emphasis his allegiance to that great tribunal in the performance of its constitutional duties. Lincoln replied that he also bowed to the Dred Scott decision in the specific case; but he repudiated it as a binding rule in political action. [81] His point seemed more obscure than was usual with him, and not satisfactory as an answer to Douglas. But as matter of fact no one was deceived by the amusing adage of the profession: that the courts do not *make* the law, but only *declare what it is*. Every one knew that the law was just what the judges chose from time to time to say that it was, and that if judicial *declarations* of the law were not reversed quite so often as legislative *makings* of the law were repealed, it was only because the identity of a bench is usually of longer duration than the identity of a legislative body. If the people, politically, willed the reversal of the Dred Scott decision, it was sure in time to be judicially reversed. [82]

Douglas boasted that the Democrats were a national party, whereas the "Black Republicans" were a sectional body whose creed could not be uttered south of Mason and Dixon's line. He was assiduous in fastening upon Lincoln the name of "Abolitionist," and "Black Republican," epithets so unpopular that those who held the faith often denied the title, and he only modified them by the offensive admission that Lincoln's doctrines were sometimes disingenuously weakened to suit certain audiences: "His principles in the north [of Illinois] are jet black; in the centre they are in color a decent mulatto; and in lower Egypt [83] they are almost white."

Concerning sectionalism, Lincoln countered fairly enough on his opponent by asking: Was it, then, the case that it was slavery which was national, and freedom which was sectional? Or, "Is it the true test of the soundness of a doctrine that in some places people won't let you proclaim it?" But the remainder of Douglas's assault was by no means to be disposed of by quick retort. When Lincoln was pushed to formulate accurately his views concerning the proper status of the negro in the community, he had need of all his extraordinary care in statement. Herein lay problems that were vexing many honest citizens and clever men besides himself, and were breeding much disagreement among persons who all were anti-slavery in a general way, but could by no means reach a comfortable unison concerning troublesome particulars. The "all men free and equal" of the Constitution, and the talk about human brotherhood, gave the Democrats wide scope for harassing anti-slavery men with vexatious taunts and embarrassing cross-interrogatories on practical points. "I do not question," said Douglas, "Mr. Lincoln's conscientious belief that the negro was made his equal, and hence is his brother. But for my own part, I do not regard the negro as my equal, and positively deny that he is my brother, or any kin to me whatever." He said that "the signers of the Declaration had no reference to the negro,... or any other inferior and degraded race, when they spoke of the equality of men," but meant only "white men, of European birth and descent." This topic opens the whole subject of Lincoln's political affiliations and of his opinions concerning slavery and the negro, opinions which seem to have undergone no substantial change during the interval betwixt this campaign and his election to the presidency. Some selections from what he said may sufficiently explain his position.

At Freeport, August 27, replying to a series of questions from Douglas, he declared that he had supposed himself, "since the organization of the Republican party at Bloomington, in May, 1856, bound as a party man by the platforms of the party, then and since." He said: "I do not now, nor ever did, stand in favor of the unconditional repeal of the Fugitive Slave Law." He believed that under the Constitution the Southerners were entitled to such a law; but thought that the existing law "should have been framed so as to be free from some of the objections that pertain to it, without lessening its efficiency." He would not "introduce it as a new subject of agitation upon the general question of slavery."

He should be "exceedingly sorry" ever to have to pass upon the question of admitting more slave States into the Union, and exceedingly glad to know that another never would be admitted. But "if slavery shall be kept out of the Territories during the territorial existence of any one given Territory, and then the people shall, having a fair chance and a clear field, when they come to adopt their constitution, do such an extraordinary thing as to adopt a slave constitution, uninfluenced by the actual presence of the institution among them, I see no alternative, if we own the country, but to admit them into the Union." He should also, he said, be "exceedingly glad to see slavery abolished in the District of Columbia," and he believed that Congress had "constitutional power to abolish it" there; but he would favor the measure only upon condition: "First, that the abolition should be gradual; second, that it should be on a vote of the majority of qualified voters in the District; and, third, that compensation should be made to unwilling owners." As to the abolition of the slave trade between the different States, he acknowledged that he had not considered the matter sufficiently to have reached a conclusion concerning it. But if he should think that Congress had power to effect such abolition, he should "not be in favor of the exercise of that power unless upon some conservative principle, akin to what I have said in relation to the abolition of slavery in the District of Columbia." As to the territorial controversy, he said: "I am impliedly, if not expressly, pledged to a belief in the *right* and *duty* of Congress to prohibit slavery in all the United States Territories." Concerning the acquisition of new territory he said: "I am not generally opposed to honest acquisition of territory; and in any given case I would or would not oppose such acquisition, according as I might think such acquisition would or would not aggravate the slavery question among ourselves." The statement derived its immediate importance from the well-known purpose of the administration and a considerable party in the South very soon to acquire Cuba. All these utterances were certainly clear enough, and were far from constituting Abolitionist doctrine, though they were addressed to an audience "as strongly tending to Abolitionism as any audience in the State of Illinois," and Mr. Lincoln believed that he was saying "that which, if it would be offensive to any person and render them enemies to himself, would be offensive to persons in this audience."

At Quincy Lincoln gave his views concerning Republicanism with his usual unmistakable accuracy, and certainly he again differentiated it widely from Abolitionism. The Republican party, he said, think slavery "a moral, a social, and a political wrong." Any man who does not hold this opinion "is misplaced and ought to leave us. While, on the other hand, if there be any man in the Republican party who is impatient over the necessity springing from its actual presence, and is impatient of the constitutional guarantees thrown around it, and would act in disregard of these, he, too, is misplaced, standing with us. He will find his place somewhere else; for we have a due regard ... for all these things." ... "I have always hated slavery as much as any Abolitionist,... but I have always been quiet about it until this new era of the introduction of the Nebraska bill again." He repeated often that he had "no purpose, directly or indirectly, to interfere with the institution of slavery in the States where it exists;" that he had "no lawful right to do so," and "no inclination to do so." He said that his declarations as to the right of the negro to "life, liberty, and the pursuit of happiness" were designed only to refer to legislation "about any new country which is not already cursed with the actual presence of the evil,—slavery." He denied having ever "manifested any impatience with the necessities that spring from the ... actual existence of slavery among us, where it does already exist."

He dwelt much upon the equality clause of the Declaration. If we begin "making exceptions to it, where will it stop? If one man says it does not mean a negro, why not another say it does not mean some other man?" Only within three years past had any one doubted that negroes were included by this language. But he said that, while the authors "intended to include *all* men, they did not mean to declare all men equal *in all respects*,... in color, size, intellect, moral development, or social capacity," but only "equal in certain inalienable rights." "Anything that argues me into his [Douglas's] idea of perfect social and political equality with the negro is but a specious and fantastic arrangement of words, by which a man can prove a horse chestnut to be a chestnut horse.... I have no purpose to produce political and social equality between the white and the black races. There is a physical difference between the two, which, in my judgment, will probably forever forbid their living together upon the footing of perfect equality; and inasmuch as it becomes a necessity that there must be a difference, I, as well as Judge Douglas, am in favor of the race to which I belong having the superior position.... But I hold that ... there is no reason in the world why the negro is not entitled to all the natural rights enumerated in the Declaration of Independence, the right to life, liberty, and the pursuit of happiness. I hold that he is as much entitled to these as the white man. I agree with Judge Douglas that he is not my equal in many respects, —certainly not in color, perhaps not in moral or intellectual endowment. But in the right to eat the bread, without the leave of anybody else, which his own hand earns, *he is my equal, and the equal of Judge Douglas, and the equal of every living man.*" Later at Charleston he reiterated much of this in almost identical language, and then in his turn took his fling at Douglas: "I am not in favor of making voters or jurors of negroes, nor of qualifying them to hold office, nor to intermarry with white people.... I do not understand that because I do not want a negro woman for a slave I must necessarily want her for a wife. My understanding is that I can just let her alone.... I have never had the least apprehension that I or my friends would marry negroes, if there was no law to keep them from it; but as Judge Douglas and his friends seem to be in great apprehension that *they* might, if there were no law to keep them from it, I give him the most solemn pledge that I will to the very last stand by the law of this State, which forbids the marrying of white people with negroes."

By all this it is made entirely evident that Lincoln held a faith widely different from that of the great crusading leaders of Abolitionism at the East. [84] Equally marked was the difference between him and them in the matters of temper and of the attitude taken towards opponents. The absence of any sense of personal hostility towards those who assailed him with unsparing vindictiveness was a trait often illustrated in his after life, and which was now noted with surprise, for it was rare in the excited politics of those days. In this especial campaign both contestants honestly intended to refrain from personalities, but the difference between their ways of doing so was marked. Douglas, under the temptation of high ability in that line, held himself in check by an effort which was often obvious and not always entirely successful. But Lincoln never seemed moved by the desire. "All I have to ask," he said, "is that we talk reasonably and rationally;" and again: "I hope to deal in all things fairly with Judge Douglas." No innuendo, no artifice, in any speech, gave the lie to these protestations. Besides this, his denunciations were always against *slavery*, and never against *slaveholders*. The emphasis of condemnation, the intensity of feeling, were never expended against persons. By this course, unusual among the Abolitionists, he not only lost nothing in force and impressiveness, but, on the contrary, his attack seemed to gain in effectiveness by being directed against no personal object, but exclusively against a practice. His war was against slavery, not against the men and women of the South who owned slaves. At Ottawa he read from the Peoria speech of 1854: "I have no prejudice against the Southern people. They are just what we would [should] be in their situation. If slavery did not now exist among them, they would not introduce it. If it did now exist among us, we should not instantly give it up.... It does seem to me that systems of gradual emancipation might be adopted; but for their tardiness in this, I will not undertake to judge our brethren of the South." Repeatedly he admitted the difficulty of the problem, and fastened no blame upon those Southerners who excused themselves for not expelling the evil on the ground that they did not know how to do so. At Peoria he said: "If all earthly power were given me, I should not know what to do as to the existing institution." He contributed some suggestions which certainly were nothing better than chimerical. Deportation to Africa was his favorite scheme; he also proposed that it would be "best for all concerned to have the colored population in a State by themselves." But he did not abuse men who declined to adopt his methods. Though he was dealing with a question which was arousing personal antagonisms as bitter as any that history records, yet he never condemned any one, nor ever passed judgment against his fellow men.

Diagnosis would perhaps show that the trait thus illustrated was mental rather than moral. This absence of animosity and reproach as towards individuals found its root not so much in human charity as in fairness of thinking. Lincoln's ways of mental working are not difficult to discover. He thought slowly, cautiously, profoundly, and with a most close accuracy; but above all else he *thought fairly*. This capacity far transcended, or, more correctly, differed from, what is ordinarily called the judicial habit of mind. Many men can weigh arguments without letting prejudice get into either scale; but Lincoln carried on the whole process of thinking, not only with an equal clearness of perception, but also with an entire impartiality of liking or disliking for both sides. His aim, while he was engaged in thinking, was to discover what was really true; and later when he spoke to others his purpose was to show them the truth which he had discovered, and to state to them on what grounds he believed it to be the truth; it did not involve a judgment against the individuals who failed to recognize that truth. His singular trait of impersonality was not made more apparent in any other way. His effort never was to defeat the person who happened to be his adversary, but always was to overcome the arguments of that adversary. Primarily he was discussing a topic and establishing a truth; it was only incidental that in doing these things he had to oppose a man. It is noteworthy that his opponents never charged him with misstating their case in order to make an apparently effective answer to it. On the contrary, his hope of success seemed always to lie in having both sides presented with the highest degree of clearness and honesty. He had perfect confidence in the ultimate triumph of the truth; he was always willing to tie fast to it, according as he could see it, and then to bide time with it. This being a genuine faith and not mere lip-service, he used the same arguments to others which he used to himself, and staked his final success upon the probability that what had persuaded his mind would in time persuade also the minds of other intelligent men. It has been well said of him by an excellent judge: "He loved the truth for the truth's sake. He would not argue from a false premise, or be deceived himself, or deceive others, by a false conclusion.... He did not seek to say merely the thing which was best for that day's debate, but the thing which would stand the test of time, and square itself with eternal justice.... His logic was severe and faultless. He did not resort to fallacy." [85]

To return to the points made in the debate: Douglas laid down the "great principle of non-interference and non-intervention by Congress with slavery in the States and Territories alike;" which he assured his audience would enable us to "continue at peace with one another." In the same connection he endeavored to silver-coat for Northern palates the bitter pill of the Dred Scott decision, by declaring that the people of any State or Territory might withhold that protecting legislation, those "friendly police regulations," without which slavery could not exist. But this was, indeed, a "lame, illogical, evasive answer," which enabled Lincoln to "secure an advantage in the national relations of the contest which he held to the end."

Lincoln, in replying, agreed that "all the States have the right to do exactly as they please about all their domestic relations, including that of slavery." But he said that the proposition that slavery could not enter a new country without police regulations was historically false; and that the facts of the Dred Scott case itself showed that there was "vigor enough in slavery to plant itself in a new country even against unfriendly legislation." Beyond this issue of historical fact, Douglas had already taken and still dared to maintain a position which proved to be singularly ill chosen. The right to hold slaves as property in the Territories had lately, to the infinite joy of the South, been declared by the Supreme Court to be guaranteed by the Constitution; and now Douglas had the audacity to repeat that notion of his, so abhorrent to all friends of slavery,—that this invaluable right could be made practically worthless by unfriendly local legislation, or even by the negative hostility of withholding friendly legislation! From the moment when this deadly suggestion fell from his ingenious lips, the Southern Democracy turned upon him with vindictive hate and marked him for destruction. He had also given himself into the hands of his avowed and natural enemies. The doctrine, said Mr. Lincoln, is "no less than that a thing may lawfully be driven away from a place where it has a lawful right to be." "If you were elected members of the legislature, what would be the first thing you would have to do, before entering upon your duties? *Swear to support the Constitution of the United States.* Suppose you believe, as Judge Douglas does, that the Constitution of the United States guarantees to your neighbor the right to hold slaves in that Territory,—that they are his property,—how can you clear your oaths, unless you give him such legislation as is necessary to enable him to enjoy that property? What do you understand by supporting the Constitution of a State, or of the United States? Is it not to give such constitutional helps to the rights established by that Constitution as may be practically needed?... And what I say here will hold with still more force against the judge's doctrine of 'unfriendly legislation.' How could you, having sworn to support the Constitution, and believing it guaranteed the right to hold slaves in the Territories, assist in legislation *intended to defeat that right?*" "Is not Congress itself under obligation to give legislative support to any right that is established under the United States Constitution?" Upon what other principle do "many of us, who are opposed to slavery upon principle, give our acquiescence to a Fugitive Slave Law?" Does Douglas mean to say that a territorial legislature, "by passing unfriendly laws," can "*nullify a constitutional right?*" He put to Douglas the direct and embarrassing query: "If the slaveholding citizens of a United States Territory should need and demand congressional legislation for the protection of their slave property in such Territory, would you, as a member of Congress, vote for or against such legislation?" "Repeat that," cried Douglas, ostentatiously; "I want to answer that question." But he never composed his reply.

Another kindred question had already been put by Lincoln: "Can the people of a United States Territory, in any lawful way, against the wish of any citizen of the United States, exclude slavery from its limits, prior to the formation of a State Constitution?" Friends advised him not to force this, as it seemed against the immediate policy of the present campaign. But it was never his way to subordinate his own deliberate opinion to the opinions of advisers; and on this occasion he was merciless in pressing this question. A story has been very generally repeated that he told the protesters that, whatever might be the bearing on the senatorship, Douglas could not answer that question and be elected President of the United States in 1860. "I am killing larger game," he said; "the battle of 1860 is worth a hundred of this." [86] A few legends of this kind are extant, which tend to indicate that Lincoln already had in mind the presidential nomination, and was fighting the present fight with an eye to that greater one in the near future. It is not easy to say how much credit should be given to such tales; they may not be wholly inventions, but a remark which is uttered with little thought may later easily take on a strong color in the light of subsequent developments.

In presenting the Republican side of the question Lincoln seemed to feel a duty beyond that of merely outarguing his opponent. He bore the weighty burden of a responsibility graver than personal success. He might prevail in the opinions of his fellow citizens; without this instant triumph he might so present his cause that the jury of posterity would declare that the truth lay with him; he might even convince both the present and the coming generations; and though achieving all these triumphs, he might still fall far short of the peculiar and exacting requirement of the occasion. For the winning of the senatorship was the insignificant part of what he had undertaken; his momentous charge was to maintain a grand moral crusade, to stimulate and to vindicate a great uprising in the cause of humanity and of justice. His full appreciation of this is entirely manifest in the tone of his speeches. They have an earnestness, a gravity, at times even a solemnity, unusual in such encounters in any era or before any audiences, but unprecedented "on the stump" before the uproarious gatherings of the West at that day. Repeatedly he stigmatized slavery as "a moral, a social, a political evil." Very impressively he denounced the positions of an opponent who "cared not whether slavery was voted down or voted up," who said that slavery was not to be differentiated from the many domestic institutions and daily affairs which civilized societies control by police regulations. He said that slavery could not be treated as "only equal to the cranberry laws of Indiana;" that slaves could not be put "upon a par with onions and potatoes;" that to Douglas he supposed that the institution really "looked small," but that a great proportion of the American people regarded slavery as "a vast moral evil." "The real issue in this controversy—the one pressing upon every mind—is the sentiment on the part of one class that looks upon the institution of slavery *as a wrong*, and of another class that does *not* look upon it as a wrong.... No man can logically say he does not care whether a wrong is voted up or voted down. He [Douglas] contends that whatever community wants slaves has a right to have them. So they have, if it is not a wrong. But if it is a wrong, he cannot say people have a right to do wrong. He says that, upon the score of equality, slaves should be allowed to go into a new Territory, like other property. This is strictly logical if there is no difference between it and other property.... But if you insist that one is wrong and the other right, there is no use to institute a comparison between right and wrong.... That is the real issue. That is the issue that will continue in this country when these poor tongues of Judge Douglas and myself shall be silent. It is the eternal struggle between these two principles, right and wrong, throughout the world. They are the two principles that have stood face to face from the beginning of time, and will ever continue to struggle. The one is the common right of humanity, and the other the divine right of kings. It is the same principle in whatever shape it develops itself. It is the same spirit that says: 'You work and toil and earn bread, and I'll eat it.'" "I ask you if it is not a false philosophy? Is it not a false statesmanship that undertakes to build up a system of policy upon the basis of caring nothing about *the very thing that everybody does care the most about?*"

We cannot leave these speeches without a word concerning their literary quality. In them we might have looked for vigor that would be a little uncouth, wit that would be often coarse, a logic generally sound but always clumsy,—in a word, tolerably good substance and very poor form. We are surprised, then, to find many and high excellences in art. As it is with Bacon's essays, so it is with these speeches: the more attentively they are read the more striking appears the closeness of their texture both in logic and in language. Clear thought is accurately expressed. Each sentence has its special errand, and each word its individual importance. There is never either too much or too little. The work is done with clean precision and no waste. Nowhere does one pause to seek a meaning or to recover a connection; and an effort to make out a syllabus shows that the most condensed statement has already been used. There are scintillations of wit and humor, but they are not very numerous. When Lincoln was urged to adopt a more popular style, he replied: "The occasion is too serious; the issues are too grave. I do not seek applause, or to amuse the people, but to convince them." This spirit was upon him from the beginning to the end. Had he been addressing a bench of judges, subject to a close limitation of minutes, he would have won credit by the combined economy and force which were displayed in these harangues to general assemblages. To speak of the lofty tone of these speeches comes dangerously near to the distasteful phraseology of extravagant laudation, than which nothing else can produce upon honest men a worse impression. Yet it is a truth visible to every reader that at the outset Lincoln raised the discussion to a very high plane, and held it there throughout. The truth which he had to sustain was so great that it was perfectly simple, and he had the good sense to utter it with appropriate simplicity. In no speech was there fervor or enthusiasm or rhetoric; he talked to the reason and the conscience of his auditors, not to their passions. Yet the depth of his feeling may be measured by the story that once in the canvass he said to a friend: "Sometimes, in the excitement of speaking, I seem to see the end of slavery. I feel that the time is soon coming when the sun shall shine, the rain fall, on no man who shall go forth to unrequited toil. How this will come, when it will come, by whom it will come, I cannot tell,—but that time will surely come." [87] It is just appreciation, and not extravagance, to say that the cheap and miserable little volume, now out of print, containing in bad newspaper type, "The Lincoln and Douglas Debates," [88] holds some of the masterpieces of oratory of all ages and nations.

The immediate result of the campaign was the triumph of Douglas, who had certainly made not only a very able and brilliant but a splendidly gallant fight, with Republicans assailing him in front and Administrationists in rear. [89] Lincoln was disappointed. His feelings had been so deeply engaged, he had worked so strenuously, and the result had been so much in doubt, that defeat was trying. But he bore it with his wonted resolute equanimity. He said that he felt "like the boy that stumped his toe, — 'it hurt too bad to laugh, and he was too big to cry.'" In fact, there were encouraging elements. [90] The popular vote stood, [91] Republicans, 126,084; Douglas Democrats, 121,940; Lecompton Democrats, 5,091. But the apportionment of districts was such that the legislature contained a majority for Douglas. [92] So the prestige of victory seemed separated from its fruits; for the nation, attentively watching this duel, saw that the new man had convinced upwards of four thousand voters more than had the great leader of the Democracy. Douglas is reported to have said that, during his sixteen years in Congress, he had found no man in the Senate whom he would not rather encounter in debate than Lincoln. If it was true that Lincoln was already dreaming of the presidency, he was a sufficiently shrewd politician to see that his prospects were greatly improved by this campaign. He had worked hard for what he had gained; he had been traveling incessantly to and fro and delivering speeches in unbroken succession during about one hundred of the hot days of the Western summer, and speeches not of a commonplace kind, but which severely taxed the speaker. After all was over, he was asked by the state committee to contribute to the campaign purse! He replied: "I am willing to pay according to my ability, but I am the poorest hand living to get others to pay. *I have been on expense* so long, without earning anything, that I am absolutely without money now for even household expenses. Still, if you can put in $250 for me,... I will allow it when you and I settle the private matter between us. This, with what I have already paid,... will exceed my subscription of $500. This, too, is exclusive of my ordinary expenses during the campaign, all of which being added to my loss of time and business bears pretty heavily upon one no better off than I am.... You are feeling badly; 'and this, too, shall pass away;' never fear."

The platform which, with such precision and painstaking, Lincoln had constructed for himself was made by him even more ample and more strong by a few speeches delivered in the interval between the close of this great campaign and his nomination by the Republicans for the presidency. In Ohio an important canvass for the governorship took place, and Douglas went there, and made speeches filled with allusions to Lincoln and the recent Illinois campaign. Even without this provocation Lincoln knew, by keen instinct, that where Douglas was, there he should be also. In no other way had he yet appeared to such advantage as in encountering "the Little Giant." To Ohio, accordingly, he hastened, and spoke at Columbus and at Cincinnati. [93] To the citizens of the latter place he said: "This is the first time in my life that I have appeared before an audience in so great a city as this. I therefore make this appearance under some degree of embarrassment." There was little novelty in substance, but much in treatment. Thus, at Cincinnati, he imagined himself addressing Kentuckians, and showed them that their next nominee for the presidency ought to be his "distinguished friend, Judge Douglas;" for "in all that there is a difference between you and him, I understand he is sincerely for you, and more wisely for you than you are for yourselves." Through him alone pro-slavery men retained any hold upon the free States of the North; and in those States, "in every possible way he can, he constantly moulds the public opinion to your ends." Ingeniously but fairly he sketched Douglas as the most efficient among the pro-slavery leaders. Perhaps the clever and truthful picture may have led Mr. Greeley and some other gentlemen at the East to suspect that they had been inconsiderate in their choice between the Western rivals; and perhaps, also, Lincoln, while addressing imaginary Kentuckians, had before his inner eye some Eastern auditors. For at the time he did not know that his voice would ever be heard at any point nearer to their ears than the hall in which he then stood. Within a few weeks, however, this unlooked-for good fortune befell. In October, 1859, he was invited to speak in the following winter in New York. That the anti-slavery men of that city wished to test him by personal observation signified that his reputation was national, and that the highest aspirations were, therefore, not altogether presumptuous. He accepted gladly, and immediately began to prepare an address which probably cost him more labor than any other speech which he ever made. He found time, however, in December to make a journey through Kansas, where he delivered several speeches, which have not been preserved but are described as "repetitions of those previously made in Illinois." Lamon tells us that the journey was an "ovation," and that "wherever Lincoln went, he was met by vast assemblages of people." The population of this agricultural State was hardly in a condition to furnish "vast assemblages" at numerous points, but doubtless the visitor received gratifying assurance that upon this battle-ground of slavery and anti-slavery the winning party warmly appreciated his advocacy of their cause.

On Saturday, February 25, 1860, Lincoln arrived in New York. On Monday his hosts "found him dressed in a sleek and shining suit of new black, covered with very apparent creases and wrinkles, acquired by being packed too closely and too long in his little valise. He felt uneasy in his new clothes and a strange place." Certainly nothing in his previous experience had prepared him to meet with entire indifference an audience of metropolitan critics; indeed, had the surroundings been more familiar, he had enough at stake to tax his equanimity when William Cullen Bryant introduced him simply as "an eminent citizen of the West, hitherto known to you only by reputation." Probably the first impression made upon those auditors by the ungainly Westerner in his outlandish garb were not the same which they carried home with them a little later. The speech was so condensed that a sketch of it is not possible. Fortunately it had the excellent quality of steadily expanding in interest and improving to the end.

Of the Dred Scott case he cleverly said that the courts had decided it *"in a sort of way;"* but, after all, the decision was "mainly based upon a mistaken statement of fact,—the statement in the opinion that 'the right of property in a slave is distinctly and expressly affirmed in the Constitution.'"

In closing, he begged the Republicans, in behalf of peace and harmony, to "do nothing through passion and ill-temper;" but he immediately went on to show the antagonism between Republican opinion and Democratic opinion with a distinctness which left no hope of harmony, and very little hope of peace. To satisfy the Southerners, he said, we must "cease to call slavery *wrong*, and join them in calling it *right*. And this must be done thoroughly,—done in *acts* as well as in *words*.... We must arrest and return their fugitive slaves with greedy pleasure. We must pull down our free-state Constitutions.... If slavery is right, all words, acts, laws, and constitutions against it are themselves wrong, and should be silenced and swept away. If it is right, we cannot object to its nationality, its universality; if it is wrong, they cannot justly insist upon its extension, its enlargement. All they ask we could readily grant, if we thought slavery right; all we ask they could as readily grant, if they thought it wrong. Their thinking it right and our thinking it wrong is the precise fact upon which depends the whole controversy. Thinking it right, as they do, they are not to blame for desiring its full recognition, as being right; but thinking it wrong, as we do, can we yield to them?... Wrong as we think slavery is, we can yet afford to let it alone where it is, because that much is due to the necessity arising from its actual presence in the nation; but can we, while our votes will prevent it, allow it to spread into the national Territories, and to overrun us here in these free States? If our sense of duty forbids this ... let us be diverted by no sophistical contrivances, such as groping for some middle ground between the right and the wrong, vain as the search for a man who should be neither a living man nor a dead man; such as a policy of 'don't care' on a question about which all true men do care; such as Union appeals beseeching true Union men to yield to Disunionists, reversing the divine rule and calling not the sinners but the righteous to repentance."

The next morning the best newspapers gave full reports of the speech, with compliments. The columns of the "Evening Post" were generously declared to be "indefinitely elastic" for such utterances; and the "Tribune" expressed commendation wholly out of accord with the recent notions of its editor. The rough fellow from the crude West had made a powerful impression upon the cultivated gentlemen of the East.

From New York Lincoln went to Massachusetts, Rhode Island, New Hampshire, and Connecticut. In this last-named State he delivered speeches which are said to have contributed largely to the Republican success in the closely contested election then at hand. In Manchester it was noticed that "he did not abuse the South, the administration, or the Democrats, or indulge in any personalities, with the exception of a few hits at Douglas's notions." [94]

These speeches of 1858, 1859, and 1860 have a very great value as contributions to history. During that period every dweller in the United States was hotly concerned about this absorbing question of slavery, advancing his own views, weighing or encountering the arguments of others, quarreling, perhaps, with his oldest friends and his nearest kindred,—for about this matter men easily quarreled and rarely compromised. Every man who fancied that he could speak in public got upon some platform in city, town, or village, and secured an audience by his topic if not by his ability; every one who thought that he could write found some way to print what he had to say upon a subject of which readers never tired; and for whatever purpose two or three men were gathered together, they were not likely to separate without a few words about North and South, pro-slavery and anti-slavery. Never was any matter more harried and ransacked by disputation. Now to all the speaking and writing of the Republicans Lincoln's condensed speeches were what a syllabus is to an elaborate discourse, what a lawyer's brief is to his verbal argument. Perhaps they may better be likened to an anti-slavery gospel; as the New Testament is supposed to cover the whole ground of Christian doctrines and Christian ethics, so that theologians and preachers innumerable have only been able to make elaborations or glosses upon the original text, so Lincoln's speeches contain the whole basis of the anti-slavery cause as maintained by the Republican party. They also set forth a considerable part of the Southern position, doubtless as fairly as the machinations of the Devil are set forth in Holy Writ. They only rather gingerly refrain from speaking of the small body of ultra-Abolitionists, —for while Lincoln was far from agreeing with these zealots, he felt that it was undesirable to widen by any excavation upon his side the chasm between them and the Republicans. So the fact is that the whole doctrine of Republicanism, as it existed during the political campaign which resulted in the election of Lincoln, also all the historical facts supporting that doctrine, were clearly and accurately stated in these speeches. Specific points were more elaborated by other persons; but every seed was to be found in this granary.

This being the case, it is worth noticing that both Lincoln and Douglas confined their disputation closely to the slavery question. Disunion and secession were words familiar in every ear, yet Lincoln referred to these things only twice or thrice, and incidentally, while Douglas ignored them. This fact is fraught with meaning. American writers and American readers have always met upon the tacit understanding that the Union was the chief cause of, and the best justification for, the war. An age may come when historians, treating our history as we treat that of Greece, stirred by no emotion at the sight of the "Stars and Stripes," moved by no patriotism at the name of the United States of America, will seek a deeper philosophy to explain this obstinate, bloody, costly struggle. Such writers may say that a rich, civilized multitude of human beings, possessors of the quarter of a continent, believing it best for their interests to set up an independent government for themselves, fell back upon the right of revolution, though they chose not to call it by that name. Now, even if it be possible to go so far as to say that every nation has always a right to preserve by force, if it can, its own integrity, certainly it cannot be stated as a further truth that no portion of a nation can ever be justified in endeavoring to obtain an independent national existence; no citizen of this country can admit this, but must say that such an endeavor is justifiable or not justifiable according as its cause and basis are right or wrong. Far down, then, at the very bottom lay the question whether the Southerners had a sufficient cause upon which to base a revolution. Now this question was hardly conclusively answered by the perfectly true statement that the North had not interfered with Southern rights. Southerners might admit this, and still believe that their welfare could be best subserved by a government wholly their own. So the very bottom question of all still remained: Was the South endeavoring to establish a government of its own for a justifiable reason and a right purpose? Now the avowed purpose was to establish on an enduring foundation a permanent slave empire; and the declared reason was, that slavery was not safe within the Union. Underneath the question of the Union therefore lay, logically, the question of slavery.

Lincoln and the other Republican leaders said that, if slavery extension was prevented, then slavery was in the way of extinction. If the assertion was true, it pretty clearly followed that the South could retain slavery only by independence and a complete imperial control within the limits of its own homogeneous nationality; for undeniably the preponderant Northern mass was becoming firmly resolved that slavery should not be extended, however it might be tolerated within its present limits. So still, by anti-slavery statement itself, the ultimate question was: whether or not the preservation of slavery was a right and sufficient cause or purpose for establishing an independent nationality. Lincoln, therefore, went direct to the logical heart of the contention, when he said that the real dispute was whether slavery was a right thing or a wrong thing. If slavery was a right thing, a Union conducted upon a policy which was believed to doom it to "ultimate extinction" was not a right thing. But if slavery was a wrong thing, a revolution undertaken with the purpose of making it perpetual was also a wrong thing. Therefore, from beginning to end, Lincoln talked about slavery. By so doing he did what he could to give to the war a character far higher even than a war of patriotism, for he extended its meaning far beyond the age and the country of its occurrence, and made of it, not a war for the United States alone, but a war for humanity, a war for ages and peoples yet to come. In like manner, he himself also gained the right to be regarded as much more than a great party leader, even more than a great patriot; for he became a champion of mankind and the defender of the chief right of man. I do not mean to say that he saw these things in this light at the moment, or that he accurately formulated the precise relationship and fundamental significance of all that was then in process of saying and doing. Time must elapse, and distance must enable one to get a comprehensive view, before the philosophy of an era like that of the civil war becomes intelligible. But the philosophy is not the less correct because those who were framing it piece by piece did not at any one moment project before their mental vision the whole in its finished proportions and relationship.

[75] As an example of Greeley's position, see letter quoted by N. and H. ii. 140, note. The fact that he was strenuously pro-Douglas and anti-Lincoln is well known. Yet afterward he said that it "was hardly in human nature" for Republicans to treat Douglas as a friend. Greeley's *American Conflict*, i. 301.

[76] Wilson, *Rise and Fall of the Slave Power*, ii. 567; for sketches of Douglas's position, see Blaine, *Twenty Years of Congress*, i. 141-144; von Holst, *Const. Hist. of U.S.* vi. 280-286; Herndon, 391-395; N. and H. ii. 138-143; Lamon, 390-395; Holland, 158. Crittenden was one of the old Whigs, who

now sorely disappointed Lincoln by preferring Douglas. N. and H. ii. 142.

[77] Several months afterward, October 25, 1858, Mr. Seward made the speech at Rochester which contained the famous sentence: "It is an irrepressible conflict between opposing and enduring forces, and it means that the United States must and will, sooner or later, become either entirely a slaveholding nation or entirely a free-labor nation." Seward's *Works*, new edition, 1884, iv. 292. But Seward ranked among the extremists and the agitators. See *Lincoln and Douglas Deb.* 244. After all, the idea had already found expression in the Richmond *Enquirer*, May 6, 1856, quoted by von Hoist, vi. 299, also referred to by Lincoln; see *Lincoln and Douglas Deb.* 262.

[78] Letter to Hon. Geo. Robertson, N. and H. i. 392; and see Lamon, 398; also see remarks of von Holst, vi. 277.

[79] *Lincoln and Douglas Deb.* 93. W.P. Fessenden, "who," says Mr. Blaine, "always spoke with precision and never with passion," expressed his opinion that if Fremont had been elected instead of Buchanan, that decision would never have been given. *Twenty Years of Congress*, i. 133.

[80] Stephen A. Douglas, Franklin Pierce, Roger B. Taney, James Buchanan.

[81] *Lincoln and Douglas Deb.* 198. At Chicago he said that he would vote for the prohibition of slavery in a new Territory "in spite of the Dred Scott decision." *Lincoln and Douglas Deb.* 20; and see the rest of his speech on the same page. The Illinois Republican Convention, June 16. 1858, expressed "condemnation of the principles and tendencies of the extra-judicial opinions of a majority of the judges," as putting forth a "political heresy." Holland, 159.

Years ago Salmon P. Chase had dared to say that, if the courts would not overthrow the pro-slavery construction of the Constitution, the people would do so, even if it should be "necessary to overthrow the courts also." Warden's *Life of Chase*, 313.

[82] For Lincoln's explanation of his position concerning the Dred Scott decision, see *Lincoln and Douglas Deb.* 20.

[83] A nickname for the southern part of Illinois.

[84] Henry Wilson has made his criticism in the words that "some of his [Lincoln's] assertions and admissions were both unsatisfactory and offensive to anti-slavery men; betrayed too much of the spirit of caste and prejudice against color, and sound harshly dissonant by the side of the Proclamation of Emancipation and the grand utterances of his later state papers." *Rise and Fall of the Slave Power*, ii. 576.

[85] Blaine, *Twenty Years of Congress*, i. 145

[86] N. and H. ii. 159, 160, 163; Arnold, 151; Lamon, 415, 416, and see 406; Holland, 189; Wilson, *Rise and Fall of the Slave Power*, ii. 576; Blaine, *Twenty Years of Congress*, i. 148.

[87] Arnold, 144. This writer speaks with discriminating praise concerning Lincoln's oratory, p. 139. It is an illustration of Lincoln's habit of adopting for permanent use any expression that pleased him, that this same phrase had been used by him in a speech made two years before this time. Holland, 151.

[88] Published in Columbus, in 1860, for campaign purposes, from copies furnished by Lincoln; see his letter to Central Exec. Comm., December 19, 1859, on fly-leaf.

[89] Many tributes have been paid to Douglas by writers who oppose his opinions; *e.g.*, Arnold says: "There is, on the whole, hardly any greater personal triumph in the history of American politics than his reëlection," pp. 149, 150; Blaine, *Twenty Years of Congress*, i. 149.

[90] See Lincoln's letter to Judd, quoted N. and H. ii. 167; also *Ibid*. 169.

[91] Raymond, 76.

[92] The Senate showed 14 Democrats, 11 Republicans; the House, 40 Democrats, 35 Republicans.

[93] In September, 1859. These are included in the volume of *The Lincoln and Douglas Debates*, printed at Columbus, 1860.

[94] *The Mirror*, quoted by Lamon, 442.

CHAPTER VI
ELECTION

Mr. J.W. Fell, a leading citizen of Illinois, says that after the debates of 1858 he urged Lincoln to seek the Republican nomination for the presidency in 1860. Lincoln, however, replied curtly that men like Seward and Chase were entitled to take precedence, and that no such "good luck" was in store for him. In March, 1859, he wrote to another person: "In regard to the other matter that you speak of, I beg that you will not give it further mention. I do not think I am fit for the presidency." He said the same to the editor of the "Central Illinois Gazette;" but this gentleman "brought him out in the issue of May 4," and "thence the movement spread rapidly and strongly." [95] In the winter of 1859-60 sundry "intimate friends," active politicians of Illinois, pressed him to consent to be mentioned as a candidate. He considered the matter over night and then gave them the desired permission, at the same time saying that he would not accept the vice-presidency.

Being now fairly started in the race, he used all his well-known skill as a politician to forward his campaign, though nothing derogatory is to be inferred from these words as to his conduct or methods. February 9, 1860, he wrote to Mr. Judd: "I am not in a position where it would hurt much for me not to be nominated on the national ticket; but I am where it would hurt some for me not to get the Illinois delegates.... Can you help me a little in this matter at your end of the vineyard?" This point of the allegiance of his own State was soon made right. The Republican State Convention met in the "Wigwam" at Decatur, May 9 and 10, 1860. Governor Oglesby, who presided, suggested that a distinguished citizen, whom Illinois delighted to honor, was present, and that he should be invited to a place on the stand; and at once, amid a tumult of applause, Lincoln was lifted over the heads of the crowd to the platform. John Hanks then theatrically entered, bearing a couple of fence rails, and a flag with the legend that they were from a "lot made by Abraham Lincoln and John Hanks in the Sangamon Bottom, in the year 1830." The sympathetic roar rose again. Then Lincoln made a "speech," appropriate to the occasion. At last, attention was given to business, and the convention resolved that Abraham Lincoln was the first choice of the Republican party of Illinois for the presidency, and instructed their delegates to the nominating convention "to use all honorable means to secure his nomination, and to cast the vote of the State as a unit for him."

With the opening of the spring of 1860 the several parties began the campaign in earnest. The Democratic Convention met first, at Charleston, April 23; and immediately the line of disruption opened. Upon the one side stood Douglas, with the moderate men and nearly all the Northern delegates, while against him were the advocates of extreme Southern doctrines, supported by the administration and by most of the delegates from the "Cotton States." The majority of the committee appointed to draft the platform were anti-Douglas men; but their report was rejected, and that offered by the pro-Douglas minority was substituted, 165 yeas to 138 nays. [96] Thereupon the delegations of Alabama, Mississippi, Florida, and Texas, and sundry delegates from other States, withdrew from the convention, [97] taking away 45 votes out of a total of 303. Those who remained declared the vote of two thirds of a full convention, *i.e.*, 202 votes, to be necessary for a choice. Then during three days fifty-seven ballots were cast, Douglas being always far in the lead, but never polling more than 152 1/2 votes. At last, on May 3, an adjournment was had until June 18, at Baltimore. At this second meeting contesting delegations appeared, and the decisions were uniformly in favor of the Douglas men, which provoked another secession of the extremist Southern men. A ballot showed 173 1/2 votes for Douglas out of a total of 191 1/2; the total was less than two thirds of the full number of the original convention, and therefore it was decided that any person receiving two thirds of the votes cast by the delegates present should be deemed the nominee. The next ballot gave Douglass 181 1/2. Herschel V. Johnson of Georgia was nominated for vice-president.

On June 28, also at Baltimore, there came together a collection composed of original seceders at Charleston, and of some who had been rejected and others who had seceded at Baltimore. Very few Northern men were present, and the body in fact represented the Southern wing of the Democracy. Having, like its competitor, the merit of knowing its own mind, it promptly nominated John C. Breckenridge of Kentucky and Joseph Lane of Oregon, and adopted the radical platform which had been reported at Charleston.

These doings opened, so that it could never be closed, that seam of which the thread had long been visible athwart the surface of the old Democratic party. The great record of discipline and of triumph, which the party had made when united beneath the dominion of imperious leaders, was over, and forever. Those questions which Lincoln obstinately and against advice had insisted upon pushing in 1858 had forced this disastrous development of irreconcilable differences. The answers, which Douglas could not shirk, had alienated the most implacable of men, the dictators of the Southern

Democracy. His "looking-both-ways" theory would not fit with their policy, and their policy was and must be immutable; modification was in itself defeat. On the other hand, what he said constituted the doctrine to which the mass of the Northern Democracy firmly held. So now, although Republicans admitted that it was "morally certain" that the Democratic party, holding together, could carry the election, [98] yet these men from the Cotton States could not take victory and Douglas together. [99] It had actually come to this, that, in spite of all that Douglas had done for the slaveholders, they now marked him for destruction at any cost. Many also believe that they had another motive; that they had matured their plans for secession; and that they did not mean to have the scheme disturbed or postponed by an ostensibly Democratic triumph in the shape of the election of Douglas.

In May the convention of the Constitutional Union party met, also at Baltimore. This organization was a sudden outgrowth designed only to meet the present emergency. Its whole political doctrine lay in the opening words of the one resolution which constituted its platform: "That it is both the part of patriotism and of duty to recognize no political principle other than the Constitution of the country, the union of the States, and the enforcement of the laws." This party gathered nearly all the peaceable elements of the community; it assumed a deprecatory attitude between angry contestants, and of course received the abuse and contempt of both; it was devoid of combative force, yet had some numerical strength. The Republicans especially mocked at these "trimmers," as if their only platform was moral cowardice, which, however, was an unfair statement of their position. The party died, of necessity, upon the day when Lincoln was elected, and its members were then distributed between the Republicans, the Secessionists, and the Copperheads. John Bell of Tennessee, the candidate for the presidency, joined the Confederacy; Edward Everett of Massachusetts, the candidate for the vice-presidency, became a Republican. The party never had a hope of electing its men; but its existence increased the chance of throwing the election into Congress; and this hope inspired exertions far beyond what its own prospects warranted.

On May 16 the Republican Convention came together at Chicago, where the great "Wigwam" had been built to hold 10,000 persons. The intense interest with which its action was watched indicated the popular belief that probably it would name the next President of the United States. Many candidates were named, chiefly Seward, Lincoln, Chase, Cameron, Edward Bates of Missouri, and William L. Dayton of New Jersey. Thurlow Weed was Seward's lieutenant. Horace Greeley, chiefly bent upon the defeat of Seward, would have liked to achieve it by the success of Bates. David Davis, aided by Judge Logan and a band of personal friends from Illinois, was manager for Lincoln. Primarily the contest lay between Seward and Lincoln, and only a dead-lock between these two could give a chance to some one of the others. But Seward's friends hoped, and Lincoln's friends dreaded, that the New Yorker might win by a rush on the first ballot. George Ashmun of Massachusetts presided. With little discussion a platform was adopted, long and ill-written, overloaded with adjectives and rhetoric, sacrificing dignity to the supreme pleasure of abusing the Democracy, but honest in stating Republican doctrines, and clearly displaying the temper of an earnest, aggressive party, hot for the fight and confident of victory. The vote of acceptance was greeted with such a cheering that "a herd of buffaloes or lions could not have made a more tremendous roaring."

The details of the brief but sharp contest for the nomination are not altogether gratifying. The partisans of Seward set about winning votes by much parading in the streets with banners and music, and by out-yelling all competitors within the walls of the convention. For this intelligent purpose they had engaged Tom Hyer, the prize fighter, with a gang of roughs, to hold possession of the Wigwam, and to howl illimitably at appropriate moments. But they had undertaken a difficult task in trying to outdo the great West, in one of its own cities, at a game of this kind. The Lincoln leaders in their turn secured a couple of stentorian yellers (one of them a Democrat), instructed them carefully, and then filled the Wigwam full actually at daybreak, while the Seward men were marching; so in the next yelling match the West won magnificently. How great was the real efficiency of these tactics in affecting the choice of the ruler of a great nation commonly accounted intelligent, it is difficult to say with accuracy; but it is certain that the expert managers spared no pains about this scenic business of "enthusiasm."

Meanwhile other work, entirely quiet, was being done elsewhere. The objection to Seward was that he was too radical, too far in advance of the party. The Bates following were pushing their candidate as a moderate man, who would be acceptable to "Union men." But Bates's chance was small, and any tendency towards a moderate candidate was likely to carry his friends to Lincoln rather than to Seward; for Lincoln was generally supposed, however erroneously, [100] to be more remote from Abolitionism than Seward was. To counteract this, a Seward delegate telegraphed to the Bates men at St. Louis that Lincoln was as radical as Seward. Lincoln, at Springfield, saw this dispatch, and at once wrote a message to David Davis: "Lincoln agrees with Seward in his irrepressible-conflict idea, and in Negro Equality; but he is opposed to Seward's Higher Law. *Make no contracts that will bind me."* He underscored the last sentence; but when his managers saw it, they recognized that such independence did not accord with the situation, and so they set it aside.

The first vote was:—

Whole number	465	
Necessary for choice	233	
William H. Seward of New York	173	1/2
Abraham Lincoln of Illinois	102	
Simon Cameron of Pennsylvania	50	1/2
Salmon P. Chase of Ohio	49	
Edward Bates of Missouri	48	
William L. Dayton of New Jersey	14	
John McLean of Ohio	12	
Jacob Collamer of Vermont	10	
Scattering	6	

The fact was, and Lincoln's friends perfectly understood it, that Cameron held that peculiar kind of power which gave him no real prospect of success, yet had a considerable salable value. Could they refrain from trying the market? They asked the owners of the 50 1/2 Cameron votes what was their price. The owners said: The Treasury Department. Lincoln's friends declared this extravagant. Then they all chaffered. Finally Cameron's men took a place in the cabinet, without further specification. Lamon says that another smaller contract was made with the friends of Caleb B. Smith. Then the Lincoln managers rested in a pleasing sense of security.

The second ballot showed slight changes:—

Seward	184	1/2
Lincoln	181	
Cameron	2	
Chase	42	1/2
Bates	5	
Dayton	10	
McLean	8	
Scattering	2	

Upon the third ballot delivery was made of what Mr. Davis had bought. That epidemic foreknowledge, which sometimes so unaccountably foreruns an event, told the convention that the decision was at hand. A dead silence reigned save for the click of the telegraphic instruments and the low scratching of hundreds of pencils checking off the votes as the roll was called. Those who were keeping the tally saw that it stood:—

Seward	180	
Lincoln	231	1/2
Chase	24	1/2
Bates	22	
Dayton	1	
McLean	5	
Scattering	1	

Cameron was out of the race; Lincoln was within 11/2 votes of the goal. Before the count could be announced, a delegate from Ohio transferred four votes to Lincoln. This settled the matter; and then other delegations followed, till Lincoln's score rose to 354. At once the "enthusiasm" of 10,000 men again reduced to insignificance a "herd of buffaloes or lions." When at last quiet was restored, William M. Evarts, who had led for Seward, offered the usual motion to make the nomination of Abraham Lincoln unanimous. It was done. Again the "tremendous roaring" arose. Later in the day the convention nominated Hannibal Hamlin [101] of Maine, on the second ballot, by 367 votes, for the vice-presidency. Then for many hours, till exhaustion brought rest, Chicago was given over to the wonted follies; cannon boomed, music resounded, and streets and barrooms were filled with the howling and drinking crowds of the intelligent promoters of one of the great moral crusades of the human race.

Lamon says that the committee deputed to wait upon Lincoln at Springfield found him "sad and dejected. The reaction from excessive joy to deep despondency—a process peculiar to his constitution—had already set in." [102] His remarks to these gentlemen were brief and colorless. His letter afterward was little more than a simple acceptance of the platform.

Since white men first landed on this continent, the selection of Washington to lead the army of the Revolution is the only event to be compared in good fortune with this nomination of Abraham Lincoln. Yet the convention deserved no credit for its action. It did not know the true ratio between Seward and Lincoln, which only the future was to make plain. By all that it did know, it ought to have given the honor to Seward, who merited it by the high offices which he had held with distinction and without blemish, by the leadership which he had acquired in the party through long-continued constancy and courage, by the force and clearness with which he had maintained its principles, by his experience and supposed natural aptitude in the higher walks of statesmanship. Yet actually by reason of these very qualifications [103] it was now admitted that the all-important "October States" of Indiana and Pennsylvania could not be carried by the Republicans if Seward were nominated; while Greeley, sitting in the convention as a substitute for a delegate from Oregon, cast as much of the weight of New York as he could lift into the anti-Seward scale. In plain fact, the convention, by its choice, paid no compliment either to Lincoln or to the voters of the party. They took him because he was "available," and the reason that he was "available" lay not in any popular appreciation of his merits, but in the contrary truth,—that the mass of people could place no intelligent estimate upon him at all, either for good or for ill. Outside of Illinois a few men, who had studied his speeches, esteemed him an able man in debate; more had a vague notion of him as an effective stump speaker of the West; far the greatest number had to find out about him. [104] In a word, Mr. Lincoln gained the nomination because Mr. Seward had been "too conspicuous," whereas he himself was so little known that it was possible for Wendell Phillips to inquire indignantly: "Who is this huckster in politics? Who is this county court advocate?" [105] For these singular reasons he was the most "available" candidate who could be offered before the citizens of the United States!

It cannot be said that the nomination was received with much satisfaction. "Honest old Abe the rail-splitter!" might sound well in the ear of the masses; but the Republican party was laden with the burden of an immense responsibility, and the men who did its thinking could not reasonably feel certain that rail-splitting was an altogether satisfactory training for the leader in such an era as was now at hand. Nevertheless, nearly [106] all came to the work of the campaign with as much zeal as if they had surely known the full value of their candidate. Shutting their minds against doubts, they made the most spirited and energetic canvass which has ever taken place in the country. The organization of the "Wide-Awake" clubs was an effective success. [107] None who saw will ever forget the spectacle presented by these processions wherein many thousands of men, singing the campaign songs, clad in uniform capes of red or white oil-cloth, each with a flaming torch or a colored lantern, marched nightly in every city and town of the North, in apparently endless numbers and with military precision, making the streets a brilliant river of variously tinted flame. Torchlight parades have become mere conventional affairs since those days, when there was a spirit in them which nothing has ever stirred more lately. They were a good preparation for the more serious marching and severer drill which were soon to come, though the Republicans scoffed at all anticipations of such a future, and sneered at the timid ones who croaked of war and bloodshed.

Almost from the beginning it was highly probable that the Republicans would win, and it was substantially certain that none of their competitors could do so. The only contrary chance was that no election might be made by the people, and that it might be thrown into Congress. Douglas with his wonted spirit made a vigorous fight, traveling to and fro, speaking constantly in the North and a few times in the South, but defiant rather than conciliatory in tone. He did not show one whit the less energy because it was obvious that he waged a contest without hope. If there were any road to Democratic success, which it now seems that there was not, it lay in uniting the sundered party. An attempt was made to arrange that whichever Democratic candidate should ultimately display the greater strength should receive the full support of the party. Projects for a fusion ticket met with some success in New York. In Pennsylvania like schemes were imperfectly successful. In other Northern States they were received with scant favor. Except some followers of Bell and Everett, men were in no temper for compromise. At the South fusion was not even attempted; the Breckenridge men would not hear of it; the voters in that section were controlled by leaders, and these leaders probably had a very distinct policy, which would be seriously interfered with by the triumph of the Douglas ticket.

The chief anxiety of Lincoln and the Republican leaders was lest some voters, who disagreed with them only on less important issues, might stay away from the polls. All the platforms, except that of the Constitutional Union party, touched upon other topics besides the question of slavery in the Territories; the tariff, native Americanism, acquisition of Cuba, a transcontinental railway, public lands, internal improvements, all found mention. The Know-Nothing party still by occasional twitchings showed that life had not quite taken flight, and endeavors were made to induce Lincoln to express his views. But he evaded it. [108] For above all else he wished to avoid the stirring of any dissension upon side issues or minor points; his hope was to see all opponents of the extension of slavery put aside for a while all other matters, refrain from discussing troublesome details, and unite for the one broad end of putting slavery where "the fathers" had left it, so that the "public mind should rest in the belief that it was in the way of ultimate extinction." He felt it to be fair and right that he should receive the votes of all anti-slavery men; and ultimately he did, with the exception only of the thorough-going Abolitionists.

It was not so very long since he had spoken of the Abolitionist leaders as "friends;" but they did not reciprocate the feeling, nor indeed could reasonably be expected to do so, or to vote the Republican ticket. They were even less willing to vote it with Lincoln at the head of it than if Seward had been there. [109]   But Republicanism itself under any leader was distinctly at odds with their views; for when they said "*abolition*" they meant accurately what they said, and abolition certainly was impossible under the Constitution. The Republicans, and Lincoln personally, with equal directness acknowledged the supremacy of the Constitution. Lincoln, therefore, plainly asserted a policy which the Abolitionists equally plainly condemned. In their eyes, to be a party to a contract maintaining slavery throughout a third of a continent was only a trifle less criminal than aiding to extend it over another third. Yet it should be said that the Abolitionists were not all of one mind, and some voted the Republican ticket as being at least a step in the right direction. Joshua R. Giddings was a member of the Republican Convention which nominated Lincoln. But Wendell Phillips, always an extremist among extremists, published an article entitled "Abraham Lincoln, the Slave-hound of Illinois," whereof the keynote was struck in this introductory sentence: "We gibbet a Northern hound to-day, side by side with the infamous Mason of Virginia." Mr. Garrison, a man of far larger and sounder intellectual powers than belonged to Phillips, did not fancy this sort of diatribe, though five months earlier he had accused the Republican party of "slavish subserviency to the Union," and declared it to be "still insanely engaged in glorifying the Union and pledging itself to frown upon all attempts to dissolve it." Undeniably men who held these views could not honestly vote for Mr. Lincoln.

The popular vote and the electoral vote were as follows: [110]   —

Li: Abraham Lincoln, Illinois.
Do: Stephen A. Douglas, Illinois.
Br: John C. Breckenridge, Kentucky.
Be: John Bell, Tennessee.

	Popular Vote				Electoral Vote			
	Li	Do	Br	Be	Li	Do	Br	Be
Maine	62,811	26,693	6,368	2,046	8	—	—	—
New Hampshire	37,519	25,881	2,112	441	5	—	—	—
Vermont	33,808	6,849	218	1,969	5	—	—	—
Massachusetts	106,533	34,372	5,939	22,231	13	—	—	—
Rhode Island	12,244	[B] 7,707	—	—	4	—	—	—
Connecticut	43,792	15,522	14,641	3,291	6	—	—	—
New York	362,646	[B] 312,510	—	—	35	—	—	—
New Jersey	58,324	[B] 62,801	—	—	4	3	—	—
Pennsylvania	268,030	16,765	[B] 178,871	12,776	27	—	—	—
Delaware	3,815	1,023	7,337	3,864	—	—	3	—
Maryland	2,294	5,966	42,482	41,760	—	—	8	—
Virginia	1,929	16,290	74,323	74,681	—	—	—	15
North Carolina	—	2,701	48,539	44,990	—	—	10	—
South Carolina [A]	—	—	—	—	—	—	8	—
Georgia	—	11,590	51,889	42,886	—	—	10	—
Florida	—	367	8,543	5,437	—	—	3	—
Alabama	—	13,651	48,831	27,875	—	—	9	—
Mississippi	—	3,283	40,797	25,040	—	—	7	—
Louisiana	—	7,625	22,861	20,204	—	—	6	—
Texas	—	—	47,548	[B] 15,438	—	—	4	—
Arkansas	—	5,227	28,732	20,094	—	—	4	—
Missouri	17,028	58,801	31,317	58,372	—	9	—	—
Tennessee	—	11,350	64,709	69,274	—	—	—	12
Kentucky	1,364	25,651	53,143	66,058	—	—	—	12
Ohio	231,610	187,232	11,405	12,194	23	—	—	—
Michigan	88,480	65,057	805	405	6	—	—	—
Indiana	139,033	115,509	12,295	5,306	13	—	—	—
Illinois	172,161	160,215	2,404	4,913	11	—	—	—
Wisconsin	86,110	65,021	888	161	5	—	—	—
Minnesota	22,069	11,920	748	62	4	—	—	—
Iowa	70,409	55,111	1,048	1,763	4	—	—	—
California	39,173	38,516	34,334	6,817	4	—	—	—
Oregon	5,270	3,951	5,006	183	3	—	—	—
Totals	1,866,452	1,375,157	847,953	590,631	180	12	72	39

[A] By legislature.

[B] Fusion electoral tickets.

Messrs. Nicolay and Hay say that Lincoln was the "indisputable choice of the American people," and by way of sustaining the statement say that, if the "whole voting strength of the three opposing parties had been united upon a single candidate, Lincoln would nevertheless have been chosen with only a trifling diminution of his electoral majority." [111] It might be better to say that Lincoln was the "indisputable choice" of the electoral college. The "American people" fell enormously short of showing a majority in his favor. His career as president was made infinitely more difficult as well as greatly more creditable to him by reason of the very fact that he was *not* the choice of the American people, but of less than half of them,—and this, too, even if the Confederate States be excluded from the computation. [112]

The election of Lincoln was "hailed with delight" by the extremists in South Carolina; for it signified secession, and the underlying and real desire of these people was secession, and not either compromise or postponement. [113]

[95] Lamon, 422.

[96] The majority report was supported by 15 slave States and 2 free States, casting 127 electoral votes; the minority report was supported by 15 free States, casting 176 electoral votes. N. and H. ii. 234.

[97] This action was soon afterward approved in a manifesto signed by Jefferson Davis, Toombs, Iverson, Slidell, Benjamin, Mason, and others. *Ibid.* 245.

[98] Greeley's *Amer. Conflict*, i. 326.

[99] *Ibid.* i. 306, 307.

[100] Mr. Blaine says that Lincoln "was chosen in spite of expressions far more radical than those of Mr. Seward." *Twenty Years of Congress*, i. 169.

[101] "In strong common sense, in sagacity and sound judgment, in rugged integrity of character, Mr. Hamlin has had no superior among public men." Blaine, *Twenty Years of Congress*, i. 170.

[102] Lamon, 453.

[103] McClure adds, or rather mentions as the chief cause, Seward's position on the public-school question in New York. *Lincoln and Men of War-Times*, 28, 29.

[104] "To the country at large he was an obscure, not to say an unknown man." *Life of W.L. Garrison*, by his children, iii. 503.

[105] *Life of W.L. Garrison*, by his children, iii. 503.

[106] See remarks of McClure, *Lincoln and Men of War-Times*, 28, 29.

[107] See N. and H. ii. 284 n.

[108] See letter of May 17, 1859, to Dr. Canisius, Holland, 196; N. and H. ii. 181.

[109] *Life of W.L. Garrison*, by his children, iii. 502.

[110] This table is taken from Stanwood's *History of Presidential Elections*.

[111] N. and H. iii. 146.

[112] The total popular vote was 4,680,193. Lincoln had 1,866,452. In North Carolina, Georgia, Florida, Alabama, Mississippi, Louisiana, Texas, Arkansas, and Tennessee, no vote was cast for the Lincoln ticket; in Virginia only 1929 voted it. Adding the total popular vote of all these States (except the 1929), we get 854,775; deducting this from the total popular vote leaves a balance of 3,825,418, of which one half is 1,912,709; so that even outside of the States of the Confederacy Lincoln did not get one half of the popular vote. South Carolina is not included in any calculation concerning the popular vote, because she chose electors by her legislature.

[113] Letter of Henry A. Wise of Virginia, May 28, 1858, quoted N. and H. ii. 302 n.

CHAPTER VII
INTERREGNUM

For a while now the people of the Northern States were compelled passively to behold a spectacle which they could not easily reconcile with the theory of the supreme excellence and wisdom of their system of government. Abraham Lincoln was chosen President of the United States November 6, 1860; he was to be inaugurated March 4, 1861. During the intervening four months the government must be conducted by a chief whose political creed was condemned by an overwhelming majority of the nation. [114] The situation was as unfair for Mr. Buchanan as it was hurtful for the people. As head of a republic, or, in the more popular phrase, as the chief "servant of the people," he must respect the popular will, yet he could not now administer the public business according to that will without being untrue to all his own convictions, and repudiating all his trusted counselors. In a situation so intrinsically false efficient government was impossible, no matter what was the strength or weakness of the hand at the helm. Therefore there was every reason for displacing Buchanan from control of the national affairs in the autumn, and every reason against continuing him in that control through the winter; yet the law of the land ordained the latter course. It seemed neither sensible nor even safe. During this doleful period all descriptions of him agree: he seemed, says Chittenden, "shaken in body and uncertain in mind,... an old man worn out by worry;" while the Southerners also declared him as "incapable of purpose as a child." To the like purport spoke nearly all who saw him.

During the same time Lincoln's position was equally absurd and more trying. After the lapse of four months he was, by the brief ceremony of an hour, to become the leader of a great nation under an exceptionally awful responsibility; but during those four months he could play no other part than simply to watch, in utter powerlessness, the swift succession of crowding events, which all were tending to make his administration of the government difficult, or even impossible. Throughout all this long time, the third part of a year, which statutes scarcely less venerable than the Constitution itself freely presented to the disunion leaders, they safely completed their civil and military organization, while the Northerners, under a ruler whom they had discredited, but of whom they could not get rid, were paralyzed for all purposes of counter preparation.

As a trifling compensation for its existence this costly interregnum presents to later generations a curious spectacle. A volume might be made of the public utterances put forth in that time by men of familiar names and more or less high repute, and it would show many of them in most strange and unexpected characters, so entirely out of keeping with the years which they had lived before, and the years which they were to live afterward, that the reader would gaze in hopeless bewilderment. In the "solid" South, so soon to be a great rebelling unit, he would find perhaps half of the people opposed to disunion; in the North he would hear everywhere words of compromise and concession, while coercion would be mentioned only to be denounced. If these four months were useful in bringing the men of the North to the fighting point, on the other hand they gave an indispensable opportunity for proselyting, by whirl and excitement, great numbers at the South. Even in the autumn of 1860 and in the Gulf States secession was still so much the scheme of leaders that there was no popular preponderance in favor of disunion doctrines. In evidence of this are the responses of governors to a circular letter of Governor Gist of South Carolina, addressed to them October 5, 1860, and seeking information as to the feeling among the people. From North Carolina, Louisiana, Georgia, and Alabama came replies that secession was not likely to be favorably received. Mississippi was non-committal. Louisiana, Georgia, and Alabama desired a convention of the discontented States, and might be influenced by its action. North Carolina, Louisiana, and Alabama would oppose forcible coercion of a seceding State. Florida alone was rhetorically belligerent. These reports were discouraging in the ears of the extremist governor; but against them he could set the fact that the disunionists had the advantage of being the aggressive, propagandist body, homogeneous, and pursuing an accurate policy in entire concert. They were willing to take any amount of pains to manipulate and control the election of delegates and the formal action of conventions, and in all cases except that of Texas the question was conclusively passed upon by conventions. By every means they "fired the Southern heart," which was notoriously combustible; they stirred up a great tumult of sentiment; they made thunderous speeches; they kept distinguished emissaries moving to and fro; they celebrated each success with an uproar of cannonading, with bonfires, illuminations, and processions; they appealed to those chivalrous virtues supposed to be peculiar to Southerners; they preached devotion to the State, love of the state flag, generous loyalty to sister slave-communities; sometimes they used insult, abuse, and intimidation; occasionally they argued seductively. Thus Mr. Cobb's assertion, that "we can make better terms out of the Union than in it," was, in the opinion of Alexander H. Stephens, the chief influence which carried Georgia out of the Union. In the main, however, it was the principle of state sovereignty and state patriotism which proved the one entirely trustworthy influence to bring over the reluctant. "I abhor disunion, but I go with my State," was the common saying; and the States were under skillful and resolute leadership. So, though the popular discontent was far short of the revolutionary point, yet individuals, one after another, yielded to that sympathetic, emotional instinct which tempts each man to fall in with the big procession. In this way it was that during the Buchanan interregnum the people of the Gulf States became genuinely fused in rebellion.

It is not correct to say that the election of Lincoln was the cause of the Rebellion; it was rather the signal. To the Southern leaders, it was the striking of the appointed hour. His defeat would have meant only postponement. South Carolina led the way. On December 17, 1860, her convention came together, the Palmetto flag waving over its chamber of conference, and on December 20 it issued its "Ordinance." [115] This declared that the Ordinance of May 23, 1788, ratifying the Constitution, is "hereby repealed," and the "Union now subsisting between South Carolina and other States, under the name of the United States of America, is hereby dissolved." A Declaration of Causes said that South Carolina had "resumed her position among the nations of the world as a separate and independent State." The language used was appropriate for the revocation of a power of attorney. The people hailed this action with noisy joy, unaccompanied by any regret or solemnity at the severance of the old relationship. The newspapers at once began to publish "Foreign News" from the other States. The new governor, Pickens, a fiery Secessionist, and described as one "born insensible to fear,"—presumably the condition of most persons at that early period of existence,—had already suggested to Mr. Buchanan the impropriety of reinforcing the national garrisons in the forts in Charleston harbor. He now accredited to the President three commissioners to treat with him for the delivery of the "forts, magazines, lighthouses, and other real estate, with their appurtenances, in the limits of South Carolina; and also for an apportionment of the public debt, and for a division of all other property held by the government of the United States as agent of the Confederate States of which South Carolina was recently a member." This position, as of the dissolution of a copartnership, or the revocation of an agency, and an accounting of debts and assets, was at least simple; and by way of expediting it an appraisal of the "real estate" and "appurtenances" within the state limits had been made by the state government. Meanwhile there was in the harbor of Charleston a sort of armed truce, which might at any moment break into war. Major Anderson in Fort Moultrie, and the state commander in the city, watched each other like two suspicious animals, neither sure when the other will spring. In short, in all the overt acts, the demeanor and the language of this excitable State, there was such insolence, besides hostility, that her emissaries must have been surprised at the urbane courtesy with which they were received, even by a President of Mr. Buchanan's views.

After the secession of South Carolina the other Gulf States hesitated briefly. Mississippi followed first; her convention assembled January 7, 1861, and on January 9 passed the ordinance, 84 yeas to 15 nays, subsequently making the vote unanimous. The Florida convention met January 3, and on January 10 decreed the State to be "a sovereign and independent nation," 62 yeas to 7 nays. The Alabama convention passed its ordinance on January 11 by 61 yeas to 39 nays; the President announced that the idea of reconstruction must be forever "dismissed." Yet the northern part of the State appeared to be substantially anti-secession. In Georgia the Secessionists doubted whether they could control a convention, yet felt obliged to call one. Toombs, Cobb, and Iverson labored with tireless zeal throughout the State; but in spite of all their proselyting, Unionist feeling ran high and debate was hot. The members from the southern part of the State ventured to menace and dragoon those from the northern part, who were largely Unionists. The latter retorted angrily; a schism and personal collisions were narrowly avoided. Alexander H. Stephens spoke for the Union with a warmth and logic not surpassed by anything that was said at the North. He and Herschel V. Johnson both voted against secession; yet, on January 18, when the vote was taken, it showed 208 yeas against 89 nays. On January 26 Louisiana followed, the vote of the convention being 113 yeas to 17 nays; but it refused to submit the ordinance to the people for ratification. The action of Texas, the only other State which seceded prior to the inauguration of Lincoln, was delayed until February 1. There Governor Houston was opposing secession with such vigor as remained to a broken old man, whereby he provoked Senator Iverson to utter the threat of assassination: "Some Texan Brutus may arise to rid his country of this old hoary-headed traitor." But in the convention, when it came to voting, the yeas were 166, the nays only 7.

By the light that was in him Mr. Buchanan was a Unionist, but it was a sadly false and flickering light, and beneath its feeble illumination his steps staggered woefully. For two months he diverged little from the path which the Secessionist leaders would have marked out for him, had they controlled his movements. At the time of the election his cabinet was:—

Lewis Cass of Michigan, secretary of state.

Howell Cobb of Georgia, secretary of the treasury.

John B. Floyd of Virginia, secretary of war.

Isaac Toucey of Connecticut, secretary of the navy.

Jacob Thompson of Mississippi, secretary of the interior.

Aaron V. Brown of Tennessee, postmaster-general.

Jeremiah S. Black of Pennsylvania, attorney-general.

Of these men Cobb, Floyd, and Thompson were extreme Secessionists. Many felt that Cobb should have been made President of the Southern Confederacy instead of Davis. In December Thompson went as commissioner from Mississippi to North Carolina to persuade that State to secede, and did not resign his place in the cabinet because, as he said, Mr. Buchanan approved his mission.

Betwixt his own predilections and the influence of these advisers Mr. Buchanan composed for the Thirty-sixth Congress a message which carried consternation among all Unionists. It was of little consequence that he declared the present situation to be the "natural effect" of the "long-continued and intemperate interference" of the Northern people with slavery. But it was of the most serious consequence that, while he condemned secession as unconstitutional, he also declared himself powerless to prevent it. His duty "to take care that the laws be faithfully executed" he knew no other way to perform except by aiding federal officers in the performance of their duties. But where, as in South Carolina, the federal officers had all resigned, so that none remained to be aided, what was he to do? This was practically to take the position that half a dozen men, by resigning their offices, could make the preservation of the Union by its chief executive impossible! [116] Besides this, Mr. Buchanan said that he had "no authority to decide what should be the relations between the Federal government and South Carolina." He afterward said that he desired to avoid a collision of arms "between this and any other government." He did not seem to reflect that he had no right to recognize a State of the Union as being an "other government," in the sense in which he used the phrase, and that, by his very abstention from the measures necessary for maintaining unchanged that relationship which had hitherto existed, he became a party to the establishment of a new relationship, and that, too, of a character which he himself alleged-to be unconstitutional. In truth, his chief purpose was to rid himself of any responsibility and to lay it all upon Congress. Yet he was willing to advise Congress as to its powers and duties in the business which he shirked in favor of that body, saying that the power to coerce a seceding State had not been delegated to it, and adding the warning that "the Union can never be cemented by the blood of its citizens shed in civil war." So the nation learned that its ruler was of opinion that to resist the destruction of its nationality was both unlawful and inexpedient.

If the conclusions of the message aroused alarm and indignation, its logic excited ridicule. Senator Hale gave a not unfair synopsis: The President, he said, declares: 1. That South Carolina has just cause for seceding. 2. That she has no right to secede. 3. That we have no right to prevent her from seceding; and that the power of the government is "a power to do nothing at all." Another wit said that Buchanan was willing to give up a *part* of the Constitution, and, if necessary, the *whole*, in order to preserve the *remainder*! But while this message of Mr. Buchanan has been bitterly denounced, and with entire justice, from the hour of its transmission to the present day, yet a palliating consideration ought to be noted: he had little reason to believe that, if he asserted the right and duty of forcible coercion, he would find at his back the indispensable force, moral and physical, of the people. Demoralization at the North was widespread. After the lapse of a few months this condition passed, and then those who had been beneath its influence desired to forget the humiliating fact, and hoped that others might either forget or never know the measure of their weakness. In order that they might save their good names, it was natural that they should seek to suppress all evidence which had not already found its way upon the public record; but enough remains to show how grievously for a while the knees were weakened under many who enjoy—and rightfully, by reason of the rest of their lives—the reputation of stalwart patriots. For example, late in October, General Scott suggested to the President a division of the country into four separate confederacies, roughly outlining their boundaries. Scott was a dull man, but he was the head of the army and enjoyed a certain prestige, so that it was impossible to say that his notions, however foolish in themselves, were of no consequence. But if the blunders of General Scott could not fatally wound the Union cause, the blunders of Horace Greeley might conceivably do so. If there had been in the Northern States any newspaper—apart from Mr. Garrison's "Liberator"—which was thoroughly committed to the anti-slavery cause, it was the New York "Tribune," under the guidance of that distinguished editor. Republicans everywhere throughout the land had been educated by his teachings, and had become accustomed to take a large part of their knowledge and their opinions in matters political from his writings. It was a misfortune for Abraham Lincoln, which cannot be overrated, that from the moment of his nomination to the day of his death the "Tribune" was largely engaged in criticising his measures and in condemning his policy.

No sooner did all that, which Mr. Greeley had been striving during many years to bring about, seem to be on the point of consummation, than the demoralized and panic-stricken reformer became desirous to undo his own achievements, and to use for the purpose of effecting a sudden retrogression all the influence which he had gained by bold leadership. November 9, 1860, it was appalling to read in the editorial columns of his sheet, that "if the Cotton States shall decide that they can do better out of the Union than in it, we insist on letting them go in peace;" that, while the "Tribune" denied the right of nullification, yet it would admit that "to withdraw from the Union is quite another matter;" that "whenever a considerable section of our Union shall deliberately resolve to go out, we shall resist all coercive measures designed to keep it in." [117] At the end of another month the "Tribune's" famous editor was still in the same frame of mind, declaring himself "averse to the employment of military force to fasten one section of our confederacy to the other," and saying that, "if eight States, having five millions of people, choose to separate from us, they cannot be permanently withheld from so doing by federal cannon." On December 17 he even said that the South had as good a right to secede from the Union as the colonies had to secede from Great Britain, and that he "would not stand up for coercion, for subjugation," because he did not "think it would be just." On February 23, 1861, he said that if the Cotton States, or the Gulf States, "choose to form an independent nation, they have a clear moral right to do so," and if the "great body of the Southern people" become alienated from the Union and wish to "escape from it, we will do our best to forward their views." A volume could be filled with the like writing of his prolific pen at this time, and every sentence of such purport was the casting of a new stone to create an almost impassable obstruction in the path along which the new President must soon endeavor to move. Thurlow Weed, editor of the Albany "Evening Journal," and the confidential adviser of Seward, wrote in favor of concessions; he declared that "a victorious party can afford to be tolerant;" and he advocated a convention to revise the Constitution, on the ground that, "after more than seventy years of wear and tear, of collision and abrasion, it should be no cause of wonder that the machinery of government is found weakened, or out of repair, or even defective." Frequently he uttered the wish, vague and of fine sound, but enervating, that the Republicans might "meet secession as patriots and not as partisans." On November 9 the Democratic New York "Herald," discussing the election of Lincoln, said: "For far less than this our fathers seceded from Great Britain;" it also declared coercion to be "out of the question," and laid down the principle that each State possesses "the right to break the tie of the confederacy, as a nation might break a treaty, and to repel coercion as a nation might repel invasion."

Local elections in New York and Massachusetts "showed a striking and general reduction of Republican strength." In December the mayor of

Philadelphia, though that city had polled a heavy Republican majority, told a mass meeting in Independence Square that denunciations of slavery were inconsistent with national brotherhood, and "must be frowned down by a just and law-abiding people." The Bell and Everett men, generally, desired peace at any price. The business men of the North, alarmed at the prospect of disorder, became loudly solicitous for concession, compromise, even surrender. [118] In Democratic meetings a threatening tone was adopted. One proposal was to reconstruct the Union, leaving out the New England States. So late even as January 21, 1861, before an immense and noteworthy gathering in New York, an orator ventured to say: "If a revolution of force is to begin, it shall be inaugurated at home;" and the words were cheered. The distinguished Chancellor Walworth said that it would be "as brutal to send men to butcher our own brothers of the Southern States as it would be to massacre them in the Northern States." When DeWitt Clinton's son, George, spoke of secession as "rebellion," the multitude hailed the word with cries of dissent. Even at Faneuil Hall, in Boston, "a very large and respectable meeting" was emphatically in favor of compromise. It was impossible to measure accurately the extent and force of all this demoralization; but the symptoms were that vast numbers were infected with such sentiments, and that they would have been worse than useless as backers of a vigorous policy on the part of the government.

With the North wavering and ready to retreat, and the South aggressive and confident, it was exacting to expect Mr. Buchanan to stand up for a fight. Why should he, with his old-time Democratic principles, now by a firm, defiant attitude precipitate a crisis, possibly a civil war, when Horace Greeley and Wendell Phillips were conspicuously running away from the consequences of their own teachings, and were loudly crying "Peace! peace!" after they themselves had long been doing all in their power to bring the North up to the fighting point? When these leaders faced to the rear, it was hard to say who could be counted upon to fill the front rank. In truth, it was a situation which might have discouraged a more combative patriot than Buchanan. Meanwhile, while the Northerners talked chiefly of yielding, the hot and florid rhetoric of the Southern orators, often laden with contemptuous insult, smote with disturbing menace upon the ears even of the most courageous Unionists. It was said at the South and feared at the North that secession had a "Spartan band in every Northern State," and that blood would flow in Northern cities at least as soon and as freely as on the Southern plantations, if forcible coercion should be attempted. Was it possible to be sure that this was all rodomontade? To many good citizens there seemed some reason to think that the best hope for avoiding the fulfillment at the North of these sanguinary threats might lie in the probability that the anti-slavery agitators would not stand up to encounter a genuinely mortal peril.

When the Star of the West retired, a little ignominiously, from her task of reinforcing Fort Sumter, Senator Wigfall jeered insolently. "Your flag has been insulted," he said; "redress it if you dare! You have submitted to it for two months, and you will submit forever.... We have dissolved the Union; mend it if you can; cement it with blood; try the experiment!" Mr. Chestnut of South Carolina wished to "unfurl the Palmetto flag, fling it to the breeze ... and ring the clarion notes of defiance in the ears of an insolent foe." Such bombastic but confident language, of which a great quantity was uttered in this winter of 1860-61, may exasperate or intimidate according to the present temper of the opponent whose ear it assaults; for a while the North was more in condition to be awestruck than to be angered. Her spokesmen failed to answer back, and left her to listen not without anxiety to fierce predictions that Southern flags would soon be floating over the dome of the Capitol and even over Faneuil Hall, if she should be so imprudent as to test Southern valor and Southern resources.

Matters looked even worse for the Union cause in Congress than in the country. Occasionally some irritated Northern Republican shot out words of spirit; but the prevalent desire was for conciliation, compromise, and concession, while some actually adopted secession doctrines. For example, Daniel E. Sickles, in the House, threatened that the secession of the Southern States should be followed by that of New York city; and in fact the scheme had been recommended by the Democratic mayor, Fernando Wood, in a message to the Common Council of the city on January 6; and General Dix conceived it to be a possibility. In the Senate Simon Cameron declared himself desirous to preserve the Union "by any sacrifice of feeling, and I may say of principle." A sacrifice of political principle by Cameron was not, perhaps, a serious matter; but he intended the phrase to be emphatic, and he was a leading Republican politician, had been a candidate for the presidential nomination, and was dictator in Pennsylvania. Even Seward, in the better days of the middle of January, felt that he could "afford to meet prejudice with conciliation, exaction with concession which surrenders no principle, and violence with the right hand of peace;" and he was "willing, after the excitement of rebellion and secession should have passed away, to call a convention for amending the Constitution."

This message of Buchanan marked the lowest point to which the temperature of his patriotism fell. Soon afterward, stimulated by heat applied from outside, it began to rise. The first intimation which impressed upon his anxious mind that he was being too acquiescent towards the South came from General Cass. That steadfast Democrat, of the old Jacksonian school, like many of his party at the North, was fully as good a patriot and Union man as most of the Republicans were approving themselves to be during these winter months of vacillation, alarm, and compromise. In November he was strenuously in favor of forcibly coercing a seceding State, but later assented to the tenor of Mr. Buchanan's message. The frame of mind which induced this assent, however, was transitory; for immediately he began to insist upon the reinforcement of the garrisons of the Southern forts, and on December 13 he resigned because the President refused to accede to his views. A few days earlier Howell Cobb had had the grace to resign from the Treasury, which he left entirely empty. In the reorganization Philip F. Thomas of Maryland, a Secessionist also, succeeded Cobb; Judge Black was moved into the State Department; and Edwin M. Stanton of Pennsylvania followed Black as attorney-general. Mr. Floyd, than whom no Secessionist has left a name in worse odor at the North, had at first advised against any "rash movement" in the way of secession, on the ground that Mr. Lincoln's administration would "fail, and be regarded as impotent for good or evil, within four months after his inauguration." None the less he had long been using his official position in the War Department to send arms into the Southern States, and to make all possible arrangements for putting them in an advantageous position for hostilities. Fortunately about this time the famous defalcation in the Indian Department, in which he was guiltily involved, destroyed his credit with the President, and at the same time he quarreled with his associates concerning Anderson's removal to Fort Sumter. On December 29 he resigned, and the duties of his place were laid for a while upon Judge Holt, the postmaster-general.

On Sunday morning, December 30, there was what has been properly called a cabinet crisis. The South Carolina commissioners, just arrived in Washington, were demanding recognition, and to treat with the government as if they were representatives of a foreign power. The President declined to receive them in a diplomatic character, but offered to act as go-between betwixt them and Congress. The President's advisers, however, were in a far less amiable frame of mind, for their blood had been stirred wholesomely by the secession of South Carolina and the presence of these emissaries with their insolent demands. Mr. Black, now at the head of the State Department, had gone through much the same phases of feeling as General Cass. In November he had been "emphatic in his advocacy of coercion," but afterward had approved the President's message and even declared forcible coercion to be *"ipso facto* an expulsion" of the State from the Union; since then he had drifted back and made fast at his earlier moorings. On this important Sunday morning Mr. Buchanan learned with dismay that either his reply to the South Carolinians must be substantially modified, or Mr.

Black and Mr. Stanton would retire from the cabinet. Under this pressure he yielded. Mr. Black drafted a new reply to the commissioners, Mr. Stanton copied it, Holt concurred in it, and, in substance, Mr. Buchanan accepted it. This affair constituted, as Messrs. Nicolay and Hay well say, "the President's virtual abdication," and thereafterward began the "cabinet régime." Upon the commissioners this chill gust from the North struck so disagreeably that, on January 2, they hastened home to their "independent nation." From this time forth the South covered Mr. Buchanan with contumely and abuse; Mr. Benjamin called him "a senile executive, under the sinister influence of insane counsels;" and the poor old man, really wishing to do right, but stripped of friends and of his familiar advisers, and confounded by the views of new counselors, presented a spectacle for pity.

On January 8 Mr. Thompson, secretary of the interior, resigned, and the vacancy was left unfilled. A more important change took place on the following day, when Mr. Thomas left the Treasury Department, and the New York bankers, whose aid was essential, forced the President, sorely against his will, to give the place to General John A. Dix. This proved an excellent appointment. General Dix was an old Democrat, but of the high-spirited type; he could have tolerated secession by peaceable agreement, but rose in anger at menaces against the flag and the Union. He conducted his department with entire success, and also rendered to the country perhaps the greatest service that was done by any man during that winter. On January 29 he sent the telegram which closed with the famous words: "If any one attempts to haul down the American flag, shoot him on the spot." [119] This rung out as the first cheering, stimulating indication of a fighting temper at the North. It was a tonic which came at a time of sore need, and for too long a while it remained the solitary dose!

So much of the President's message as concerned the condition of the country was referred in the House to a Committee of Thirty-three, composed by appointing one member from each State. Other resolutions and motions upon the same subject, to the number of twenty-five, were also sent to this committee. It had many sessions from December 11 to January 14, but never made an approach to evolving anything distantly approaching agreement. When, on January 14, the report came, it was an absurd fiasco: it contained six propositions, of which each had the assent of a majority of a quorum; but seven minority reports, bearing together the signatures of fourteen members, were also submitted; and the members of the seceding States refused to act. The only actual fruit was a proposed amendment to the Constitution: "That no amendment shall be made to the Constitution which will authorize or give to Congress the power to abolish or interfere, within any State, with the domestic institutions thereof, including that of persons held to labor or service by the laws of said State." In the expiring hours of the Thirty-sixth Congress this was passed by the House, and then by the Senate, and was signed by the President. Lincoln, in his inaugural address, said of it: "Holding such a provision to be now constitutional law, I have no objection to its being made express and irrevocable." This view of it was correct; it had no real significance, and the ill-written sentence never disfigured the Constitution; it simply sank out of sight, forgotten by every one.

Collaterally with the sitting of this House committee, a Committee of Thirteen was appointed in the Senate. To these gentlemen also "a string of Union-saving devices" was presented, but on the last day of the year they reported that they had "not been able to agree upon any general plan of adjustment."

The earnest effort of the venerable Crittenden to Affect a compromise aroused a faint hope. But he offered little else than an extension westward of the Missouri Compromise line; and he never really had the slightest chance of effecting that consummation, which in fact *could not be* effected. His plan was finally defeated on the last evening of the session.

Collaterally with these congressional debates there were also proceeding in Washington the sessions of the Peace Congress, another futile effort to concoct a cure for an incurable condition. It met on February 4, 1861, but only twenty-one States out of thirty-four were represented. The seven States which had seceded said that they could not come, being "Foreign Nations." Six other States [120] held aloof. Those Northern States which sent delegates selected "their most conservative and compromising men," and so great a tendency towards concession was shown that Unionists soon condemned the scheme as merely a deceitful cover devised by the Southerners behind which they could the more securely carry on their processes of secession. These gentlemen talked a great deal and finally presented a report or plan to Congress five days before the end of the session; the House refused to receive it, the Senate rejected it by 7 ayes to 28 nays. The only usefulness of the gathering was as evidence of the unwillingness of the South to compromise. In fact the Southern leaders were entirely frank and outspoken in acknowledging their position; they had said, from the beginning, that they did not wish the Committee of Thirty-three to accomplish anything; and they had endeavored to dissuade Southerners from accepting positions upon it. Hawkins of Florida said that "the time of compromise had passed forever." South Carolina refused to share in the Peace Congress, because she did "not deem it advisable to initiate negotiations when she had no desire or intention to promote the object in view." Governor Peters of Mississippi, in poetic language, suggested another difficulty: "When sparks cease to fly upwards," he said, "Comanches respect treaties, and wolves kill sheep no more, the oath of a Black Republican might be of some value as a protection to slave property." Jefferson Davis contemptuously stigmatized all the schemes of compromise as "quack nostrums," and he sneered justly enough at those who spun fine arguments of legal texture, and consumed time "discussing abstract questions, reading patchwork from the opinions of men now mingled with the dust."

It is not known by what logic gentlemen who held these views defended their conduct in retaining their positions in the government of the nation for the purpose of destroying it. Senator Yulee of Florida shamelessly gave his motive for staying in the Senate: "It is thought we can keep the hands of Mr. Buchanan tied and disable the Republicans from effecting any legislation which will strengthen the hands of the incoming administration." Mr. Toombs of Georgia, speaking and voting at his desk in the Senate, declared himself "as good a rebel and as good a traitor as ever descended from Revolutionary loins," and said that the Union was already dissolved,—by which assertion he made his position in the Senate absolutely indefensible. The South Carolina senators resigned before their State ordained itself a "foreign nation," and incurred censure for being so "precipitate." In a word, the general desire was to remain in office, hampering and obstructing the government, until March 4, 1861, and at a caucus of disunionists it was agreed to do so. But the pace became too rapid, and resignations followed pretty close upon the formal acts of secession.

On the same day on which the Peace Congress opened its sessions in Washington, there came together at Montgomery, in Alabama, delegates from six States for the purpose of forming a Southern Confederacy. On the third day thereafter a plan for a provisional government, substantially identical with the Constitution of the United States, was adopted. On February 9 the oath of allegiance was taken, and Jefferson Davis and Alexander H. Stephens were elected respectively President and Vice-President. On February 13 the military and naval committees were directed to report plans for organizing an army and navy. Mr. Davis promptly journeyed to Montgomery, making on the way many speeches, in which he told his hearers that no plan for a reconstruction of the old Union would be entertained; and promised that those who should interfere with the new nation would have to "smell Southern powder and to feel Southern steel." On February 18 he was inaugurated, and in his address again referred to the "arbitrament of the sword." Immediately afterward he announced his cabinet as follows:—

Robert Toombs of Georgia, secretary of state.
C.G. Memminger of South Carolina, secretary of the

treasury.

L.P. Walker of Alabama, secretary of war.

S.R. Mallory of Florida, secretary of the navy.

J.H. Reagan of Texas, postmaster-general.

Judah P. Benjamin of Louisiana, attorney-general.

On March 11 the permanent Constitution was adopted. [121] Thus the machine of the new government was set in working order. Mr. Greeley gives some interesting figures showing the comparative numerical strength of the sections of the country at this time: [122] —

The free population of the seven States which had seceded, was	2,656,948
The free population of the eight slave States [123] which had not seceded, was	5,633,005
Total	8,289,953
The slaves in the States of the first list were	2,312,046
The slaves in the States of the second list were	1,638,297
Total of slaves	3,950,343
The population of the whole Union by the census of 1860, was	31,443,321

The disproportion would have discouraged the fathers of the new nation, if they had anticipated that the North would be resolute in using its overwhelming resources. But how could they believe that this would be the case when they read the New York "Tribune" and the reports of Mr. Phillips's harangues?

On February 13 the electoral vote was to be counted in Congress. Rumors were abroad that the Secessionists intended to interfere with this by tumults and violence; but the evidence is insufficient to prove that any such scheme was definitely matured; it was talked of, but ultimately it seems to have been laid aside with a view to action at a later date. Naturally enough, however, the country was disquieted. In the emergency the action of General Scott was watched with deep anxiety. A Southerner by birth and by social sympathies, he had been expected by the Secessionists to join their movement. But the old soldier—though broken by age and infirmities, and though he had proposed the folly of voluntarily quartering the country, like the corpse of a traitor—had his patriotism and his temper at once aroused when violence was threatened. On and after October 29 he had repeatedly advised reinforcement of the Southern garrisons; though it must be admitted, in Buchanan's behalf, that the general made no suggestion as to how or where the troops could be obtained for this purpose. In the same spirit he now said, with stern resolution, that there should be ample military preparations to insure both the count and the inauguration; and he told some of the Southerners that he would blow traitors to pieces at the cannon's mouth without hesitation. Disturbed at his vehemence, they denounced him bitterly, and sent him frequent notices of assassination. Floyd distributed orders concerning troops and munitions directly from the War Department, and carefully concealed them from the general who was the head of the army. But secrecy and intimidation were in vain. The aged warrior was fiercely in earnest; if there was going to be any outbreak in Washington he was going to put it down with bullets and bayonets, and he gathered his soldiers and instructed his officers accordingly. But happily the preparation of these things was sufficient to render the use of them unnecessary. When the day came Vice-President Breckenridge performed his duty, however unwelcome, without flinching. He presided over the joint session and conducted the count with the air of a man determined to enforce law and order, and at the close declared the election of Abraham Lincoln and Hannibal Hamlin.

Still only the smaller crisis had been passed. Much more alarming stories now flew from mouth to mouth, — of plots to seize the capital and to prevent the inauguration, even to assassinate Lincoln on his journey to Washington. How much foundation there was for these is not accurately known. That the idea of capturing Washington had fascinated the Southern fancy is certain. "I see no reason," said Senator Iverson, "why Washington city should not be continued the capital of the Southern Confederacy." The Richmond "Examiner" railed grossly: "That filthy cage of unclean birds must and will assuredly be purified by fire.... Our people can take it, — they will take it.... Scott, the arch-traitor, and Lincoln, the beast, combined, cannot prevent it. The 'Illinois Ape' must retrace his journey more rapidly than he came." The abundant talk of this sort created uneasiness; and Judge Holt said that there was cause for alarm. But a committee of Congress reported that, though it was difficult to speak positively, yet they found no evidence sufficient to prove "the existence of a secret organization." Alexander H. Stephens has denied that there was any intention to attack the city, and probably the notion of seizure did not pass beyond the stage of talk.

But the alleged plot to assassinate Mr. Lincoln was more definite. He had been spending the winter quietly in Springfield, where he had been overrun by visitors, who wished to look at him, to advise him, and to secure promises of office; fortunately the tedious procession had lost part of its offensiveness by touching his sense of humor. Anxious people made well-meaning but useless efforts to induce him to say something for effect upon the popular mind; but he resolutely and wisely maintained silence. His position and opinions, he said, had already been declared in his speeches with all the clearness he could give to them, and the people had appeared to understand and approve them. He could not improve and did not desire to change these utterances. Occasionally he privately expressed his dislike to the conceding and compromising temper which threatened to undo, for an indefinite future, all which the long and weary struggle of anti-slavery men had accomplished. In this line he wrote a letter of protest to Greeley, which inspired that gentleman to a singular expression of sympathy; let the Union go to pieces, exclaimed the emotional editor, let presidents be assassinated, let the Republican party suffer crushing defeat, but let there not be "another nasty compromise." To Mr. Kellogg, the Illinoisian on the House Committee of Thirty-three, Lincoln wrote: "Entertain no proposition for a compromise in regard to the extension of slavery. The instant you do, they have us under again; all our labor is lost, and sooner or later must be done over again." He repeated almost the same words to E.B. Washburne, a member of the House. Duff Green tried hard to get something out of him for the comfort of Mr. Buchanan, but failed to extort more than commonplace generalities. To Seward he wrote that he did not wish to interfere with the present status, or to meddle with slavery as it now lawfully existed. To like purport he wrote to Alexander H. Stephens, induced thereto by the famous Union speech of that gentleman. He eschewed hostile feeling, saying: "I never have been, am not now, and probably never shall be, in a mood of harassing the people, either North or South." Nevertheless, while he said that all were "brothers of a common country," he was perfectly resolved that the country should remain "common," even if the bond of brotherhood had to be riveted by force. He admitted that this necessity would be "an ugly point;" but he was perfectly clear that "the right of a State to secede is not an open or debatable question." He desired that General Scott should be prepared either to "hold or retake" the Southern forts, if need should be, at or after the inauguration; but on his journey to Washington he said to many audiences that he wished no war and no bloodshed, and that these evils could be avoided if people would only "keep cool" and "keep their temper, on both sides of the line."

On Monday, February 11, 1861, Mr. Lincoln spoke to his fellow citizens of Springfield a very brief farewell, so solemn as to sound ominous in the ears of those who know what afterward occurred. It was arranged that he should stop at various points upon the somewhat circuitous route which had been laid out, and that he should arrive in Washington on Saturday, February 23. The programme, was pursued accurately till near the close;

he made, of course, many speeches, but none added anything to what was already known as to his views.

Meantime the thick rumors of violence were bringing much uneasiness to persons who were under responsibilities. Baltimore was the place where, and its villainous "Plug Uglies" were the persons by whom, the plot, if there was one, was to be executed. Mr. Felton, president of the Philadelphia, Wilmington and Baltimore Railroad Company, engaged Allan Pinkerton to explore the matter, and the report of this skillful detective indicated a probability of an attack with the purpose of assassination. At that time the cars were drawn by horses across town from the northern to the southern station, and during the passage an assault could be made with ease and with great chance of success. As yet there was no indication that the authorities intended to make, even if they could make, [124] any adequate arrangements for the protection of the traveler. At Philadelphia Mr. Lincoln was told of the fears of his friends, and talked with Mr. Pinkerton, but he refused to change his plan. On February 22 he was to assist at a flag-raising in Philadelphia, and was then to go on to Harrisburg, and on the following day he was to go from there to Baltimore. He declined to alter either route or hours.

But other persons besides Mr. Felton had been busy with independent detective investigations, the result of which was in full accord with the report of Mr. Pinkerton. On February 22 Mr. Frederick W. Seward, sent by his father and General Scott, both then at Washington, delivered to Mr. Lincoln, at Philadelphia, the message that there was "serious danger" to his life if the time of his passage through Baltimore should be known. Yet Lincoln still remained obdurate. He declared that if an escorting delegation from Baltimore should meet him at Harrisburg, he would go on with it. But at Harrisburg no such escort presented itself. Then the few who knew the situation discussed further as to what should be done, Norman B. Judd being chief spokesman for evading the danger by a change of programme. Naturally the objection of seeming timid and of exciting ridicule was present in the minds of all, and it was put somewhat emphatically by Colonel Sumner. Mr. Lincoln at last settled the dispute; he said: "I have thought over this matter considerably since I went over the ground with Pinkerton last night. The appearance of Mr. Frederick Seward, with warning from another source, confirms Mr. Pinkerton's belief. Unless there are some other reasons besides fear of ridicule, I am disposed to carry out Judd's plan."

This plan was accordingly carried out with the success which its simplicity insured. Mr. Lincoln and his stalwart friend, Colonel Lamon, slipped out of a side door to a hackney carriage, were driven to the railway station, and returned by the train to Philadelphia. Their departure was not noticed, but had it been, news of it could not have been sent away, for Mr. Felton had had the telegraph wires secretly cut outside the town. He also ordered, upon a plausible pretext, that the southward-bound night train on his road should be held back until the arrival of this train from Harrisburg. Mr. Lincoln and Colonel Lamon passed from the one train to the other without recognition, and rolled into Washington early on the following morning. Mr. Seward and Mr. Washburne met Lincoln at the station and went with him to Willard's Hotel. Soon afterward the country was astonished, and perhaps some persons were discomfited, as the telegraph carried abroad the news of his arrival.

Those who were disappointed at this safe conclusion of his journey, if in fact there were any such, together with many who would have contemned assassination, at once showered upon him sneers and ridicule. They said that Lincoln had put on a disguise and had shown the white feather, when there had been no real danger. But this was not just. Whether or not there was the completed machinery of a definite, organized plot for assault and assassination is uncertain; that is to say, this is not *proved*; yet the evidence is so strong that the majority of investigators seem to agree in the opinion that *probably* there was a plan thoroughly concerted and ready for execution. Even if there was not, it was very likely that a riot might be suddenly started, which would be as fatal in its consequences as a premeditated scheme. But, after all, the question of the plot is one of mere curiosity and quite aside from the true issue. That issue, so far as it presented itself for determination by Mr. Lincoln, was simply whether a case of such probability of danger was made out that as a prudent man he should overrule the only real objection, — that of exciting ridicule, — and avoid a peril which the best judges believed to exist, and which, if it did exist, involved consequences of immeasurable seriousness not only to himself but to the nation. For a wise man only one conclusion was possible. The story of the disguise was a silly slander, based upon the trifling fact that for this night journey Lincoln wore a traveling cap instead of his hat.

Lincoln's own opinion as to the danger is not quite clear. [125] He said to Mr. Lossing that, after hearing Mr. Seward, he believed "such a plot to be in existence." But he also said: "I did not then, nor do I now, believe I should have been assassinated, had I gone through Baltimore as first contemplated; but I thought it wise to run no risk, where no risk was necessary."

The reflection can hardly fail to occur, how grossly unfair it was that Mr. Lincoln should be put into the position in which he was put at this time, and then that fault should be found with him even if his prudence was overstrained. Many millions of people in the country hated him with a hatred unutterable; among them might well be many fanatics, to whom assassination would seem a noble act, many desperadoes who would regard it as a pleasing excitement; and he was to go through a city which men of this stamp could at any time dominate. The custom of the country compelled this man, whom it had long since selected as its ruler, to make a journey of extreme danger without any species of protection whatsoever. So far as peril went, no other individual in the United States had ever, presumably, been in a peril like that which beset him; so far as safeguards went, he had no more than any other traveler. A few friends volunteered to make the journey with him, but they were useless as guardians; and he and they were so hustled and jammed in the railway stations that one of them actually had his arm broken. This extraordinary spectacle may have indicated folly on the part of the nation which permitted it, but certainly it did not involve the disgrace of the individual who had no choice about it. The people put Mr. Lincoln in a position in which he was subjected to the most appalling, as it is the most vague, of all dangers, and then left him to take care of himself as best he could. It was ungenerous afterward to criticise him for exercising prudence in the performance of that duty which he ought never to have been called upon to perform at all. [126]

Immediately after his arrival in Washington Mr. Lincoln received a visit from the members of the Peace Congress. Grotesque and ridiculous descriptions of him, as if he had been a Caliban in education, manners, and aspect, had been rife among Southerners, and the story goes that the Southern delegates expected to be at once amused and shocked by the sight of a clodhopper whose conversation would be redolent of the barnyard, not to say of the pigsty. Those of them who had any skill in reading character were surprised,— as the tradition is,—discomfited, even a little alarmed, at what in fact they beheld; for Mr. Lincoln appeared before them a self-possessed man, expressing to them such clear convictions and such a distinct and firm purpose as compelled them into new notions of his capacity and told them of much trouble ahead. His remark to Mr. Rives, coming from one who spoke accurately, had an ominous sound in rebellious ears: "My course is as plain as a turnpike road. It is marked out by the Constitution. I am in no doubt which way to go." The wiser Southerners withdrew from this reception quite sober and thoughtful, with some new ideas about the man with whom their relationship seemed on the verge of becoming hostile. After abundant allowance is made for the enthusiasm of Northern admirers, it remains certain that Lincoln bore well this severe ordeal of criticism on the part of those who would have been glad to despise him. Ungainly they saw him, but not undignified, and the strange impressive sadness seldom dwelt so strikingly upon his face as at this time, as though all the weight of misery, which the millions of his fellow citizens were to endure throughout the coming years, already burdened the soul of the ruler who had been chosen to play the most responsible part in the crisis and the anguish.

March 4, 1861, inauguration day, was fine and sunny. If there had ever been any real danger of trouble, the fear of it had almost entirely subsided. Northerners and Southerners had found out in good season that General Scott was not in a temporizing mood; he had in the city two batteries, a few companies of regulars,—653 men, exclusive of some marines,—and the corps of picked Washington Volunteers. He said that this force was all he wanted. President Buchanan left the White House in an open carriage, escorted by a company of sappers and miners under Captain Duane. At Willard's Hotel Mr. Lincoln entered the carriage, and the two gentlemen passed along the avenue, through crowds which cheered but made no disturbance, to the Capitol. General Scott with his regulars marched, "flanking the movement, in parallel streets." His two batteries, while not made unpleasantly conspicuous, yet controlled the plateau which extends before the east front of the Capitol. Mr. Lincoln was simply introduced by Senator Baker of Oregon, and delivered his inaugural address. His voice had great carrying capacity, and the vast crowd heard with ease a speech of which every sentence was fraught with an importance and scrutinized with an anxiety far beyond that of any other speech ever delivered in the United States. At its close the venerable Chief Justice Taney administered the oath of office, thereby informally but effectually reversing the most famous opinion delivered by him during his long incumbency in his high office. .

The inaugural address was simple, earnest, and direct, unincumbered by that rhetorical ornamentation which the American people have always admired as the highest form of eloquence. Those Northerners who had expected magniloquent periods and exaggerated outbursts of patriotism were disappointed; and as they listened in vain for the scream of the eagle, many grumbled at the absence of what they conceived to be *force*. Yet the general feeling was of satisfaction, which grew as the address was more thoroughly studied. The Southerners, upon their part, looking anxiously to see whether or not they must fight for their purpose, construed the words of the new President correctly. They heard him say: "The union of these States is perpetual." "No State upon its own mere motion can lawfully get out of the Union." "I shall take care, as the Constitution itself expressly enjoins upon me, that the laws of the Union be faithfully executed in all the States." He also declared his purpose "to hold, occupy, and possess the property and places belonging to the government, and to collect the duties and imposts." These sentences made up the issue directly with secession, and the South, reading them, knew that, if the North was ready to back the President, war was inevitable; none the less so because Mr. Lincoln closed with patriotic and generous words: "We are not enemies, but friends. We must not be enemies. Though passion may have strained, it must not break our bonds of affection."

Until after the election of Mr. Lincoln in November, 1860, the sole issue between the North and the South, between Republicans on the one hand and Democrats and Compromisers on the other, had related to slavery. Logically, the position of the Republicans was impregnable. Their platforms and their leaders agreed that the party intended strictly to respect the Constitution, and not to interfere at all with slavery in the States within which it now lawfully existed. They said with truth that they had in no case deprived the slaveholding communities of their rights, and they denied the truth of the charge that they cherished an inchoate design to interfere with those rights; adding very truly that, at worst, a mere design, which did not find expression in an overt act, could give no right of action to the South. Mr. Lincoln had been most explicit in declaring that the opposition to slavery was not to go beyond efforts to prevent its *extension*, which efforts would be wholly within the Constitution and the law. He repeated these things in his inaugural.

But while these incontrovertible allegations gave the Republicans a logical advantage of which they properly made the most, the South claimed a right to make other collateral and equally undeniable facts the ground of action. The only public matter in connection with which Mr. Lincoln had won any reputation was that of slavery. No one could deny that he had been elected because the Republican party had been pleased with his expression of opinion on this subject. Now his most pointed and frequently reiterated expression of that opinion was that slavery was a "moral, social, and political evil;" and this language was a fair equivalent of the statement of the Republican platform of 1856, classing Slavery and Mormonism together, as "twin relics of barbarism." That the North was willing, or would long be willing, to remain in amicable social and political bonds with a moral, social, and political evil, and a relic of barbarism, was intrinsically improbable, and was made more improbable by the symptoms of the times. [127] Indeed, Mr. Seward had said, in famous words, that his section would not play this unworthy part; he had proclaimed already the existence of an "irrepressible conflict;" and therefore the South had the word of the Republican leader that, in spite of the Republican respect for the law, an anti-slavery crusade was already in existence. The Southern chiefs distinctly recognized and accepted this situation. [128] There was an avowed Northern condemnation of their institution; there was an acknowledged "conflict." Such being the case, it was the opinion of the chief men at the South that the position taken by the North, of strict performance of clear constitutional duties concerning an odious institution, would not suffice for the safe perpetuation of that institution. [129] This, their judgment, appeared to be in a certain way also the judgment of Mr. Lincoln; for he also conceived that to put slavery where the "fathers" had left it was to put it "in the way of ultimate extinction;" and he had, in the most famous utterance of his life, given his forecast of the future to the effect that the country would in time be "all free." The only logical deduction was that he, and the Republican party which had agreed with him sufficiently to make him president, believed that the South had no lawful recourse by which this result, however unwelcome or ruinous, could in the long run and the fullness of time be escaped. Under such circumstances Southern political leaders now decided that the time for separation had come. In speaking of their scheme they called it "secession," and said that secession was a lawful act because the Constitution was a compact revocable by any of the parties. They might have called it "revolution," [130] and have defended it upon the general right of any large body of people, dissatisfied with the government under which they find themselves, to cast it off. But, if the step was *revolution*, then the burden of proof was upon them; whereas they said that *secession* was their lawful right, without any regard whatsoever to the motive which induced them to exercise it. [131] Such was the character of the issue between the North and the South prior to the first ordinance of secession. The action of South Carolina, followed by the other Gulf States, at once changed that issue, shifting it from pro-slavery versus anti-slavery to union versus disunion. This alteration quickly compelled great numbers of men, both at the North and at the South, to reconsider and, upon a new issue, to place themselves also anew.

It has been said by all writers that in the seven seceding States there was, in the four months following the election, a very large proportion of "Union men." The name only signified that these men did not think that the present inducements to disunion were sufficient to render it a wise measure. It did not signify that they thought disunion unlawful, unconstitutional, and treasonable. When, however, state conventions decided the question of advisability against their opinions, and they had to choose between allegiance to the State and allegiance to the Union, they immediately adhered to the State, and this none the less because they feared that she had taken an ill-advised step. That is to say, at the South a "Union man" *wished* to preserve the Union, whereas at the North a "Union man" recognized a supreme *obligation* to do so.

While the South, by political alchemy, was becoming solidified and homogeneous, a corresponding change was going on at the North. In that section the great numbers—of whom some would have re-made the Constitution, others would have agreed to peaceable separation, and still others would have made any concession to retain the integrity of the Union—now saw that these were indeed, as Jefferson Davis had said, "quack nostrums," and that the choice lay between permitting a secession accompanied with insulting menaces and some degree of actual violence, and maintaining the Union by coercion. In this dilemma great multitudes of Northern Democrats, whose consciences had never been in the least disturbed by the existence of slavery in the country or even by efforts to extend it, became "Union men" in the Northern sense of the word, which made it about equivalent to coercionists. Their simple creed was the integrity and perpetuity of the nation.

Mr. Lincoln showed in his inaugural his accurate appreciation of the new situation. Owing all that he had become in the world to a few anti-slavery speeches, elevated to the presidency by votes which really meant little else than hostility to slavery, what was more natural than that he should at this moment revert to this great topic and make the old dispute the main part and real substance of his address? But this fatal error he avoided. With unerring judgment he dwelt little on that momentous issue which had only just been displaced, and took his stand fairly upon that still more momentous one which had so newly come up. He spoke for the Union; upon that basis a united North *ought* to support him; upon that basis the more northern of the slave States might remain loyal. As matter of fact, Union had suddenly become the real issue, but it needed at the hands of the President to be publicly and explicitly announced as such; this recognition was essential; he gave it on this earliest opportunity, and the announcement was the first great service of the new Republican ruler. It seems now as though he could hardly have done otherwise, or have fallen into the error of allying himself with bygone or false issues. It may be admitted that he could not have passed this new one by; but the important matter was that of proportion and relation, and in this it was easy to blunder. In truth it was a crisis when blundering was so easy that nearly all the really able men of the North had been doing it badly for three or four months past, and not a few of them were going to continue it for two or three months to come. Therefore the sound conception of the inaugural deserves to be considered as an indication, one among many, of Lincoln's capacity for seeing with entire distinctness the great main fact, and for recognizing it as such. Other matters, which lay over and around such a fact, side issues, questions of detail, affairs of disguise or deception, never confused or misled him. He knew with unerring accuracy where the biggest fact lay, and he always anchored fast to it and stayed with it. For many years he had been anchored to anti-slavery; now, in the face of the nation, he shifted his anchorage to the Union; and each time he held securely.

[114] Breckenridge was the legitimate representative of the administrationists, and his ticket received only 847,953 votes out of 4,680,193. Douglas and Buchanan were at open war.

[115] See remarks of Mr. Elaine upon use of this word. *Twenty Years of Congress*, i. 219.

[116] But it should be said that Attorney-General Black supported these views in a very elaborate opinion, which he had furnished to the President, and which was transmitted to Congress at the same time with the message.

[117] Greeley afterwards truly said that his journal had plenty of company in these sentiments, even among the Republican sheets. *Amer. Conflict*, i. 359. Reference is made in the text to the utterances of the *Tribune* more because it was so prominent and influential than because it was very peculiar in its position.

[118] Wilson, *Rise and Fall of Slave Power*, iii. 63-69; N. and H. in. 255. See account of "the Pine Street meeting," New York, in Dix's *Memoirs of Dix*, i. 347.

[119] For an account of this by General Dix himself, see *Memoirs of John A. Dix*, by Morgan Dix, i. 370-373.

[120] Arkansas, California, Michigan, Minnesota, Oregon, and Wisconsin

[121] It differed from that of the United States very little, save in containing a distinct recognition of slavery, and in being made by the States instead of by the people.

[122] *American Conflict*, i. 351.

[123] This includes Delaware, 110,420, and Maryland, 599,846.

[124] Marshal Kane and most of the police were reported to be Secessionists. Pinkerton, *Spy of the Rebellion*, 50, 61.

[125] Lamon says that Mr. Lincoln afterwards regretted this journey, and became convinced "that he had committed a grave mistake." Lamon, 527. So also McClure, 45, 48.

[126] For accounts of this journey and statements of the evidence of a plot, see Schouler, *Hist. of Mass. in Civil War*, i. 59-65 (account by Samuel M. Felton, Prest. P.W. & B.R.R. Co.); N. and H. iii. ch. 19 and 20; Chittenden, *Recoll. of Lincoln*, x.; Holland, 275; Arnold, 183-187; Lamon, ch. xx. (this account ought to be, and doubtless is, the most trustworthy); Herndon, 492 (a bit of gossip which sounds improbable); Pinkerton, *Spy of the Rebellion*, 45-103. On the anti-plot side of the question the most important evidence is the little volume, *Baltimore and the Nineteenth of April, 1861*, by George William Brown. This witness, whose strict veracity is beyond question, was mayor of the city. One of his statements, especially, is of the greatest importance. It is obvious that, if the plot existed, one of two things ought to occur on the morning of February 23, viz.: either the plotters and the mobsmen should know that Mr. Lincoln had escaped them, or else they should be at the station at the hour set for his arrival. In fact they were not at the station; there was no sudden assault on the cars, nor other indication of assassins and a mob. Had they, then, received knowledge of what had occurred? Those who sustain the plot-theory say that the news had spread through the city, so that all the assassins and the gangs of the "Plug Uglies" knew that their game was up. This was *possible*, for Mr. Lincoln had arrived in the Washington station a few minutes after six o'clock in the morning, and the train which was expected to bring him to Baltimore did not arrive in Baltimore until half after eleven o'clock. But, on the other hand, the news was not dispatched from Washington immediately upon his arrival; somewhat later, though still early in the morning, the detectives telegraphed to the friends of Mr. Lincoln, but in cipher. Just at what time intelligible telegrams, which would inform the public, were sent out cannot be learned; but upon any arrangement of hours it is obvious that the time was exceedingly short for distributing the news throughout the lower quarters of Baltimore by word of mouth, and there is no pretense of any publication. But while the believers in

the plot say, nevertheless, that this had been done and that the story of the journey had spread through the city so that all the assassins and "Plug Uglies" knew it in time to avoid assembling at the railway station about eleven o'clock, yet it appears that Mr. Brown, the mayor, knew nothing about it. On the contrary, he tells us that in anticipation of Mr. Lincoln's arrival he, "as mayor of the city, accompanied by the police commissioners and supported by a strong force of police, was at the Calvert Street station on Saturday morning, February 23, at 11.30 o'clock ... ready to receive with due respect the incoming President. An open carriage was in waiting, in which I was to have the honor of escorting Mr. Lincoln through the city to the Washington station, and of sharing in any danger which he might encounter. It is hardly necessary to say that I apprehended none." To the "great astonishment" of Mr. Brown, however, the train brought only "Mrs. Lincoln and her three sons," and "it was then announced that he had passed through the city *incognito* in the night train." This is a small bit of evidence to set against the elaborate stories of the believers in the plot, yet to some it will seem like the little obstruction which suffices to throw a whole railway train from the track. I would rather let any reader, who is sufficiently interested to examine the matter, reach his own conclusion, than endeavor to furnish one for him; for I think that a dispute more difficult of really conclusive settlement will not easily be found.

[127] Some of the Southern members of Congress collected and recited sundry noteworthy utterances of Republicans concerning slavery, and certainly there was little in them to induce a sense of security on the part of slaveholders. Wilson, *Rise and Fall of Slave Power*, iii. 97, 154.

[128] Toombs declared, as Lincoln had said, that what was wanted was that the North should *call slavery right*. Wilson, *Rise and Fall of Slave Power*, iii. 76. Stephens declared the "corner-stone" of the new government to be "the great truth that the negro is not equal to the white man; that slavery ... is his natural and normal condition;" and said that it was the first government "in the history of the world based upon this great physical, philosophical, and moral truth."

N. and H. iii. 203; and see his letter to Lincoln, *ibid.* 272, 273. Mississippi, in declaring the causes of her secession, said: "Our position is thoroughly identical with the institution of slavery,—the greatest material interest in the world." N. and H. iii. 201. Senator Mason of Virginia said: "It is a war of sentiment, of opinion; a war of one form of society against another form of society." Wilson, *Rise and Fall of Slave Power*, iii. 26. Green of Missouri ascribed the trouble to the "vitiated and corrupted state of public sentiment." *Ibid.* 23. Iverson of Georgia said it was the "public sentiment" at the North, not the "overt acts" of the Republican administration, that was feared; and said that there was ineradicable enmity between the two sections, which had not lived together in peace, were not so living now, and could not be expected to do so in the future. *Ibid.* 17.

[129] Historians generally seem to admit that the South had to choose between making the fight now, and seeing its favorite institution gradually become extinct.

[130] Sometimes, though very rarely, the word was used.

[131] See Lincoln's message to Congress, July 4, 1861.

CHAPTER VIII
THE BEGINNING OF WAR

From the inaugural ceremonies Lincoln drove quietly back through Pennsylvania Avenue and entered the White House, the President of the United States,—alas, united no longer. Many an anxious citizen breathed more freely when the dreaded hours had passed without disturbance. But burdens a thousand fold heavier than any which were lifted from others descended upon the new ruler. Save, however, that the thoughtful, far-away expression of sadness had of late seemed deeper and more impressive than ever before, Lincoln gave no sign of inward trouble. His singular temperament armed him with a rare and peculiar strength beneath responsibility and in the face of duty. He has been seen, with entire tranquillity, not only seeking, but seeming to assume as his natural due or destiny, positions which appeared preposterously out of accord alike with his early career and with his later opportunities for development. In trying to explain this, it is easier to say what was *not* the underlying quality than what it was. Certainly there was no taint whatsoever of that vulgar self-confidence which is so apt to lead the "free and equal" citizens of the great republic into grotesque positions. Perhaps it was a grand simplicity of faith; a profound instinctive confidence that by patient, honest thinking it would be possible to know the right road, and by earnest enduring courage to follow it. Perhaps it was that so-called divine inspiration which seems always a part of the highest human fitness. The fact which is distinctly visible is, that a fair, plain and honest method of thinking saved him from the perplexities which beset subtle dialecticians in politics and in constitutional law. He had lately said that his course was "as plain as a turnpike road;" it was, to execute the public laws.

His duty was simple; his understanding of it was unclouded by doubt or sophistry; his resolution to do it was firm; but whether his hands would be strengthened sufficiently to enable him to do it was a question of grave anxiety. The president of a republic can do everything if the people are at his back, and almost nothing if the people are not at his back. Where, then, were now the people of the United States? In seven States they were openly and unitedly against him; in at least seven more they were under a very strong temptation to range themselves against him in case of a conflict; and as for the Republican States of the North, on that fourth day of March, 1861, no man could say to what point they would sustain the administration. There had as yet come slight indications of any change in the conceding, compromising temper of that section. Greeley and Seward and Wendell Phillips, representative men, were little better than Secessionists. The statement sounds ridiculous, yet the proof against each comes from his own mouth. The "Tribune" had retracted none of those disunion sentiments, of which examples have been given. Even so late as April 10, 1861, Mr. Seward wrote officially to Mr. C.F. Adams, minister to England: "Only an imperial and despotic government could subjugate thoroughly disaffected and insurrectionary members of the state. This federal, republican country of ours is, of all forms of government, the very one which is the most unfitted for such a labor." He had been and still was favoring delay and conciliation, in the visionary hope that the seceders would follow the scriptural precedent of the prodigal son. On April 9 the rumor of a fight at Sumter being spread abroad, Mr. Phillips said: [132] "Here are a series of States, girding the Gulf, who think that their peculiar institutions require that they should have a separate government. They have a right to decide that question without appealing to you or me.... Standing with the principles of '76 behind us, who can deny them the right?... Abraham Lincoln has no right to a soldier in Fort Sumter.... There is no longer a Union.... Mr. Jefferson Davis is angry, and Mr. Abraham Lincoln is mad, and they agree to fight.... You cannot go through Massachusetts and recruit men to bombard Charleston or New Orleans.... We are in no condition to fight.... Nothing but madness can provoke war with the Gulf States;"—with much more to the same effect.

If the veterans of the old anti-slavery contest were in this frame of mind in April, Lincoln could hardly place much dependence upon the people at large in March. If he could not "recruit men" in Massachusetts, in what State could he reasonably expect to do so? Against such discouragement it can only be said that he had a singular instinct for the underlying popular feeling, that he could scent it in the distance and in hiding; moreover, that he was always willing to run the chance of any consequences which might follow the performance of a clear duty. Still, as he looked over the dreary Northern field in those chill days of early March, he must have had a marvelous sensitiveness in order to perceive the generative heat and force in the depths beneath the cheerless surface and awaiting only the fullness of the near spring season to burst forth in sudden universal vigor. Yet such was his knowledge and such his faith concerning the people that we may fancy, if we will, that he foresaw the great transformation. But there were still other matters which disturbed him. Before his inauguration, he had heard much of his coming official isolation. One of the arguments reiterated alike by Southern Unionists and by Northerners had been that the Republican President would be powerless, because the Senate, the House, and the Supreme Court were all opposed to him. But the supposed lack of political sympathy on the part of these bodies, however it might beget anxiety for the future, was for the present of much less moment than another fact, viz., that none of the distinguished men, leaders in his own party, whom Lincoln found about him at Washington, were in a frame of mind to assist him efficiently. If all did not actually distrust his capacity and character,—which, doubtless, many honestly did,—at least they were profoundly ignorant concerning both. Therefore they could not yet, and did not, place genuine, implicit confidence in him; they could not yet, and did not, advise and aid him at all in the same spirit and with the same usefulness as later they were able to do. They were not to blame for this; on the contrary, the condition had been brought about distinctly against their will, since certainly few of them had looked with favor upon the selection of an unknown, inexperienced, ill-educated man as the Republican candidate for the presidency. How much Lincoln felt his loneliness will never be known; for, reticent and self-contained at all times, he gave no outward sign. That he felt it less than other men would have done may be regarded as certain; for, as has already appeared to some extent, and as will appear much more in this narrative, he was singularly self-reliant, and, at least in appearance, was strangely indifferent to any counsel or support which could be brought to him by others. Yet, marked as was this trait in him, he could hardly have been human had he not felt oppressed by the personal solitude and political isolation of his position when the responsibility of his great office rested newly upon him. Under all these circumstances, if this lonely man moved slowly and cautiously during the early weeks of his administration, it was not at his door that the people had the right to lay the reproach of weakness or hesitation.

Mr. Buchanan, for the convenience of his successor, had called an extra session of the Senate, and on March 5 President Lincoln sent in the nominations for his cabinet. All were immediately confirmed, as follows:—

William H. Seward, New York, secretary of state.
Salmon P. Chase, Ohio, secretary of the treasury.
Simon Cameron, Pennsylvania, secretary of war.
Gideon Welles, Connecticut, secretary of the navy.
Caleb B. Smith, Indiana, secretary of the interior.
Edward Bates, Missouri, attorney-general.
Montgomery Blair, Maryland, postmaster-general.

It is matter of course that a cabinet slate should fail to give general satisfaction; and this one encountered fully the average measure of criticism.

The body certainly was somewhat heterogeneous in its composition, yet the same was true of the Republican party which it represented. Nor was it by any means so heterogeneous as Mr. Lincoln had designed to have it, for he had made efforts to place in it a Southern spokesman for Southern views; and he had not desisted from the purpose until its futility was made apparent by the direct refusal of Mr. Gilmer of North Carolina, and by indications of a like unwillingness on the part of one or two other Southerners who were distantly sounded on the subject. Seward, Chase, Bates, and Cameron were the four men who had manifested the greatest popularity, after Lincoln, in the national convention, and the selection of them, therefore, showed that Mr. Lincoln was seeking strength rather than amity in his cabinet; for it was certainly true that each one of them had a following which was far from being wholly in sympathy with the following of any one of the others. The President evidently believed that it was of more importance that each great body of Northern men should feel that its opinions were fairly presented, than that his cabinet officers should always comfortably unite in looking at questions from one and the same point of view. Judge Davis says that Lincoln's original design was to appoint Democrats and Republicans alike to office. He carried this theory so far that the radical Republicans regarded the make-up of the cabinet as a "disgraceful surrender to the South;" while men of less extreme views saw with some alarm that he had called to his advisory council four ex-Democrats and only three ex-Whigs, a criticism which he met by saying that he himself was an "old-line Whig" and should be there to make the parties even. On the other hand, the Republicans of the middle line of States grumbled much at the selection of Bates and Blair as representatives of their section.

The cabinet had not been brought together without some jarring and friction, especially in the case of Cameron. On December 31 Mr. Lincoln intimated to him that he should have either the Treasury or the War Department, but on January 3 requested him to "decline the appointment." Cameron, however, had already mentioned the matter to many friends, without any suggestion that he should not be glad to accept either position, and therefore, even if he were willing to accede to the sudden, strange, and unexplained request of Mr. Lincoln, he would have found it difficult to do so without giving rise to much embarrassing gossip. Accordingly he did not decline, and thereupon ensued much wire-pulling. Pennsylvania protectionists wanted Cameron in the Treasury, and strenuously objected to Chase as an ex-Democrat of free-trade proclivities. On the other hand, Lincoln gradually hardened into the resolution that Chase should have the Treasury. He made the tender, and it was accepted. He then offered consolation to Pennsylvania by giving the War portfolio to Cameron, which was accepted with something of chagrin. How far this Cameron episode was affected by the bargain declared by Lamon to have been made at Chicago cannot be told. Other biographers ignore this story, but I do not see how the direct testimony furnished by Lamon and corroborated by Colonel McClure can justly be treated in this way; neither is the temptation so to treat it apparent, since the evidence entirely absolves Lincoln from any complicity at the time of making the alleged "trade," while he could hardly be blamed if he felt somewhat hampered by it afterward.

Seward also gave trouble which he ought not to have given. On December 8 Lincoln wrote to him that he would nominate him as secretary of state. Mr. Seward assented and the matter remained thus comfortably settled until so late as March 2, 1861, when Seward wrote a brief note asking "leave to withdraw his consent." Apparently the Democratic complexion of the cabinet, and the suggestions of suspicious friends, made him fear that his influence in the ministry would be inferior to that of Chase. Coming at this eleventh hour, which already had its weighty burden of many anxieties, this brief destructive note was both embarrassing and exasperating. It meant the entire reconstruction of the cabinet. Never did Lincoln's tranquil indifference to personal provocation stand him in better stead than in this crisis,—for a crisis it was when Seward, in discontent and distrust, desired to draw aloof from the administration. He held the note of the recalcitrant politician for two days unanswered, then he wrote a few lines: "Your note," he said, "is the subject of the most painful solicitude with me; and I feel constrained to beg that you will countermand the withdrawal. The public interest, I think, demands that you should; and my personal feelings are deeply enlisted in the same direction." These words set Mr. Seward right again; on March 5 he withdrew his letter of March 2, and in a few hours was appointed.

Immediately after the installation of the new government three commissioners from the Confederacy came to Washington, and requested an official audience. They said that seven States of the American Union had withdrawn therefrom, had reassumed sovereign power, and were now an independent nation in fact and in right; that, in order to adjust upon terms of amity and good-will all questions growing out of this political separation, they were instructed to make overtures for opening negotiations, with the assurance that the Confederate government earnestly desired a peaceful solution and would make no demand not founded in strictest justice, neither do any act to injure their late confederates. From the Confederate point of view these approaches were dignified and conciliatory; from the Northern point of view they were treasonable and insolent. Probably the best fruit which Mr. Davis hoped from them was that Mr. Seward, who was well known to be desirous of finding some peace-assuring middle course, might be led into a discussion of the situation, inevitably provoking divisions in the cabinet, in the Republican party, and in the country. But though Seward's frame of mind about this time was such as to put him in great jeopardy of committing hurtful blunders, he was fortunate enough to escape quite doing so. To the agent of the commissioners he replied that he must "consult the President," and the next day he wrote, in terms of personal civility, that he could not receive them. Nevertheless they remained in Washington a few weeks longer, gathering and forwarding to the Confederate government such information as they could. In this they were aided by Judge Campbell of Alabama, a Secessionist, who still retained his seat upon the bench of the Supreme Court. This gentleman now became a messenger between the commissioners and Mr. Seward, with the purpose of eliciting news and even pledges from the latter for the use of the former. His errands especially related to Fort Sumter, and he gradually drew from Mr. Seward strong expressions of opinion that Sumter would in time be evacuated, even declarations substantially to the effect that this was the arranged policy of the government. Words which fell in so agreeably with the wishes of the judge and the commissioners were received with that warm welcome which often outruns correct construction, and later were construed by them as actual assurances, at least in substance, whereby they conceived themselves to have been "abused and overreached," and they charged the government with "equivocating conduct." In the second week in April, contemporaneously with the Sumter crisis, they addressed to Mr. Seward a high-flown missive of reproach, in which they ostentatiously washed the hands of the South, as it were, and shook from their own departing feet the dust of the obdurate North, where they had not been met "in the conciliatory and peaceful spirit" in which they had come. They invoked "impartial history" to place the responsibility of blood and mourning upon those who had denied the great fundamental doctrine of American liberty; and they declared it "clear that Mr. Lincoln had determined to appeal to the sword to reduce the people of the Confederate States to the will of the section or party whose President he is." In this dust-cloud of glowing rhetoric vanished the last deceit of peaceful settlement.

About the same time, April 13, sundry commissioners from the Virginia convention waited upon Lincoln with the request that he would communicate the policy which he intended to pursue towards the Confederate States. Lincoln replied with a patient civility that cloaked satire: "Having at the beginning of my official term expressed my intended policy as plainly as I was able, it is with deep regret and some mortification I now learn that there is great and injurious uncertainty in the public mind as to what that policy is, and what course I intend to pursue." To this ratification of the plain position taken in his inaugural, he added that he might see fit to repossess himself of the public property, and that possibly he might withdraw the mail service from the seceding States.

The inauguration of Mr. Lincoln was followed by a lull which endured for several weeks. A like repose reigned contemporaneously in the Confederate States. For a while the people in both sections received with content this reaction of quiescence. But as the same laws of human nature were operative equally at the North and at the South, it soon came about that both at the North and at the South there broke forth almost simultaneously strong manifestations of impatience. The genuine President at Washington and the sham President at Montgomery were assailed by the like pressing demand: Why did they not do something to settle this matter? Southern irascibility found the situation exceedingly trying. The imposing and dramatic attitude of the Confederate States had not achieved an appropriate result. They had organized a government and posed as an independent nation, but no power in the civilized world had yet recognized them in this character; on the contrary, Abraham Lincoln, living hard by in the White House, was explicitly denying it, contumaciously alleging himself to be their lawful ruler, and waiting with an exasperating patience to see what they were really going to do in the business which they had undertaken. They must make some move or they would become ridiculous, and their revolution would die and their confederacy would dissolve from sheer inanition. The newspapers told their leaders this plainly; and a prominent gentleman of Alabama said to Mr. Davis: "Sir, unless you sprinkle blood in the face of the people of Alabama, they will be back in the Union in ten days." On the other hand, the people of the North were as energetic as the sons of the South were excitable, and with equal urgency they also demanded a conclusion. If the Union was to be enforced, why did not Mr. Lincoln enforce it? How long did he mean placidly to suffer treason and a rival government to rest undisturbed within the country?

With this state of feeling growing rapidly more intense in both sections, action was inevitable. Yet neither leader wished to act first, even for the important purpose of gratifying the popular will. As where two men are resolved to fight, yet have an uneasy vision of a judge and jury in waiting for them, each seeks to make the other the assailant and himself to be upon his defense, so these two rulers took prudent thought of the tribunal of public sentiment not in America alone but in Europe also, with perhaps a slight forward glance towards posterity. If Mr. Lincoln did not like to "invade" the Southern territory, Mr. Davis was equally reluctant to make the Southern "withdrawal" actively belligerent through operations of military offense.

Both men were capable of statesmanlike waiting to score a point that was worth waiting for; Davis had been for years biding the ripeness of time, but Lincoln had the capacity of patience beyond any precedent on record.

The spot where the strain came, where this question of the first blow must be settled, was at Fort Sumter, in the mid-throat of Charleston harbor. On December 27, 1860, by a skillful movement at night, Major Anderson, the commander at Fort Moultrie, had transferred his scanty force from that dilapidated and untenable post on the shore to the more defensible and more important position of Fort Sumter. Thereafter a precarious relationship betwixt peace and war had subsisted between him and the South Carolinians. It was distinctly understood that, sooner or later, by negotiation or by force, South Carolina intended to possess herself of this fortress. From her point of view it certainly was preposterous and unendurable that the key to her chief harbor and city should be permanently held by a "foreign" power. Gradually she erected batteries on the neighboring mainland, and kept a close surveillance upon the troops now more than half besieged in the fort.

Under the Buchanan régime the purpose of the United States government had been less plain than it became after Mr. Lincoln's accession; for Buchanan had not the courage either to order a surrender, or to provoke real warfare by reinforcing the place. In vain did the unfortunate Major Anderson seek distinct instructions; the replies which he received were contradictory and more obscure than Delphic oracles. This unfair, vacillating, and contemptible conduct indicated the desire to lay upon him alone the whole responsibility of the situation, with a politic and selfish reservation to the government of the advantage of disavowing and discrediting him, whatever he might do. On January 9 a futile effort at communication was made by the steamer Star of the West; it failed, and left matters worse rather than better. On March 3, 1861, the Confederate government put General Beauregard in command at Charleston, thereby emphasizing the resolution to have Sumter ere long. Such was the situation on March 4, when Mr. Lincoln came into control and declared a policy which bound him to "hold, occupy, and possess" Sumter. On the same day there came a letter from Major Anderson, describing his position. There were shut up in the fort together a certain number of men and a certain quantity of biscuit and of pork; when the men should have eaten the biscuit and the pork, which they would probably do in about four weeks, they would have to go away. The problem thus became direct, simple, and urgent.

Lincoln sought an opinion from Scott, and was told that "evacuation seems almost inevitable." He requested a more thorough investigation, and a reply to specific questions: "To what point of time can Anderson maintain his position in Sumter? Can you, with present means, relieve him in that time? What additional means would enable you to do so?" The general answered that four months would be necessary to prepare the naval force, and an even longer time to get together the 5000 regular troops and 20,000 volunteers that would be needed, to say nothing of obtaining proper legislation from Congress. Equally discouraging were the opinions of the cabinet officers. On March 15 Lincoln put to them the question: "Assuming it to be possible to now provision Fort Sumter, under all the circumstances is it wise to attempt it?" Only Chase and Blair replied that it would be wise; Seward, Cameron, Wells, Smith, and Bates were against it.

The form of this question indicated that Lincoln contemplated a possibility of being compelled to recede from the policy expressed in his inaugural. Yet it was not his temperament to abandon a purpose deliberately matured and definitely announced, except under absolute necessity. To determine now this question of necessity he sent an emissary to Sumter and another to Charleston, and meantime stayed offensive action on the part of the Confederates by authorizing Seward to give assurance through Judge Campbell that no provisioning or reinforcement should be attempted without warning. Thus he secured, or continued, a sort of truce, irregular and informal, but practical. Meantime he was encouraged by the earnest propositions of Mr. G.V. Fox, until lately an officer of the navy, who was ready to undertake the relief of the fort. Eager discussions ensued, wherein naval men backed the project of Mr. Fox, and army men condemned it. Such difference of expert opinion was trying, for the problem was of a kind which Mr. Lincoln's previous experience in life did not make it easy for him to solve with any confidence in the correctness of his own judgment.

Amid this puzzlement day after day glided by, and the question remained unsettled. Yet during this lapse of time sentiment was ripening, and perhaps this was the real purpose of Lincoln's patient waiting. On March 29 his ministers again put their opinions in writing, and now Chase, Welles, and Blair favored an effort at reinforcement; Bates modified his previous opposition so far as to say that the time had come either to evacuate or relieve the fort; Smith favored evacuation, but only on the ground of military necessity; and Seward alone advocated evacuation in part on the ground of policy; he deemed it unwise to "provoke a civil war," especially "in rescue of an untenable position."

Was it courtesy or curiosity that induced the President to sit and listen to this warm debate between his chosen advisers? They would have been angry had they known that they were bringing their counsel to a chief who had already made his decision. They did not yet know that upon every occasion of great importance Lincoln would make up his mind for and by himself, yet would not announce his decision, or save his counselors the trouble of counseling, until such time as he should see fit to act. So in this instance he had already, the day before the meeting of the cabinet, directed Fox to draw up an order for such ships, men, and supplies as he would require, and when the meeting broke up he at once issued formal orders to the secretaries of the navy and of war to enter upon the necessary preparation.

Contemporaneously with this there was also undertaken another enterprise for the relief of Fort Pickens at Pensacola. It was, however, kept so strictly secret that the President did not even communicate it to Mr. Welles. Apparently his only reason for such extreme reticence lay in the proverb: "If you wish your secret kept, keep it." But proverbial wisdom had an unfortunate result upon this occasion. Both the President and Mr. Welles set the eye of desire upon the warship Powhatan, lying in New York harbor. The secretary designed her for the Sumter fleet; the President meant to send her to Pensacola. Of the Sumter expedition she was an absolutely essential part; for the Pensacola plan she was not altogether indispensable.

On April 6 Captain Mercer, on board the Powhatan as his flagship, and on the very point of weighing anchor to sail in command of the Sumter reinforcement, under orders from Secretary Welles, was astounded to find himself dispossessed and superseded by Lieutenant Porter, who suddenly came upon the deck bringing an order signed by the President himself. A few hours later, at Washington, a telegram startled Mr. Welles with the news. Utterly confounded, he hastened, in the early night-time, to the White House, and obtained an audience of the President. Then Mr. Lincoln learned what a disastrous blunder he had made; greatly mortified, he requested Mr. Seward to telegraph with all haste to New York that the Powhatan must be immediately restored to Mercer for Sumter. Lieutenant Porter was already far down the bay, when he was overtaken by a swift tug bringing this message. But unfortunately Mr. Seward had so phrased the dispatch that it did not purport to convey an order either from the President or the secretary of the navy, and he had signed his own name: "Give up the Powhatan to Mercer. SEWARD." To Porter, hurriedly considering this unintelligible occurrence, it seemed better to go forward under the President's order than to obey the order of an official who had no apparent authority to command him. So he steamed on for Pensacola.

On April 8, discharging the obligation of warning, Mr. Lincoln notified General Beauregard that an attempt would be made to put provisions into Sumter, but not at present to put in men, arms, or ammunition, unless the fort should be attacked. Thereupon Beauregard, at two o'clock P.M. on April 11, sent to Anderson a request for a surrender. Anderson refused, remarking incidentally that he should be starved out in a few days. At 3.20

A.M., on April 12, Beauregard notified Anderson that he should open fire in one hour. That morning the occupants of Sumter, 9 commissioned officers, 68 non-commissioned officers and privates, 8 musicians, and 43 laborers, breakfasted on pork and water, the last rations in the fort. Before daybreak the Confederate batteries were pouring shot and shell against the walls. Response was made from as many guns as the small body of defenders could handle. But the fort was more easily damaged than were the works on the mainland, and on the morning of the 13th, the officers' quarters having caught fire, and the magazine being so imperiled that it had to be closed and covered with earth, the fort became untenable. Early in the evening terms of capitulation were agreed upon.

Meantime three transports of the relief expedition were lying outside the bar. The first arrived shortly before the bombardment began, the other two came only a trifle later. All day long these vessels lay to, wondering why the Powhatan did not appear. Had she been there upon the critical night of the 12th, the needed supplies could have been thrown into the fort, for the weather was so dark that the rebel patrol was useless, and it was actually believed in Charleston that the relief had been accomplished. But the Powhatan was far away steaming at full speed for Pensacola. For this sad blunder Lincoln generously, but fairly enough, took the blame to himself. The only excuse which has ever been advanced in behalf of Mr. Lincoln is that he allowed himself to be led blindfold through this important business by Mr. Seward, and that he signed such papers as the secretary of state presented to him without learning their purport and bearing. But such an excuse, even if it can be believed, seems fully as bad as the blunder which it is designed to palliate.

Other blame also has been laid upon Lincoln on the ground that he was dilatory in reaching the determination to relieve the fort. That the decision should have been reached and the expedition dispatched more promptly is entirely evident; but whether or not Lincoln was in fault is quite another question. Three facts are to be considered: 1. The highest military authority in the country advised him, a civilian, that evacuation was a necessity. 2. Most of his ministers were at first against reinforcement, and they never unanimously recommended it; especially his secretary of state condemned it as bad policy. 3. The almost universal feeling of the people of the North, so far as it could then be divined, was compromising, conciliatory, and thoroughly opposed to any act of war. Under such circumstances it was rather an exhibition of independence and courage that Lincoln reached the conclusion of relieving the fort at all, than it was a cause of fault-finding that he did not come to the conclusion sooner. He could not know in March how the people were going to feel after the 13th of April; in fact, if they had fancied that he was provoking hostilities, their feeling might not even then have developed as it did. Finally, he gained his point in forcing the Confederacy into the position of assailant, and there is every reason to believe that he bought that point cheaply at the price of the fortress.

The news of the capture of Sumter had an instant and tremendous effect. The States which had seceded were thrown into a pleasurable ferment of triumph; the Northern States arose in fierce wrath; the Middle States, still balancing dubiously between the two parties, were rent with passionate discussion. For the moment the North seemed a unit; there had been Southern sympathizers before, and Southern sympathizers appeared in considerable numbers later, but for a little while just now they were very scarce. Douglas at once called upon the President, and the telegraph carried to his numerous followers throughout the land the news that he had pledged himself "to sustain the President in the exercise of all his constitutional functions to preserve the Union, and maintain the government, and defend the Federal capital." By this prompt and generous action he warded off the peril of a divided North. Douglas is not in quite such good repute with posterity as he deserves to be; his attitude towards slavery was bad, but his attitude towards the country was that of a zealous patriot. His veins were full of fighting blood, and he was really much more ready to go to war for the Union than were great numbers of Republicans whose names survive in the strong odor of patriotism. During the presidential campaign he had been speaking out with defiant courage regardless of personal considerations, and in this present juncture he did not hesitate an instant to bring to his successful rival an aid which at the time and under the circumstances was invaluable.

In every town and village there were now mass meetings, ardent speeches, patriotic resolutions, a confusing stir and tumult of words that would become deeds as fast as definite plans could furnish opportunity. The difficulty lay in utilizing this abundant, this exuberant zeal. Historians say rhetorically that the North sprang to arms; and it really would have done so if there had been any arms to spring to; but muskets were scarce, and that there were any at all was chiefly due to the fact that antiquated and unserviceable weapons had been allowed to accumulate undestroyed. Moreover, no one knew even the manual of arms; and there were no uniforms, or accoutrements, or camp equipment of any sort. There was, however, the will which makes the way. Simultaneously with the story of Sumter came also the President's proclamation of April 15. He called for seventy-five thousand volunteers to serve for three months,—an insignificant body of men, as it now seems, and a period of time not sufficient to change them from civilians into soldiers. Yet for the work immediately visible the demand seemed adequate. Moreover, as the law stood, a much longer term could not have been named, [133] and an apparently disproportionate requisition in point of numbers might have been of injurious effect; for nearly every one was cheerfully saying that the war would be no such very great affair after all. In his own mind the President may or may not have forecast the future more accurately than most others were doing; but his idea plainly was to ask no more than was necessary for the visible occasion. He stated that the troops would be used to "repossess the forts, places, and property which had been seized from the Union," and that great care would be taken not to disturb peaceful citizens. Amid all the prophesying and theorizing, and the fanciful comparisons of the respective fighting qualities of the Northern and Southern populations, a sensible remark is attributed to Lincoln: "We must not forget that the people of the seceded States, like those of the loyal States, are American citizens with essentially the same characteristics and powers. Exceptional advantages on one side are counterbalanced by exceptional advantages on the other. We must make up our minds that man for man the soldier from the South will be a match for the soldier from the North, and *vice versa*." This was good common sense, seasonably offsetting the prevalent but foolish notion that the Southerners were naturally a better fighting race than the Northerners. Facts ultimately sustained Lincoln's just estimate of equality; for though the North employed far greater numbers than did the South, it was because the North had the burdens of attack and conquest upon exterior lines of great extent, because it had to detail large bodies of troops for mere garrison and quasi-police duty, and because during the latter part of the war it took miserable throngs of bounty-bought foreigners into its ranks. Man for man, as Lincoln said at the outset, the war proved that Northern Americans and Southern Americans were closely matched. [134]

By the same instrument the President summoned Congress to assemble in extra session on July 4. It seemed a distant date; and many thought that the Executive Department ought not to endeavor to handle alone all the possible novel developments of so long a period. But Mr. Lincoln had his purposes. By July 4 he and circumstances, together, would have wrought out definite conditions, which certainly did not exist at present; perhaps also, like most men who find themselves face to face with difficult practical affairs, he dreaded the conclaves of the law-makers; but especially he wished to give Kentucky a chance to hold a special election for choosing members of this Congress, because the moral and political value of Kentucky could hardly be overestimated, and the most tactful manoeuvring was necessary to control her.

The Confederate cabinet was said to have greeted Mr. Lincoln's proclamation with "bursts of laughter." The governors of Kentucky, North Carolina, Arkansas, Tennessee, and Missouri telegraphed that no troops would be furnished by their respective States, using language clearly designed to be offensive and menacing. The Northern States, however, responded promptly and enthusiastically. Men thronged to enlist. Hundreds of thousands offered themselves where only 75,000 could be accepted. Of the human raw material there was excess; but discipline and equipment could not be created by any measure of mere willingness. Yet there was great need of dispatch. Both geographically and politically Washington lay as an advanced outpost in immediate peril. General Scott had been collecting the few companies within reach; but all, he said on April 8, "may be too late for this place." By April 15, however, he believed himself able to hold the city till reinforcements should arrive. The total nominal strength of the United States army, officers and men, was only 17,113, of whom not two thirds could be counted upon the Union side, and even these were scattered over a vast expanse of country, playing police for Indians, and garrisoning distant posts. Rumors of Southern schemes to attack Washington caused widespread alarm; the government had no more definite information than the people, and all alike feared that there was to be a race for the capital, and that the South, being near and prepared, would get there first. As matter of fact, the Southern leaders had laid no military plan for this enterprise, and the danger was exaggerated. The Northerners, however, did not know this, and made desperate haste.

The first men to arrive came from Philadelphia, 460 troops, as they were called, though they came "almost entirely without arms." In Massachusetts, Governor Andrew, an anti-slavery leader, enthusiastic, energetic, and of great executive ability, had been for many months preparing the militia for precisely this crisis, weeding out the holiday soldiers and thoroughly equipping his regiments for service in the field. For this he had been merrily ridiculed by the aristocracy of Boston during the winter; but inexorable facts now declared for him and against the local aristocrats. On April 15 he received the call from Washington, and immediately sent forth his own summons through the State. All day on the 16th, amid a fierce northeasterly storm, the troops poured into Boston, and by six o'clock on that day three full regiments were ready to start. [135] Three days before this the governor had asked Secretary Cameron for 2000 rifled muskets from the national armory at Springfield, in the State. The secretary refused, and the governor managed to supply his regiment with the most improved arms [136] without aid from the national government. On the forenoon of the 17th, the Sixth Regiment started for Washington. Steamers were ready to take it to Annapolis; but the secretary of war, with astonishing ignorance of facts easily to be known, ordered it to come through Baltimore. Accordingly the regiment reached Baltimore on the 19th, the anniversary of the battle of Lexington. Seven companies were transported in horse-cars from the northern to the southern station without serious hindrance; but then the tracks of the street railway were torn up, and the remaining four companies had to leave the cars and march. A furious mob of "Plug Uglies" and Secessionists assailed them with paving-stones, brickbats, and pistol-shots. The mayor and the marshal of the police force performed fairly their official duty, but were far from quelling the riot. The troops, therefore, thrown on their own resources, justifiably fired upon their assailants. The result of the conflict was that 4 soldiers were killed and 36 were wounded, and of the rioters 12 were killed, and the number of wounded could not be ascertained. The troops reached Washington at five o'clock in the afternoon, the first armed rescuers of the capital; their presence brought a comforting sense of relief, and they were quartered in the senate chamber itself.

What would be the effect of the proclamation, of the mustering of troops in the capital, and of the bloodshed at Baltimore upon the slave States which still remained in the Union, was a problem of immeasurable importance. The President, who had been obliged to take the responsibility of precipitating the crisis in these States, appreciated more accurately than any one else the magnitude of the stake involved in their allegiance. He watched them with the deepest anxiety, and brought the utmost care and tact of his nature to the task of influencing them. The geographical position of Maryland, separating the District of Columbia from the loyal North, made it of the first consequence. The situation there, precarious at best, seemed to be rendered actually hopeless by what had occurred. A tempest of uncontrollable rage whirled away the people and prostrated all Union feeling. Mayor Brown admits that "for some days it looked very much as if Baltimore had taken her stand decisively with the South;" and this was putting it mildly, when the Secessionist Marshal Kane was telegraphing: "Streets red with Maryland blood. Send express over the mountains of Maryland and Virginia for the riflemen to come without delay." Governor Hicks was opposed to secession, but he was shaken like a reed by this violent blast. Later on this same April 19, Mayor Brown sent three gentlemen to President Lincoln, bearing a letter from himself, in which he said that it was "not possible for more soldiers to pass through Baltimore unless they fight their way at every step." That night he caused the northward railroad bridges to be burned and disabled; and soon afterward the telegraph wires were cut.

The President met the emergency with coolness and straightforward simplicity, abiding firmly by his main purpose, but conciliatory as to means.

He wrote to the governor and the mayor: "For the future troops *must* be brought here, but I make no point of bringing them *through* Baltimore;" he would "march them *around* Baltimore," if, as he hoped, General Scott should find it feasible to do so. In fulfillment of this promise he ordered a detachment, which had arrived at a station near Baltimore, to go all the way back to Philadelphia and come around by water. He only demurred when the protests were extended to include the whole "sacred" soil of Maryland,—for it appeared that the presence of slavery accomplished the consecration of soil! His troops, he said, could neither fly over the State, nor burrow under it; therefore they must cross it, and the Marylanders must learn that "there was no piece of American soil too good to be pressed by the foot of a loyal soldier on his march to the defense of the capital of his country." For a while, however, until conditions in Baltimore changed, Eastern regiments came by way of Annapolis, though with difficulty and delay. Yet, even upon this route, conflict was narrowly avoided.

Soon, however, these embarrassments came to an end, and the President's policy was vindicated by its fruits. It had been strictly his own; he alone ruled the occasion, and he did so in the face of severe pressure to do otherwise, some of which came even from members of his cabinet. Firmness, reasonableness, and patience brought things right; Lincoln spoke sensibly to the Marylanders, and gave them time to consider the situation. Such treatment started a reaction; Unionism revived and Unionists regained courage. Moreover, the sure pressure of material considerations was doing its work. Baltimore, as an isolated secession outpost, found, even in the short space of a week, that business was destroyed and that she was suffering every day financial loss. In a word, by the end of the month, "the tide had turned." Baltimore, if not quite a Union city, at least ceased to be secessionist. On May 9 Northern troops passed unmolested through it. On May 13 General Butler with a body of troops took possession of Federal Hill, which commands the harbor and city, and fortified it. If the Baltimore question was still open at that time, this settled it. Early in the same month the state legislature came together, Mr. Lincoln refusing to accept the suggestion of interfering with it. This body was by no means Unionist, for it "protested against the war as unjust and unconstitutional, announced a determination to take no part in its prosecution, and expressed a desire for the immediate recognition of the Confederate States." Yet practically it put a veto on secession by voting that it was inexpedient to summon a convention; it called on all good citizens "to abstain from violent and unlawful interference with the troops." Thus early in May this brand, though badly scorched, was saved from the conflagration; and its saving was a piece of good fortune of which the importance cannot be exaggerated;

for without Maryland Washington could hardly have been held, and with the national capital in the hands of the rebels European recognition probably could not have been prevented. These momentous perils were in the mind of the administration during those anxious days, and great indeed was the relief when the ultimate turn of affairs became assured. For a week officials in Washington were painfully taught what it would mean to have Baltimore a rebel city and Maryland a debatable territory and battle-ground. For a week Mr. Lincoln and his advisers lived almost in a state of siege; they were utterly cut off from communication with the North; they could get no news; they could not learn what was doing for their rescue, nor how serious were the obstructions in the way of such efforts; in place of correct information they heard only the most alarming rumors. In a word, they were governing a country to which they really had no access. The tension of those days was awful; and it was with infinite comfort that they became certain that, whatever other strain might come, this one at least could not be repeated. Henceforth the loyalty of Maryland, so carefully nurtured, gradually grew in strength to the end. Many individuals long remained in their hearts disloyal, and thousands [137] joined the Confederate ranks; but they had to leave their State in order to get beneath a secessionist standard, for Maryland was distinctly and conclusively in the Union.

The situation, resources, and prestige of Virginia made her next to Maryland in importance among the doubtful States. Her Unionists were numerically preponderant; and accordingly the convention, which assembled early in January, was opposed to secession by the overwhelming majority of 89 to 45. But the Secessionists here as elsewhere in the South were propagandists, fiery with enthusiasm and energy, and they controlled the community although they were outnumbered by those who held, in a more quiet way, contrary opinions. When the decisive conflict came it was short and sharp and carried with a rush. By intrigue, by menace, by passionate appeals seasonably applied with sudden intensity of effort at the time of the assault upon Sumter, the convention was induced to pass an ordinance of secession. Those who could not bring themselves to vote in the affirmative were told that they might "absent themselves or be hanged." On the other hand, there were almost no lines along which the President could project any influence into the State to encourage the Union sentiment. He sought an interview with a political leader, but the gentleman only sent a substitute, and the colloquy amounted to nothing. He fell in with the scheme of General Scott concerning Robert E. Lee, which might have saved Virginia; but this also miscarried. General Lee has always been kindly spoken of at the North, whether deservedly or not is a matter not to be discussed here. Only a few bare facts and dates can be given: April 17, by a vote of 88 to 55, the dragooned convention passed an "ordinance to repeal the ratification of the Constitution of the United States," but provided that this action should for the present be kept secret, and that it might be annulled by the people at a popular voting, which should be had upon it on the fourth Thursday in May. The injunction of secrecy was immediately broken, and before the polls were to be opened for the balloting Virginia was held by the military forces of the Confederacy, so that the vote was a farce. April 18 Mr. F.P. Blair, Jr., had an interview in Washington with Lee, in which he intimated to Lee that the President and General Scott designed to place him in command of the army which had just been summoned. [138] Accounts of this conversation, otherwise inconsistent, all agree that Lee expressed himself as opposed to secession, [139] but as unwilling to occupy the position designed for him, because he "could take no part in an invasion of the Southern States." April 20 he tendered his resignation of his commission in the army, closing with the words, "Save in defense of my native State, I never desire again to draw my sword." [140] On April 22-23 he was appointed to, and accepted, the command of the state forces. In so accepting he said: "I devote myself to the service of my native State, in whose behalf alone will I ever again draw my sword." [141] April 24 a military league was formed between Virginia and the Confederate States, and her forces were placed under the command of Jefferson Davis; also an invitation was given, and promptly accepted, to make Richmond the Confederate capital. May 16 Virginia formally entered the Confederacy, and Lee became a general—the third in rank—in the service of the Confederate States, though the secession of his State was still only inchoate and might never become complete, since the day set for the popular vote had not arrived, and it was still a possibility that the Unionists might find courage to go to the polls. Thus a rapid succession of events settled it that the President could save neither Virginia nor Robert E. Lee for the Union. Yet the failure was not entire. The northwestern counties were strongly Union in their proclivities, and soon followed to a good end an evil example; for they in turn seceded from Virginia, established a state government, sought admission into the Union, and became the State of West Virginia.

Next in order of importance came Kentucky. The Secessionists, using here the tactics so successful in other States, endeavored to drive through by rush and whirl a formal act of secession. But the Unionists of Kentucky were of more resolute and belligerent temper than those of Georgia and Virginia, and would not submit to be swept away by a torrent really of less volume than their own. [142] Yet in spite of the spirited head thus made by the loyalists the condition in the State long remained such as to require the most skillful treatment by the President; during several critical weeks one error of judgment, a single imprudence, upon his part might have proved fatal. For the condition was anomalous and perplexing, and the conflict of opinion in the State had finally led to the evolution of a theory or scheme of so-called "neutrality." A similar notion had been imperfectly developed in Maryland, when her legislature declared that she would take no part in a war. The idea was illogical to the point of absurdity, for by it the "neutral" State would at once stay in the Union and stand aloof from it. Neutrality really signified a refusal to perform those obligations which nevertheless were admitted to be binding, and it made of the State a defensive barrier for the South, not to be traversed by Northern troops on an errand of hostility against Confederate Secessionists. It was practical "non-coercion" under a name of fairer sound, and it involved the inconsequence of declaring that the dissolution of an indissoluble Union should not be prevented; it was the proverbial folly of being "for the law but ag'in the enforcement of it." In the words of a resolution passed by a public meeting in Louisville: it was the "duty" of Kentucky to maintain her "independent position," taking sides neither with the administration nor with the seceding States, *but with the Union against them both.*

Nevertheless, though both logic and geography made neutrality impracticable, yet at least the desire to be neutral indicated a wavering condition, and therefore it was Mr. Lincoln's task so to arrange matters that, when the State should at last see that it could by no possibility avoid casting its lot with one side or the other, it should cast it with the North. For many weeks the two Presidents played the game for this invaluable stake with all the tact and skill of which each was master. It proved to be a repetition of the fable of the sun and the wind striving to see which could the better make the traveler take off his cloak, and fortunately the patience of Mr. Lincoln represented the warmth of the sun. He gave the Kentuckians time to learn by observation and the march of events that neutrality was an impossibility, also to determine with which side lay the probable advantages for themselves; also he respected the borders of the State during its sensitive days, though in doing so he had to forego some military advantages of time and position. Deliberation brought a sound conclusion. Kentucky never passed an ordinance of secession, but maintained her representation in Congress and contributed her quota to the armies; and these invaluable results were largely due to this wise policy of the President. Many of her citizens, of course, fought upon the Southern side, as was the case in all these debatable Border States, where friends and even families divided against each other, and each man placed himself according to his own convictions. It may seem, therefore, in view of this individual independence of action, that the ordinance of secession was a formality which would not have greatly affected practical conditions; and many critics of Mr. Lincoln at the time could not appreciate the value of his "border-state policy," and thought that he was making sacrifices and paying prices wholly against wisdom, and out of proportion to anything that could be gained thereby. But he understood the situation and comparative values correctly. Loyalty to the State governed multitudes; preference of the State over the United States cost the nation vast numbers of would-be Unionists in the seceding States, and in fact made secession possible; and the same feeling, erroneous though it was from the Unionist point of view, yet saved for the Unionist party very great numbers in these doubtful States which never in fact seceded. Mr. Davis appreciated this just as much as Mr. Lincoln did; both were shrewd men, and were wasting no foolish efforts when they strove so hard to carry or to prevent formal state action. They appreciated very well that success in passing an ordinance would gain for the South throngs of adherents whose allegiance was, by their peculiar political creed, due to the winner in this local contest.

In Tennessee the Unionist majority, as indicated early in February, was overwhelming. Out of a total vote of less than 92,000, more than 67,000 opposed a state convention. The mountaineers of the eastern region especially were stalwart loyalists, and later held to their faith through the severe ordeal of a peculiarly cruel invasion. But the political value of these scattered settlements was small; and in the more populous parts the Secessionists pursued their usual aggressive and enterprising tactics with success. Ultimately the governor and the legislature despotically compelled secession. It was not decreed by a popular vote, not even by a convention, but by votes of the legislature cast in secret session, a proceeding clearly *ultra vires* of that body. Finally, on June 8, when a popular vote was taken, the State was in the military control of the Confederacy.

Very similar was the case of North Carolina. The people of the uplands, like their neighbors of Tennessee, were Unionists, and in the rest of the State there was a prevalent Union sentiment; but the influence of the political leaders, their direct usurpations of power, and the customary energetic propagandism, ultimately won. After a convention had been once voted down by popular vote, a second effort to bring one together was successfully made, and an ordinance of secession was passed on May 20. Arkansas was swept along with the stream, seceding on May 6, although prior to that time the votes both for holding a state convention and afterward in the convention itself had shown a decided Unionist preponderance. These three States, Tennessee, North Carolina, and Arkansas, were entirely beyond the reach of the President. He had absolutely no lines of influence along which he could work to restrain or to guide them.

Missouri had a career peculiar to herself. In St. Louis there was a strong Unionist majority, and especially the numerous German population was thoroughly anti-slavery, and was vigorously led by F.P. Blair, Jr. But away from her riverfront the State had a sparse population preserving the rough propensities of frontiersmen; these men were not unevenly divided between loyalty and secession and they were an independent, fighting set of fellows, each one of whom intended to follow his own fancy. The result was that Missouri for a long while carried on a little war of her own within her own borders, on too large a scale to be called "bushwhacking," and yet with a strong flavor of that irregular style of conflict. The President interested himself a good deal in the early efforts of the loyalists, and amid a puzzling snarl of angry "personal politics" he tried to extend to them aid and countenance, though with imperfect success. It was fortunate that Missouri was away on the outskirts, for she was the most vexatious and perplexing part of the country. Her population had little feeling of state allegiance, or, indeed, of any allegiance at all, but what small amount there was fell upon the side of the Union; for though the governor and a majority of the legislature declared for secession, yet the state convention voted for the Union by a large majority. It is true that a sham convention passed a sham ordinance, but this had no weight with any except those who were already Secessionists.

Thus by the close of May, 1861, President Lincoln looked forth upon a spectacle tolerably definite at last, and certainly as depressing as ever met the eyes of a great ruler. Eleven States, with area, population, and resources abundant for constituting a powerful nation and sustaining an awful war, were organized in rebellion; their people were welded into entire unity of feeling, were enthusiastically resolute, and were believed to be exceptionally good fighters. The population of three Border States was divided between loyalty and disloyalty. The Northern States, teeming with men and money, had absolutely no experience whatsoever to enable them to utilize their vast resources with the promptitude needful in the instant emergency. There was a notion, prevalent even among themselves, that they were by temperament not very well fitted for war; but this fancy Mr. Lincoln quietly set aside, knowing better. He also had confidence in the efficiency of Northern men in practical affairs of any kind whatsoever, and he had not to tax his patience to see this confidence vindicated. His appeal for military support seemed the marvelous word of a magician, and wrought instant transformation throughout the vast loyal territory. One half of the male population began to practice the manual, to drill, and to study the text-books of military science; the remainder put at least equal energy into the preparations for equipment; every manufacturer in the land set the proverbial Yankee enterprise and ingenuity at work in the adaptation of his machinery to the production of munitions of war and all the various outfit for troops. Every foundry, every mill, and every shipyard was at once diverted from its accustomed industries in order to supply military demands; patriotism and profit combined to stimulate sleepless toil and invention. In a hard-working community no one had ever before worked nearly so hard as now. The whole North was in a ferment, and every human being strained his abilities of mind and of body to the utmost in one serviceable direction or another; the wise and the foolish, the men of words and the men of deeds, the projectors of valuable schemes and the venders of ridiculous inventions, the applicants for military commissions and the seekers after the government's contracts, all hustled and crowded each other in feverish eagerness to get at work in the new condition of things. It was going to take time for all this energy to produce results, — yet not a very long time; the President had more patience than would be needed, and the spirit of his people reassured him. If the lukewarm, compromising temper of the past winter had caused him to feel any lurking anxious doubts as to how the crisis would be met, such illusive mists were now cleared away in a moment before the sweeping gale of patriotism.

[132] At New Bedford, in a lecture "which was interrupted by frequent hisses." Schouler, *Hist. of Mass. in the Civil War*, i. 44-47.

[133] The Act of 1795 only permitted the use of the militia until thirty days after the next session of Congress; this session being now summoned for July 4, the period of service extended only until August 3.

[134] When General Grant took command of the Eastern armies he said that the country should be cautioned against expecting too great success, because the loyal and rebel armies were made up of men of the same race, having about the same experience in war, and neither able justly to claim any great superiority over the other in endurance, courage, or discipline. Chittenden, *Recoll.* 320.

[135] The third, fourth, and sixth. Schouler, *Mass. in the Civil War*, i. 52.

[136] Schouler, *Mass. in the Civil War*, i. 72.

[137] Mayor Brown thinks that the estimate of these at 20,000 is too great. Brown, *Baltimore and Nineteenth April, 1861,* p. 85.

[138] N. and H. iv. 98; Chittenden, 102; Lee's biographer, Childe, says that "President Lincoln offered him the effective command of the Union Army," and that Scott "conjured him ... not to quit the army." Childe, *Lee,* 30.

[139] Shortly before this time he had written to his son that it was "idle to talk of secession," that it was "nothing but revolution" and "anarchy." N. and H. iv. 99.

[140] Childe, *Lee,* 32; Mr. Childe, p. 33, says that Lee's resignation was accepted on the 20th (the very day on which his letter was dated!), so that he "ceased to be a member of the United States Army" before he took command of the state forces. *Per contra,* N. and H. iv. 101.

[141] Childe, *Lee,* 34.

[142] Greeley in his *Amer. Conflict,* i. 349, says that the "open Secessionists were but a handful." This, however, is clearly an exaggerated statement.

CHAPTER IX
A REAL PRESIDENT, AND NOT A REAL BATTLE

The capture of Fort Sumter and the call for troops established one fact. There was to be a war. The period of speculation was over and the period of action had begun. The transition meant much. The talking men of the country had not appeared to advantage during the few months in which they had been busy chiefly in giving weak advice and in concocting prophecies. They now retired before the men of affairs, who were to do better. To the Anglo-Saxon temperament it was a relief to have done with waiting and to begin to do something. Activity cleared the minds of men, and gave to each his appropriate duty.

The gravity of the crisis being undeniable, the people of the North queried, with more anxiety than ever before, as to what kind of a chief they had taken to carry them through it. But the question which all asked none could answer. Mr. Lincoln had achieved a good reputation as a politician and a stump speaker. Whatever a few might *think*, this was all that any one *knew*. The narrow limitations of his actual experience certainly did not encourage a belief in his probable fitness to encounter duties more varied, pressing, numerous, novel, and difficult than had ever come so suddenly to confound any ruler within recorded time. Later on, when it was seen with what rare capacity he met demands so exacting, many astonished and excitable observers began to cry out that he was inspired. This, however, was sheer nonsense. That the very peculiar requirements of these four years found a president so well responding to them may be fairly regarded, by those who so please, as a specific Providential interference,—a striking one among many less striking. But, in fact, nothing in Mr. Lincoln's life requires, for its explanation, the notion of divine inspiration. His doings, one and all, were perfectly intelligible as the outcome of honesty of purpose, strong common sense, clear reasoning powers, and a singular sagacity in reading the popular mind. Intellectually speaking, a clear and vigorous thinking capacity was his chief trait. This sounds commonplace and uninteresting, but a more serviceable qualification could not have been given him. The truth is, that it was part of the good fortune of the country that the President was not a brilliant man. Moreover, he was cool, shrewd, dispassionate, and self-possessed, and was endowed really in an extraordinary degree with an intermingling of patience and courage, whereby he was enabled both to await and to endure results. Above all he was a masterful man; not all the time and in small matters, and not often in an opinionated way; but, from beginning to end, whenever he saw fit to be master, master he was. [143]

This last fact, when it became known, answered another question which people were asking: In whose hands were the destinies of the North to be? In those of Mr. Lincoln? or in those of the cabinet? or in those of influential advisers, something like what have been called "favorites" in Europe, and "kitchen cabinet" in the more homely phrase of the United States? The early impression was that Mr. Lincoln did not know a great deal. How could he? Where and how could he have learned much? It must be admitted that it was entirely natural that his advisers, and other influential men concerned in public affairs, should adopt and act upon the theory that Mr. Lincoln, emerging so sharply from such a past as his had been, into such a crisis as was now present, must need a vast amount of instruction, guidance, suggestion. Accordingly there were many gentlemen who stood ready, not to say eager, to supply these fancied wants, and who could have supplied them very well had they existed. Therefore one of the first things which Mr. Lincoln had to do was, without antagonizing Mr. Seward and Mr. Chase, to indicate to them that they were to be not only in name but also in rigid fact his secretaries, and that he was in fact as well as by title President. This delicate business was done so soon as opportunity offered, not in any disguised way but with plain simplicity. Mr. Chase never took the disposition quite pleasantly. He managed his department with splendid ability, but in the personal relation of a cabinet adviser upon the various matters of governmental policy he was always somewhat uncomfortable to get along with, inclined to fault-finding, ever ready with discordant suggestions, and in time also disturbed by ambition.

Mr. Seward behaved far better. After the question of supremacy had been settled, though in a way quite contrary to his anticipation, he frankly accepted the subordinate position, and discharged his duties with hearty good-will. Indeed, this settlement had already come, before the time which this narrative has reached; but the people did not know it; it was a private matter betwixt the two men who had been parties to it. Only Mr. Lincoln and Mr. Seward knew that the secretary had suggested his willingness to run the government for the President, and that the President had replied that he intended to run it himself. It came about in this way: on April 1 Mr. Seward presented, in writing, "Some thoughts for the President's consideration." He opened with the statement, not conciliatory, that "We are at the end of a month's administration, and yet without a policy, either domestic or foreign." He then proceeded to offer suggestions for each. For the "policy at home" he proposed, as the "ruling idea:" "Change the question before the public from one upon slavery, or about slavery, for a question upon Union or Disunion." It was odd and not complimentary that he should seem to forget or ignore that precisely this thing had already been attempted by Mr. Lincoln in his inaugural address. Also within a few days, as we all know now, events were to show that the attempt had been successful. Further comment upon the domestic policy of Mr. Seward is, therefore, needless. But his scheme "For Foreign Nations" is more startling:—

"I would demand explanations from Spain and France categorically at once.

"I would seek explanations from Great Britain and Russia, and send agents into Canada, Mexico, and Central America, to rouse a vigorous spirit of independence on this continent against European intervention.

"And, if satisfactory explanations are not received from Spain and France,

"Would convene Congress and declare war against them.

"But whatever policy we adopt, there must be an energetic prosecution of it.

"For this purpose it must be somebody's business to pursue and direct it incessantly.

"Either the President must do it himself, and be all the while active in it, or

"Devolve it on some member of his cabinet.

"Once adopted, debates on it must end, and all agree and abide.

" It is not in my especial province.

"But I neither seek to evade nor assume responsibility."

Suggestions so wild could not properly constitute material for "consideration" by the President; but much consideration on the part of students of those times and men is provoked by the fact that such counsel emanated from such a source. The secretary of state, heretofore the most distinguished leader in the great Republican movement, who should by merit of actual achievement have been the Republican candidate for the presidency, and who was expected by a large part of the country to save an ignorant president from bad blunders, was advancing a proposition to create pretexts whereby to force into existence a foreign war upon a basis which was likely to set one half of the civilized world against the other half. The purpose for which he was willing to do this awful thing was: to paralyze for a while domestic discussions, and to undo and leave to be done anew by the next generation all that vast work which he himself, and the President whom he advised, and the leaders of the great multitude whom they both represented, had for years been engaged in prosecuting with all the might that was in them. But the explanation is simple: like many another at that trying moment, the secretary was smitten with sudden panic at the condition which had been brought about so largely by his own efforts. It was strictly a panic, for it passed away rapidly as panics do.

The biographer of Mr. Seward may fairly enough glide lightly over this episode, since it was nothing more than an episode; but one who writes of Mr. Lincoln must, in justice, call attention to this spectacle of the sage statesman from whom, if from any one, this "green hand," this inexperienced President, must seek guidance, thus in deliberate writing pointing out a course which was ridiculous and impossible, and which, if it had been possible, would have been an intolerably humiliating retreat. The anxious people, who thought that their untried President might, upon the worst estimate of his own abilities, get on fairly well by the aid of wise and skilled advisers, would have been aghast had they known that, inside of the government, the pending question was: not whether Mr. Lincoln would accept sound instruction, but whether he would have sense to recognize bad advice, and independence to reject it. Before Mr. Seward went to bed on that night of April 1, he was perhaps the only man in the country who knew the solution of this problem. But he knew it, for Mr. Lincoln had already answered his letter. It had not taken the President long! The secretary's extraordinary offer to assume the responsibility of pursuing and directing the policy of the government was rejected within a few hours after it was made; rejected not offensively, but briefly, clearly, decisively, and without thanks. Concerning the proposed policies, domestic and foreign, the President said as little as was called for; he actually did not even refer to the scheme for inaugurating gratuitously a war with a large part of Europe, in order for a while to distract attention from slavery.

To us, to-day, it seems that the President could not have missed a course so obvious; yet Mr. Seward, who suggested the absurdity, was a great statesman. In truth, the President had shown not only sense but nerve. For the difference between Seward's past opportunities and experience and his own was appreciated by him as fully as by any one. He knew perfectly well that what seemed the less was controlling what seemed the greater when he overruled his secretary. It took courage on the part of a thoughtful man to put himself in such a position. Other solemn reflections also could not be avoided. Not less interested than any other citizen in the fate of the nation, he had also a personal relation to the ultimate event which was exclusively his own. For he himself might be called, in a certain sense, the very cause of rebellion; of course the people who had elected him carried the real responsibility; but he stood as the token of the difference, the concrete provocation to the fight. The South had said: *Abraham Lincoln* brings secession. It was frightful to think that, as he was in fact the signal, so posterity might mistake him for the very cause of the rending of a great nation, the failure of a grand experiment. It might be that this destiny was before him, for the outcome of this struggle no one could foretell; it might be his sad lot to mark the end of the line of Presidents of the United States. Lincoln was not a man who could escape the full weight of these reflections, and it is to be remembered that all actions were taken beneath that weight. It was a strong man, then, who stood up and said, This is my load and I will carry it; and who did carry it, when others offered to shift much of it upon their own shoulders; also who would not give an hour's thought to a scheme which promised to lift it away entirely, and to leave it for some other who by and by should come after him.

It is worth while to remember that Mr. Lincoln was the most advised man, often the worst advised man, in the annals of mankind. The torrent must have been terribly confusing! Another instance deserves mention: shortly before Mr. Seward's strange proposal, Governor Hicks, distracted at the tumult in Maryland, had suggested that the quarrel between North and South should be referred to Lord Lyons as arbitrator! It was difficult to know whether to be amused or resentful before a proposition at once so silly and so ignominious. Yet it came from an important official, and it was only one instance among thousands. With war as an actuality, such vagaries as those of Hicks and Seward came sharply to an end. People wondered and talked somewhat as to how long hostilities would last, how much they would cost, how they would end; and were not more correct in these speculations than they had been in others. But though the day of gross absurdities was over, the era of advice endured permanently. That peculiar national trait whereby every American knows at least as much on every subject whatsoever as is known by any other living man, produced its full results during the war. Every clergyman and humanitarian, every village politician and every city wire-puller, every one who conned the maps of Virginia and imbibed the military wisdom of the newspapers, every merchant who put his name to a subscription paper, considered it his privilege and his duty to set the President right upon every question of moral principle, of politics, of strategy, and of finance. In one point of view it was not flattering that he should seem to stand in need of so much instruction; and this was equally true whether it came bitterly, as criticism from enemies, or sugar-coated, as advice from friends. That friends felt obliged to advise so much was in itself a criticism. Probably, however, Mr. Lincoln was not troubled by this view, for he keenly appreciated the idiosyncrasies as well as the better qualities of the people. They, however, were a long while in understanding him sufficiently to recognize that there was never a man whom it was less worth while to advise.

Business crowded upon Mr. Lincoln, and the variety and novelty of it was without limit. On April 17 Jefferson Davis issued a proclamation offering "letters of marque and reprisal" to owners of private armed vessels. Two days later the President retorted by proclaiming a blockade of Confederate ports. [144] Of course this could not be made effective upon the moment. On March 4 the nominal total of vessels in the navy was 90. Of these, 69 were classed as "available;" but only 42 were actually in commission; and even of these many were in Southern harbors, and fell into the hands of the Confederates; many more were upon foreign and distant stations. Indeed, the dispersion was so great that it was commonly charged as having been intentionally arranged by secessionist officials under Mr. Buchanan. Also, at the very moment when this proclamation was being read throughout the country, the great navy yard of Gosport, at Norfolk, Virginia, "always the favored depot" of the government, with all its workshops and a great store of cannon and other munitions, was passing into the hands of the enemy. Most of the vessels and some other property were destroyed by Federals before the seizure was consummated; nevertheless, the loss was severe. Moreover, even had all the vessels of the regular navy been present, they would have had other duties besides lying off Southern ports. Blockading squadrons, therefore, had to be improvised, and orders at once issued for the purchase and equipment of steam vessels from the merchant marine and the coasting service. Fortunately the summer season was at hand, so that these makeshifts were serviceable for many months, during which better craft were rapidly got together by alteration and building. Three thousand miles of coast and many harbors were included within the blockade limits, and were distributed into departments under different commanders. Each commander was instructed to declare his blockade in force as soon as he felt able to make it tolerably effective, with the expectation of rapidly improving its efficiency. The beginning was, therefore, ragged, and was naturally criticised in a very jealous and hostile spirit by those foreign nations who suffered by it. Dangerous disputes threatened to arise, but were fortunately escaped, and in a surprisingly short time "Yankee" enterprise made the blockade too thorough for question.

Amid the first haste and pressure it was ingeniously suggested that, since the government claimed jurisdiction over the whole country and recognized only a rebellion strictly so called, therefore the President could by proclamation simply *close* ports at will. Secretary Welles favored this course, and in the extra session of the summer of 1861 Congress passed a bill giving authority to Mr. Lincoln to pursue it, in his discretion. Mr. Seward, with better judgment, said that it might be legal, but would certainly be unwise. The position probably could have been successfully maintained by lawyers before a bench of judges; but to have relied upon it in the teeth of the commercial interests and unfriendly sentiment of England and France would have been a fatal blunder. Happily it was avoided; and the President had the shrewdness to keep within a line which shut out technical discussion. Already he saw that, so far as relations with foreigners were concerned, the domestic theory of a rebellion, pure and simple, must be very greatly modified. In a word, that which began as rebellion soon developed into civil war; the two were closely akin, but with some important differences.

Nice points of domestic constitutional law also arose with the first necessity for action, opening the broad question as to what course should be pursued in doubtful cases, and worse still in those cases where the government could not fairly claim the benefit of a real doubt. The plain truth was that, in a condition faintly contemplated in the Constitution, many things not permitted by the Constitution must be done to preserve the Constitution. The present crisis had been very scantily and vaguely provided for by "the fathers." The instant that action became necessary to save the Union under the Constitution, it was perfectly obvious that the Constitution must be stretched, transcended, and most liberally interlined, in a fashion which would furnish annoying arguments to the disaffected. The President looked over the situation, and decided, in the proverbial phrase, to take the bull by the horns; that which clearly ought to be done he would do, law or no law, doubt or no doubt. He would have faith that the people would sustain him; and that the courts and the lawyers, among whose functions it is to see to it that laws and statutes do not interfere too seriously with the convenience of the community, would arrive, in what subtle and roundabout way they might choose, at the conclusion that whatever must be done might be done. These learned gentlemen did their duty, and developed the "war powers" under the Constitution in a manner equally ingenious, comical, and sensible. But the fundamental basis was, that necessity knows no law; every man in the country knew this, but the well-intentioned denied it, as matter of policy, while the ill-intentioned made such use of the opportunities thus afforded to them as might have been expected. Among the "war Democrats," however, there was at least ostensible liberality.

An early question related to the writ of habeas corpus. The Maryland legislature was to meet on April 26, 1861, and was expected to guide the

State in the direction of secession. Many influential men urged the President to arrest the members before they could do this. He, however, conceived such an interference with a state government, in the present condition of popular feeling, to be impolitic. "We cannot know in advance," he said, "that the action will not be lawful and peaceful;" and he instructed General Scott to watch them, and, in case they should make a movement towards arraying the people against the United States, to counteract it by "the bombardment of their cities, and, in the extremest necessity, the suspension of the writ of habeas corpus." This intimation that the suspension of the venerated writ was a measure graver than even bombarding a city, surely indicated sufficient respect for laws and statutes. The legislators restrained their rebellious ardor and proved the wisdom of Mr. Lincoln's moderation. In the autumn, however, the crisis recurred, and then the arrests seemed the only means of preventing the passage of an ordinance of secession. Accordingly the order was issued and executed. Public opinion upheld it, and Governor Hicks afterward declared his belief that only by this action had Maryland been saved from destruction.

The privilege of habeas corpus could obviously, however, be made dangerously serviceable to disaffected citizens. Therefore, April 27, the President instructed General Scott: "If at any point on or in the vicinity of any military line which is now, or which shall be, used between the city of Philadelphia and the city of Washington, you find it necessary to suspend the writ of habeas corpus for the public safety, you ... are authorized to suspend that writ." Several weeks elapsed before action was taken under this authority. Then, on May 25, John Merryman, recruiting in Maryland for the Confederate service, was seized and imprisoned in Fort McHenry. Chief Justice Taney granted a writ of habeas corpus. General Cadwalader replied that he held Merryman upon a charge of treason, and that he had authority under the President's letter to suspend the writ. The chief justice thereupon issued against the general an attachment for contempt, but the marshal was refused admittance to the fort. The chief justice then filed with the clerk, and also sent to the President, his written opinion, in which he said: "I understand that the President not only claims the right to suspend the writ of habeas corpus at his discretion, but to delegate that discretionary power to a military officer;" whereas, according to the view of his honor, the power did not lie even with the President himself, but only with Congress. Warming to the discussion, he used pretty strong language, to the effect that, if authority intrusted to other departments could thus "be usurped by the military power at its discretion, the people ... are no longer living under a government of laws; but every citizen holds life, liberty, and property at the will and pleasure of the army officer in whose military district he may happen to be found." It was unfortunate that the country should hear such phrases launched by the chief justice against the President, or at least against acts done under orders of the President. Direct retort was of course impossible, and the dispute was in abeyance for a short time. [145] But the predilections of the judicial hero of the Dred Scott decision were such as to give rise to grave doubts as to whether or not the Union could be saved by any process which would not often run counter to his ideas of the law; therefore in this matter the President continued to exercise the useful and probably essential power, though taking care, for the future, to have somewhat more regard for form. Thus, on May 10, instead of simply writing a letter, he issued through the State Department a proclamation authorizing the Federal commander on the Florida coast, "if he shall find it necessary, to suspend there the writ of habeas corpus."

In due time the assembling of Congress gave Mr. Lincoln the opportunity to present his side of the case. In his message he said that arrests, and suspension of the writ, had been made "very sparingly;" and that, if authority had been stretched, at least the question was pertinent: "Are all the laws but one to go unexecuted, and the government itself to go to pieces, lest that one be violated?" He, however, believed that in fact this question was not presented, and that the law had not been violated. "The provision of the Constitution, that the privilege of the writ of habeas corpus shall not be suspended unless when, in cases of rebellion or invasion, the public safety may require it, is equivalent to a provision that such privilege may be suspended when, in cases of rebellion or invasion, the public safety does require it." As between Congress and the executive, "the Constitution itself is silent as to which or who is to exercise the power; and as the provision was plainly made for a dangerous emergency it cannot be believed that the framers of the instrument intended that in every case the danger should run its course until Congress could be called together, the very assembling of which might be prevented, as was intended in this case by the rebellion."

If it was difficult, it was also undesirable to confute the President's logic. The necessity for military arrests and for indefinite detention of the arrested persons was undeniable. Congress therefore recognized the legality of what had been done, and the power was frequently exercised thereafter, and to great advantage. Of course mistakes occurred, and subordinates made some arrests which had better have been left unmade; but these bore only upon discretion in individual cases, not upon inherent right. The topic, however, was in itself a tempting one, not only for the seriously disaffected, but for the far larger body of the quarrelsome, who really wanted the government to do its work, yet maliciously liked to make the process of doing it just as difficult and as disagreeable as possible. Later on, when the malcontent class acquired the organization of a distinct political body, no other charge against the administration proved so plausible and so continuously serviceable as this. It invited to florid declamation profusely illustrated with impressive historical allusions, and to the free use of vague but grand and sonorous phrases concerning "usurpation," "the subjection of the life, liberty, and property of every citizen to the mere will of a military commander," and other like terrors. Unfortunately men much more deserving of respect than the Copperheads, men of sound loyalty and high ability, but of anxious and conservative temperament, were led by their fears to criticise severely arrests of men who were as dangerous to the government as if they had been soldiers of the Confederacy.

May 3, 1861, by which time military exigencies had become better understood, Mr. Lincoln called "into the service of the United States 42,034 volunteers," and directed that the regular army should be increased by an aggregate of 22,714 officers and enlisted men. More suggestive than the mere increase was the fact that the volunteers were now required "to serve for a period of three years, unless sooner discharged." The opinion of the government as to the magnitude of the task in hand was thus for the first time conveyed to the people. They received it seriously and without faltering.

July 4, 1861, the Thirty-seventh Congress met in extra session, and the soundness of the President's judgment in setting a day which had at first been condemned as too distant was proved. In the interval, nothing had been lost which could have been saved by the sitting of Congress; while, on the other hand, the members had had the great advantage of having time to think soberly concerning the business before them, and to learn the temper and wishes of their constituents.

Mr. Lincoln took great pains with his message, which he felt to be a very important document. It was his purpose to say simply what events had occurred, what questions had been opened, and what necessities had arisen; to display the situation and to state facts fairly and fully, but not apparently to argue the case of the North. Yet it was essential for him so to do this that no doubt could be left as to where the right lay. This peculiar process of argument by statement had constituted his special strength at the bar, and he now gave an excellent instance of it. He briefly sketched the condition of public affairs at the time when he assumed the government; he told the story of Sumter, and of the peculiar process whereby Virginia had been linked to the Confederacy. With a tinge of irony he remarked that, whether the sudden change of feeling among the members of the Virginian Convention was "wrought by their great approval of the assault upon

Sumter, or their great resentment at the government's resistance to that assault, is not definitely known."

He explained the effect of the neutrality theory of the Border States. "This," he said, "would be disunion completed. Figuratively speaking, it would be the building of an impassable wall along the line of separation, — and yet not quite an impassable one, for under the guise of neutrality it would tie the hands of the Union men, and freely pass supplies to the insurrectionists.... At a stroke it would take all the trouble off the hands of secession, except what proceeds from the external blockade." It would give to the disunionists "disunion, without a struggle of their own."

Of the blockade and the calls for troops, he said: "These measures, whether strictly legal or not, were ventured upon under what appeared to be a popular demand and a public necessity, trusting then, as now, that Congress would ratify them." At the same time he stated the matter of the suspension of the writ of habeas corpus, which has been already referred to.

Speaking of the doctrine that secession was lawful under the Constitution, and that it was not rebellion, he made plain the genuine significance of the issue thus raised: "It presents ... the question whether a Constitutional Republic or Democracy, a government of the people by the same people, can or cannot maintain its territorial integrity against its own domestic foes. It presents the question whether discontented individuals, too few in numbers to control the administration according to the organic law in any case, can always, upon the pretenses made in this case, or any other pretenses, or arbitrarily without any pretense, break up their government, and thus practically put an end to free government upon the earth. It forces us to ask: Is there in all Republics this inherent fatal weakness? Must a government of necessity be too strong for the liberties of its own people, or too weak to maintain its own existence?" The Constitution of the Confederacy was a paraphrase with convenient adaptations of the Constitution of the United States. A significant one of these adaptations was the striking out of the first three words, "We, the people," and the substitution of the words, "We, the deputies of the sovereign and independent States." "Why," said Mr. Lincoln, "why this deliberate pressing out of view the rights of men and the authority of the people? This is essentially a people's contest. On the side of the Union it is a struggle for maintaining in the world that form and substance of government whose leading object is to elevate the condition of men ... to afford to all an unfettered start and a fair chance in the race of life.... This is the leading object of the government for whose existence we contend. I am most happy to believe that the plain people understand and appreciate this."

Many persons, not gifted with the power of thinking clearly, were disturbed at what seemed to them a purpose to "invade" and to "subjugate" sovereign States,—as though a government could invade its own country or subjugate its own subjects! These phrases, he said, were producing "uneasiness in the minds of candid men" as to what would be the course of the government toward the Southern States after the suppression of the rebellion. The President assured them that he had no expectation of changing the views set forth in his inaugural address; that he desired "to preserve the government, that it may be administered for all as it was administered by the men who made it. Loyal citizens everywhere have a right to expect this,... and the government has no right to withhold or neglect it. It is not perceived that in giving it there is any coercion, any conquest, or any subjugation."

In closing he said that it was with the deepest regret that he had used the war power; but "in defense of the government, forced upon him, he could but perform this duty or surrender the existence of the government." Compromise would have been useless, for "no popular government can long survive a marked precedent that those who carry an election can only save the government from immediate destruction by giving up the main point upon which the people gave the election." To those who would have had him compromise he explained that only the people themselves, not their servants, can safely reverse their own deliberate decisions. He had no power to agree to divide the country which he had the duty to govern. "As a private citizen the executive could not have consented that these institutions shall perish; much less could he, in betrayal of so vast and so sacred a trust as these free people have confided to him. He felt that he had no moral right to shrink, nor even to count the chances of his own life in what might follow."

The only direct request made in the message was that, to make "this contest a short and decisive one," Congress would "place at the control of the government for the work at least 400,000 men, and $400,000,000. That number of men is about one tenth of those of proper ages within the regions where apparently all are willing to engage, and the sum is less than a twenty-third part of the money value owned by the men who seem ready to devote the whole."

The message was well received by the people, as it deserved to be.

The proceedings of Congress can only be referred to with brevity. Yet a mere recital of the names of the more noteworthy members of the Senate and the House must be intruded, if merely for the flavor of reminiscence which it will bring to readers who recall those times. In the Senate, upon the Republican side, there were: Lyman Trumbull from Illinois, James Harlan and James W. Grimes from Iowa, William P. Fessenden from Maine, Charles Sumner and Henry Wilson from Massachusetts, Zachariah Chandler from Michigan, John P. Hale from New Hampshire, Benjamin F. Wade from Ohio, and John Sherman, who was elected to fill the vacancy created by the appointment of Salmon P. Chase to the Treasury Department, David Wilmot from Pennsylvania, filling the place of Simon Cameron, Henry B. Anthony from Rhode Island, Andrew Johnson from Tennessee, Jacob Collamer from Vermont, and James R. Doolittle from Wisconsin. On the Democratic side, there were: James A. McDougall of California, James A. Bayard and William Saulsbury of Delaware, Jesse D. Bright of Indiana, who was expelled February 5, 1862, John C. Breckenridge of Kentucky, who a little later openly joined the Secessionists, and was formally expelled December 4, 1861; he was succeeded by Garrett Davis, an "American or Old Line Whig," by which name he and two senators from Maryland preferred to be described; James W. Nesmith of Oregon. Lane and Pomeroy, the first senators from the free State of Kansas, were seated. In the House Galusha A. Grow of Pennsylvania, who had lately knocked down Mr. Keitt of South Carolina in a fisticuff encounter on the floor of the chamber, was chosen speaker, over Francis P. Blair, Jr., of Missouri. Thaddeus Stevens of Pennsylvania was the most prominent man in the body. Among many familiar names in running down the list the eye lights upon James E. English of Connecticut; E.B. Washburne, Isaac N. Arnold, and Owen Lovejoy of Illinois; Julian, Voorhees, and Schuyler Colfax of Indiana; Crittenden of Kentucky; Roscoe Conkling, Reuben E. Fenton, and Erastus Corning of New York; George H. Pendleton, Vallandigham, Ashley, Shellabarger, and S.S. Cox of Ohio; Covode of Pennsylvania; Maynard of Tennessee. The members came together in very good temper; and the great preponderance of Republicans secured dispatch in the conduct of business; for the cliques which soon produced intestine discomfort in that dominant party were not yet developed. No ordinary legislation was entered upon; but in twenty-nine working days seventy-six public Acts were passed, of which all but four bore directly upon the extraordinary emergency. The demands of the President were met, with additions: 500,000 men and $500,000,000 were voted; $207,000,000 were appropriated to the army, and $56,000,000 to the navy. August 6 Congress adjourned.

The law-makers were treated, during their session, to what was regarded, in the inexperience of those days, as a spectacle of real war. During a couple of months past large bodies of men had been gathering together, living in tents, shouldering guns, and taking the name of armies. General Butler was in command at Fortress Monroe, and was faced by Colonel Magruder, who held the peninsula between the York and the James rivers. Early in June the lieutenants of these two commanders performed the comical fiasco of the "battle" of Big Bethel. In this skirmish the Federal regiments fired into each other, and then retreated, while the Confederates withdrew; but in language of absurd extravagance the Confederate colonel reported that he had won a great victory, and Northern men flushed beneath the ridicule incurred by the blunder of their troops.

A smaller affair at Vienna was more ridiculous; several hundred soldiers, aboard a train of cars, started upon a reconnoissance, as if it had been a picnic. The Confederates fired upon them with a couple of small cannon, and they hastily took to the woods. When they got home they talked wisely about "masked batteries." But the shrewdness and humor of the people were not thus turned aside, and the "masked battery" long made the point of many a bitter jest.

Up the river, Harper's Ferry was held by "Stonewall" Jackson, who was soon succeeded by J.E. Johnston. Confronting and watching this force was General Patterson, at Chambersburg, Pennsylvania, with a body of men rapidly growing to considerable numbers by the daily coming of recruits. Not very far away, southeastward, the main body of the Confederate army, under Beauregard, lay at Manassas, and the main body of the Federal army, under McDowell, was encamped along the Potomac. On May 23 the Northern advance crossed that river, took possession of Arlington Heights and of Alexandria, and began work upon permanent defensive intrenchments in front of the capital.

The people of the North knew nothing about war or armies. Wild with enthusiasm and excitement, they cheered the departing regiments, which, as they vaguely and eagerly fancied, were to begin fighting at once. Yet it was true that no one would stake his money on a "football team" which should go into a game trained in a time so short as that which had been allowed for bringing into condition for the manoeuvres and battlefields of a campaign an army of thirty or forty thousand men, with staff and commissariat, and arms of infantry, cavalry, and artillery, altogether constituting an organization vast, difficult, and complex in the highest degree of human coöperation. Nevertheless "On to Richmond!" rolled up the imperious cry from every part of the North. The government, either sharing in this madness, or feeling that it must be yielded to, passed the word to the commander, and McDowell very reluctantly obeyed orders and started with his army in that direction,—not, however, with any real hope of reaching this nominal objective; for he was an intelligent man and a good soldier, and was perfectly aware of the unfitness of his army. But when, protesting, he suggested that his troops were "green," he was told to remember that the Southern troops were of the same tint; for, in a word, the North was bound to have a fight, and would by no means endure that the three months' men should come home without doing something more positive than merely preventing the capture of Washington.

On July 16, therefore, McDowell began his advance, having with him about 35,000 men, and by the 19th he was at the stream of Bull Run, behind which the Confederates lay. He planned his battle skillfully, and began his attack on the morning of the 21st. On the other hand, Beauregard was at the double disadvantage of misapprehending his opponent's purpose, and of failing to get his orders conveyed to his lieutenants until the fight was far advanced. The result was, that at the beginning of the afternoon the Federals had almost won a victory which they fully deserved. That they did not finally secure it was due to the inefficiency of General Patterson. This general had crossed the Potomac a few days before and had been instructed to watch Johnston, who had drawn back near Winchester, and either to prevent him from moving his force from the Shenandoah Valley to Manassas, or, failing this, to keep close to him and unite with McDowell. But Patterson neither detained nor followed his opponent. On July 18 Beauregard telegraphed to Johnston: "If you wish to help me, now is the time." If Patterson wished to help McDowell, then, also, was the time. The Southern general seized his opportunity, and the Northern general let his opportunity go. Johnston, uninterrupted and unfollowed by Patterson, brought his troops in from Manassas Junction upon the right wing of the Federals at the very moment and crisis when the battle was actually in the process of going in their favor. Directly all was changed. Older troops would not have stood, and these untried ones were defeated as soon as they were attacked. Speedily retreat became rout, and rout became panic. At a great speed the frightened soldiers, resolved into a mere disorganized mob of individuals, made their way back to the camps on the Potomac; many thought Washington safer, and some did not stop short of their distant Northern homes.

The Southerners, who had been on the point of running away when the Northerners anticipated them in so doing, now triumphed immoderately, and uttered boastings magniloquent enough for Homeric heroes. Yet they were, as General Johnston said, "almost as much disorganized by victory as were the Federals by defeat." Many of them also hastened to their homes, spreading everywhere the cheering tidings that the war was over and the South had won.

In point of fact, it was a stage of the war when defeat was more wholesome than victory. Fortunately, too, the North was not even momentarily discouraged. The people had sense enough to see that what had happened was precisely what should have been expected. A little humiliated at their own folly, about as much vexed with themselves as angry with their enemies, they turned to their work in a new spirit. Persistence displaced excitement, as three years' men replaced three months' men. The people settled down to a long, hard task. Besides this, they had now some idea of what was necessary to be done in order to succeed in that task. Invaluable lessons had been learned, and no lives which were lost in the war bore fruit of greater usefulness than did those which seemed to have been foolishly thrown away at Bull Run.

[143] So said Hon. George W. Julian, somewhat ruefully acknowledging that Lincoln "was always himself the President." *Polit. Recoll.* 190.

[144] South Carolina, Georgia, Alabama, Florida, Mississippi, Louisiana, and Texas were covered by this proclamation; on April 27, North Carolina and Virginia were added.

[145] For the documents in this case, and also for some of the more famous professional opinions thereon, see McPherson, *Hist, of Rebellion, 154 et seq.*; also (of course from the side of the chief justice), Tyler's *Taney,* 420-431; and see original draft of the President's message on this subject; N. and H. iv. 176.

CHAPTER X
THE FIRST ACT OF THE MCCLELLAN DRAMA

On the day after the battle of Bull Run General George B. McClellan was summoned to Washington, where he arrived on July 26. On the 25th he had been assigned to the command of the army of the Potomac. By all the light which President Lincoln had at the time of making this appointment, it seemed the best that was possible; and in fact it was so, in view of the immediate sphere of usefulness of a commanding general in Virginia. McClellan was thirty-four years old, of vigorous physique and fine address. After his graduation at West Point, in 1846, he was attached to the Engineer Corps; he served through the Mexican war, and for merit received a captaincy. In 1855 he was sent by Jefferson Davis, then secretary of war, to Europe to study the organizing and handling of armies in active service; and he was for a while at the British headquarters during the siege of Sebastopol, observing their system in operation. In January, 1857, he resigned from the army; but with the first threatenings of the civil war he made ready to play an active part. April 23, 1861, he was appointed by the governor of Ohio a major-general, with command of all the state forces. May 13, by an order from the national government, he took command of the Department of the Ohio, in which shortly afterward Western Virginia was included. He found the sturdy mountaineers of this inaccessible region for the most part loyalists, but overawed by rebel troops, and toward the close of May, upon his own sole responsibility, he inaugurated a campaign for their relief. In this he had the good fortune to be entirely successful. By some small engagements he cleared the country of armed Secessionists and returned it to the Union; and in so doing he showed energy and good tactical ability. These achievements, which later in the war would have seemed inconsiderable, now led to confidence and promotion.

In his new and exalted position McClellan became commander of a great number of men, but not of a great army. The agglomeration of civilians, who had run away from Manassas under the impression that they had fought and lost a real battle, was utterly disorganized and demoralized. Some had already reached the sweet safety of the villages of the North; others were lounging in the streets of Washington and swelling the receipts of its numerous barrooms. The majority, it is true, were in camp across the

Potomac, but in no condition to render service. All, having been enlisted for three months, now had only a trifling remnant of so-called military life before them, in which it seemed to many hardly worth while to run risks. The new call for volunteers for three years had just gone forth, and though troops began to arrive under it with surprising promptitude and many three months' men reënlisted, yet a long time had to elapse before the new levies were all on hand. Thus betwixt departing and coming hosts McClellan's duty was not to use an army, but to create one.

The task looked immeasurable, but there was a fortunate fitness for it upon both sides. The men who in this awful crisis were answering the summons of President Lincoln constituted a raw material of a kind such as never poured into any camp save possibly into that of Cromwell. For the most part they were courageous, intelligent, self-respecting citizens, who were under the noble compulsion of conscience and patriotism in leaving reputable and prosperous callings for a military career. The moral, mental, and physical average of such a body of men was a long way above that of professional armies, and insured readiness in acquiring their new calling. But admirable as were the latent possibilities, and apt as each individual might be, these multitudes arrived wholly uninstructed; few had even so much as seen a real soldier; none had any notion at all of what military discipline was, or how to handle arms, or to manoeuvre, or to take care of their health. Nor could they easily get instruction in these things, for officers knew no more than privates; indeed, for that matter, one of the great difficulties at first encountered lay in the large proportion of utterly unfit men who had succeeded in getting commissions, and who had to be toilfully eliminated.

That which was to be done, McClellan was well able to do. He had a passion for organization, and fine capacity for work; he showed tact and skill in dealing with subordinates; he had a thorough knowledge and a high ideal of what an army should be. He seemed the Genius of Order as he educated and arranged the chaotic gathering of human beings, who came before him to be transmuted from farmers, merchants, clerks, shopkeepers, and what not into soldiers of all arms and into leaders of soldiers. To that host in chrysalis he was what each skillful drill-master is to his awkward squad. Under his influence privates learned how to obey and officers how to command; each individual merged the sense of individuality in that of homogeneousness and cohesion, until the original loose association of units became one grand unit endowed with the solidarity and machine-like quality of an efficient army. Patient labor produced a result so excellent that General Meade said long afterward: "Had there been no McClellan there could have been no Grant, for the army made no essential improvement under any of his successors."

That the formation of this great complex machine was indispensable, and that it would take much time, were facts which the disaster at Bull Run had compelled both the administration and the people to appreciate moderately well. Accordingly they resolutely set themselves to be patient. The cry of "On to Richmond!" no longer sounded through the land, and the restraint imposed by the excited masses upon their own ardor was the strongest evidence of their profound earnestness. In a steady stream they poured men and material into the camps in Virginia, and they heard with satisfaction of the advance of the levies in discipline and soldierly efficiency. For a while the scene was pleasant and without danger. "It was," says Arnold, describing that of which he had been an eye-witness, "the era of brilliant reviews and magnificent military displays, of parades, festive parties, and junketings." Members of Congress found excursions to the camps attractive for themselves and their visitors. Glancing arms, new uniforms, drill, and music constituted a fine show. Thus the rest of the summer passed away, and autumn came and was passing, too. Then here and there signs of impatience began again to be manifested. It was observed with discontent that the glorious days of the Indian Summer, the perfect season for military operations, were gliding by as tranquilly as if there were not a great war on hand, and still the citizen at home read each morning in his newspaper the stereotyped bulletin, "All quiet on the Potomac;" the phrase passed into a byword and a sneer. By this time, too, to a nation which had not European standards of excellence, the army seemed to have reached a high state of efficiency, and to be abundantly able to take the field. Why did not its commander move? Amid all the drilling and band-playing the troops had been doing hard work: a chain of strong fortifications scientifically constructed had been completed around the capital, and rendered it easy of defense. It could be left in safety. Why, then, was it not left? Why did the troops still linger?

For a moment this monotony was interrupted by the ill-conducted engagement at Ball's Bluff. On October 21 nearly 2000 troops were sent across the Potomac by the local commander, with the foolish expectation of achieving something brilliant. [146] The actual result was that they were corralled in an open field; in their rear the precipitous bank dropped sharply to the river, upon which floated only the two or three little boats which had ferried them across in small parties; in front and flank from the shelter of thick woods an outnumbering force of rebels poured a steady fire upon them. They were in a cruel snare, and suffered terribly in killed and drowned, wounded and captured. The affair was, and the country at once saw that it was, a gross blunder. The responsibility lay upon General Stone and Colonel Baker. Stone, a military man by education, deserved censure, but he was treated in a manner so cruel, so unjust, and so disproportionate to his deserts, that his error has been condoned in sympathy for his wrongs. The injustice was chargeable chiefly to Stanton, in part to the Committee on the Conduct of the War. Apparently Mr. Lincoln desired to know as little as possible about a wrong which he could not set right without injury to the public interests. He said to Stanton concerning the arrest: "I suppose you have good reasons for it, and having good reasons I am glad I knew nothing of it until it was done." To General Stone himself he said that, if he should tell all he knew about it, he should not tell much. Colonel Baker, senator from Oregon, a personal friend of the President, a brilliant orator, and a man beloved and admired by all who knew him, was a favorable specimen of the great body of new civilian officers. While brimming over with gallantry and enthusiasm, he was entirely ignorant of the military art. In the conduct of this enterprise a considerable discretion had been reposed in him, and he had, as was altogether natural, failed in everything except courage. But as he paid with his life on the battlefield the penalty of his daring and his inexperience, he was thought of only with tenderness and regret.

This skirmish illustrated the scant trust which could yet be reposed in the skill and judgment of subordinate officers. The men behaved with encouraging spirit and constancy under severe trial. But could a commander venture upon a campaign with brigadier-generals and colonels so unfit to assume responsibility?

Nevertheless impatience hardly received a momentary check from this lesson. With some inconsistency, people placed unlimited confidence in McClellan's capacity to beat the enemy, but no confidence at all in his judgment as to the feasibility of a forward movement. The grumbling did not, however, indicate that faith in him was shaken, for just now he was given promotion by Mr. Lincoln, and it met with general approval. For some time past it had been a cause of discomfort that he did not get on altogether smoothly with General Scott; the elder was irascible and jealous, the younger certainly not submissive. At last, on October 31, the old veteran regretfully but quite wisely availed himself of his right to be placed upon the retired list, and immediately, November 1, General McClellan succeeded him in the distinguished position of commander-in-chief (under the President) of all the armies of the United States. On the same day Mr. Lincoln courteously hastened out to headquarters to make in person congratulations which were unquestionably as sincere as they were generous. Every one felt that a magnificent opportunity was given to a favorite general. But unfortunately among all his admirers there was not one who believed in him quite so fully as he believed in himself; he lost all sense of perspective and proportion, and felt upon a pinnacle from which he could look down even on a president. [147] Being in this masterful temper, he haughtily disregarded the growing demand for an advance. On the other hand the politicians, always eager to minister to the gratification of the people, began to be importunate; they harried the President, and went out to camp to prick their civilian spurs into the general himself. But McClellan had a soldierly contempt for such intermeddling in matters military, and was wholly unimpressible. When Senator Wade said that an unsuccessful battle was preferable to delay, for that a defeat would easily be repaired by swarming recruits, the general tartly replied that he preferred a few recruits before a victory to a great many after a defeat. But, however cleverly and fairly the military man might counter upon the politician, there was no doubt that discontent was developing dangerously. The people had conscientiously intended to do their part fully, and a large proportion of them now sincerely believed that they had done it. They knew that they had been lavish of men, money, and supplies; and they thought that they had been not less liberal of time; wherefore they rebelled against the contrary opinion of the general, whose ideal of a trustworthy army had by no means been reached, and who, being of a stubborn temperament, would not stir till it had been.

It is difficult to satisfy one's self of the real fitness of the army to move at or about this time,—that is to say, in or near the month of November, 1861,—for the evidence is mixed and conflicting. The Committee on the Conduct of the War asserted that "the army of the Potomac was well armed and equipped and had reached a high state of discipline by the last of September or first of October;" but the committee was not composed of experts. Less florid commendation is given by the Comte de Paris, of date October 15. McClellan himself said: "It certainly was not till late in November that the army was in any condition to move, nor even then were they capable of assaulting intrenched positions." At that time winter was at hand, and advance was said to be impracticable. That these statements were as favorable as possible seems probable; for it is familiar knowledge that the call for these troops did not issue until July, that at the close of November the recruits were still continuing "to pour in, to be assigned and equipped and instructed;" [148] that many came unarmed or with useless weapons; and that these "civilians, suddenly called to arms as soldiers and officers, did not take kindly to the subordination and restraints of the camp." [149] Now McClellan's temperament did not lead him to run risks in the effort to force achievements with means of dubious adequacy. His purpose was to create a machine perfect in every part, sure and irresistible in operation, and then to set it in motion with a certainty of success. He wrote to Lincoln: "I have ever regarded our true policy as being that of fully preparing ourselves, and then seeking for the most decisive results." [150] Under favoring circumstances this plan might have been the best. But circumstances were not favoring. Neither he nor the government itself, nor indeed both together, could afford long or far to disregard popular feeling. Before the close of November that popular feeling was such that the people would have endured without flinching the discouragement of a defeat, but would not endure the severe tax of inaction, and from this time forth their impatience gathered volume until it became a controlling element in the situation. Themselves intending to be reasonable, they grew more and more convinced that McClellan was unreasonable. General and people confronted each other: the North would fight, at the risk of defeat; McClellan would not fight, because he was not sure to win. Any one who comprehended the conditions, the institutions of the country, the character of the nation, especially its temper concerning the present conflict, also the necessities beneath which that conflict must be waged, if it was to be waged at all, would have seen that the people must be deferred to. The question was not whether they were right or wrong. Assuming them to be wrong, it would still be a mistake to withstand them beyond a certain point. If yielding to them should result in disastrous consequences, they must be called upon to rally, and could be trusted to do so, instructed but undismayed by their experience. All this McClellan utterly failed to appreciate, thereby leading Mr. Swinton very justly to remark that he was lacking in "the statesmanlike qualities that enter into the composition of a great general." [151]

On the other hand, no man ever lived more capable than Mr. Lincoln of precisely appreciating the present facts, or more sure to avoid those peculiar blunders which entrapped the military commander. He was very loyal in living up to his pledge to give the general full support, and by his conduct during many months to come he proved his readiness to abide to the last possible point. He knew, however, with unerring accuracy just where that last point lay, and he saw with disquietude that it was being approached too rapidly. He was getting sufficient knowledge of McClellan's character to see that the day was not distant when he must interfere. Meantime he kept his sensitive finger upon the popular pulse, as an expert physician watches a patient in a fever. With the growth of the impatience his anxiety grew, for the people's war would not be successfully fought by a dissatisfied people. Repeatedly he tested the situation in the hope that a movement could be forced without undue imprudence; but he was always met by objections from McClellan. In weighing the Northern and the Southern armies against each other, the general perhaps undervalued his own resources and certainly overvalued those of his opponent. He believed that the Confederate "discipline and drill were far better than our own;" wherein he was probably in error, for General Lee admitted that, while the Southerners would always fight well, they were refractory under discipline. Moreover, they were at this time very ill provided with equipment and transportation. Also McClellan said that the Southern army had thrown up intrenchments at Manassas and Centreville, and therefore the "problem was to attack victorious and finely drilled troops in intrenchment." But the most discouraging and inexplicable assertion, which he emphatically reiterated, concerned the relative numerical strength. He not only declared that he himself could not put into the field the numbers shown by the official returns to be with him, but also he exaggerated the Southern numbers till he became extravagant to the point of absurdity. So it had been from the outset, and so it continued to be to the time when he was at last relieved of his command. Thus, on August 15, he conceived himself to be "in a terrible place; the enemy have three or four times my force." September 9 he imagined Johnston to have 130,000 men, against his own 85,000; and he argued that Johnston could move upon Baltimore a column 100,000 strong, which he could meet with only 60,000 or 70,000. Later in October he marked the Confederates up to 150,000. He estimated his own requirement at a "total effective force" of 208,000 men, which implied "an aggregate, present and absent, of about 240,000 men." Of these he designed 150,000 as a "column of active operations;" the rest were for garrisons and guards. He said that in fact he had a gross aggregate of 168,318, and the "force present for duty was 147,695." Since the garrisons and the guards were a fixed number, the reduction fell wholly upon the movable column, and reduced "the number disposable for an advance to 76,285." Thus he made himself out to be fatally overmatched. But he was excessively in error. In the autumn Johnston's effective force was only 41,000 men, and on December 1, 1861, it was 47,000. [152]

Such comparisons, advanced with positiveness by the highest authority, puzzled Mr. Lincoln. They seemed very strange, yet he could not disprove them, and was therefore obliged to face the perplexing choice which was mercilessly set before him: "either to go into winter quarters, or to assume the offensive with forces greatly inferior in number" to what was "desirable and necessary." "If political considerations render the first course unadvisable, the second alone remains." The general's most cheering admission was that, by stripping all other armies down to the lowest numbers absolutely necessary for a strict defensive, and by concentrating all the forces of the nation and all the attention of the government upon "the vital point" in Virginia, it might yet be possible for this "main army, whose destiny it [was] to decide the controversy,... to move with a reasonable prospect of success before the winter is fairly upon us." A direct assertion of impossibility, provocative of denial or discussion, would have been less disheartening.

In passing, it may be remarked that McClellan's prevision that the ultimate arbitrament of the struggle must occur in Virginia was correct. But in another point he was wrong, and unfortunately this was of more immediate consequence, because it corroborated him in his purpose to delay till he could make success a certainty. He hoped that when he moved, he should be able to win one or two overwhelming victories, to capture Richmond, and to crush the rebellion in a few weeks. It was a brilliant and captivating programme, [153] but impracticable and undesirable. Even had the Southerners been quelled by so great a disaster,—which was not likely,—they would not have been thoroughly conquered, nor would slavery have been disposed of, and both these events were indispensable to a definitive peace between the two sections. Whether the President shared this notion of his general is not evident. Apparently he was not putting his mind upon theories reaching into the future so much as he was devoting his whole thought to dealing with the urgent problems of the present. If this was the case, he was pursuing the wise and sound course. In the situation, it was more desirable to fight a great battle at the earliest possible moment than to await a great victory many months hence.

It is commonplace wisdom that it is foolish for a civilian to undertake the direction of a war. Yet our Constitution ordains that "the President shall be commander-in-chief of the army and navy of the United States, and of the militia of the several States, when called into the actual service of the United States." It is not supposable that the delegates who suggested this function, or the people who ordained it, anticipated that presidents generally would be men skilled in military science. Therefore Mr. Lincoln could not escape the obligation on the ground of unfitness for the duty which was imperatively placed upon him. It might be true that to set him in charge of military operations was like ordering a merchant to paint a picture or a jockey to sail a ship, but it was also true that he was so set in charge. He could not shirk it, nor did he try to shirk it. In consequence hostile critics have dealt mercilessly with his actions, and the history of this winter and spring of 1861-62 is a painful and confusing story of bitter controversy and crimination. Further it is to be remembered that, apart from the obligation imposed on the President by the Constitution, it was true that if civilians could not make rapid progress in the military art, the war might as well be abandoned. They were already supposed to be doing so; General Banks, a politician, and General Butler, a lawyer, were already conducting important movements. Still it remains undeniable that finally it was only the professional soldiers who, undergoing successfully the severe test of time, composed the illustrious front rank of strategists when the close of the war left every man in his established place. In discussing this perplexing period, extremists upon one side attribute the miscarriages and failure of McClellan's campaign to ceaseless, thwarting interference by the President, the secretary of war, and other civil officials. Extremists upon the other side allege the marvel that a sudden development of unerring judgment upon every question involving the practical application of military science took place on Mr. Lincoln's part. [154] Perhaps the truth lies between the disputants, but it is not likely ever to be definitely agreed upon so long as the controversy excites interest; for the discussion bristles with *ifs*, and where this is the case no advocate can be irremediably vanquished.

It seems right, at this place, to note one fact concerning Mr. Lincoln which ought not to be overlooked and which cannot be denied. This is his entire *political unselfishness*, the rarest moral quality among men in public life. In those days of trouble and distrust slanders were rife in a degree which can hardly be appreciated by men whose experience has been only with quieter times. Sometimes purposes and sometimes methods were assailed; and those prominent in civil life, and a few also in military life, were believed to be artfully and darkly seeking to interlace their personal political fortunes in the web of public affairs, naturally subordinating the latter fabric. Alliances, enmities, intrigues, schemes, and every form of putting the interest of self before that of the nation, were insinuated with a bitter malevolence unknown except amid such abnormal conditions. The few who escaped charges of this kind were believed to cherish their own peculiar fanaticisms, desires, and purposes concerning the object and results of the struggle, which they were resolved to satisfy at almost any cost and by almost any means. While posterity is endeavoring very wisely to discredit and to forget a great part of these painful criminations, it is cheering to find that no effort has to be made to forget anything about the President. In his case injurious gossip has long since died away and been buried. Whatever may be said of him in other respects, at least the purity and the singleness of his patriotism shine brilliant and luminous through all this cloud-dust of derogation. By his position he had more at stake, both in his lifetime and before the tribunal of the future, than any other person in the country. But there was only one idea in his mind, and that was,—not that *he should save the country*, but *that the country should be saved*. Not the faintest shadow of self ever fell for an instant across this simple purpose. He was intent to play his part out faithfully, with all the ability he could bring to it; but any one else, who could, might win and wear the title of savior. He chiefly cared that the saving should be done. Never once did he manipulate any covert magnet to draw toward himself the credit or the glory of a measure or a move. To his own future he seemed to give no thought. It would be unjust to allow the dread of appearing to utter eulogy rather than historic truth to betray a biographer into overlooking this genuine magnanimity.

It was in December, 1861, that Congress created the famous Committee on the Conduct of the War, to some of whose doings it has already been necessary to allude. The gentlemen who were placed upon it were selected partly of course for political reasons, and were all men who had made themselves conspicuous for their enthusiasm and vehemence; not one of them had any military knowledge. The committee magnified its office almost beyond limit,—investigated everything; haled whom it chose to testify before it; made reports, expressed opinions, insisted upon policies and measures in matters military; and all with a dictatorial assumption and self-confidence which could not be devoid of effect, although every one knew that each individual member was absolutely without fitness for this business. So the committee made itself a great power, and therefore also a great complication, in the war machinery; and though it was sometimes useful, yet, upon a final balancing of its long account, it failed to justify its existence, as, indeed, was to have been expected from the outset. [155] In the present discussions concerning an advance of the army, its members strenuously insisted upon immediate action, and their official influence brought much strength to that side.

The first act indicating an intention on the part of the President to interfere occurred almost simultaneously with the beginning of the general's illness. About December 21, 1861, he handed to McClellan a brief memorandum: "If it were determined to make a forward movement of the army of the Potomac, without awaiting further increase of numbers or better drill and discipline, how long would it require to actually get in motion? After leaving all that would be necessary, how many troops could join the movement from southwest of the river? How many from northeast of it?" Then he proceeded briefly to hint rather than distinctly to suggest that plan of a direct advance by way of Centreville and Manassas, which later on he persistently advocated. Ten days elapsed before McClellan returned answers, which then came in a shape too curt to be respectful. Almost immediately afterward the general fell ill, an occurrence which seemed to his detractors a most aggravating and unjustifiable intervention of Nature herself in behalf of his policy of delay.

On January 10 a dispatch from General Halleck represented in his department also a condition of check and helplessness. Lincoln noted upon it: "Exceedingly discouraging. As everywhere else, nothing can be done." Yet something must be done, for the game was not to be abandoned. Under this pressure, on this same day, he visited McClellan, but could not see him;

nor could he get any definite idea how long might be the duration of the typhoid fever, the lingering and uncertain disease which had laid the general low. Accordingly he summoned General McDowell and General Franklin to discuss with him that evening the military situation. The secretaries of state and of the treasury, and the assistant secretary of war, also came. The President, says McDowell, "was greatly disturbed at the state of affairs," "was in great distress," and said that, "if something was not soon done, the bottom would be out of the whole affair; and if General McClellan did not want to use the army, he would like to '*borrow it*,' provided he could see how it could be made to do something." The two generals were directed to inform themselves concerning the "actual condition of the army," and to come again the next day. Conferences followed on January 11 and 12, Postmaster-General Blair and General Meigs being added to the council. The postmaster-general condemned a direct advance as "strategically defective," while Chase descanted on the "moral power" of a victory. The picture of the two civilians injecting their military suggestions is not reassuring. Meigs is somewhat vaguely reported to have favored a "battle in front."

McDowell and Franklin had not felt justified in communicating these occurrences to McClellan, because the President had marked his order to them "private and confidential." But the commander heard rumors of what was going forward, [156] and on January 12 he came from his sick-room to see the President; he was "looking quite well," and apparently was "able to assume the charge of the army." The apparition put a different complexion upon the pending discussions. On the 13th the same gentlemen met, but now with the addition of General McClellan. The situation was embarrassing. McClellan took scant pains to conceal his resentment. McDowell, at the request of the President, explained what he thought could be done, closing "by saying something apologetic;" to which McClellan replied, "somewhat coldly if not curtly: 'You are entitled to have any opinion you please.'" Secretary Chase, a leader among the anti-McClellanites, bluntly asked the general to explain his military plans in detail; but McClellan declined to be interrogated except by the President, or by the secretary of war, who was not present. Finally, according to McClellan's account, which differs a little but not essentially from that of McDowell, Mr. Lincoln suggested [157] that he should tell what his plans were. McClellan replied, in substance, that this would be imprudent and seemed unnecessary, and that he would only give information if the President would order him in writing to do so, and would assume the responsibility for the results. [158] McDowell adds (but McClellan does not), that the President then asked McClellan "if he had counted upon any particular time; he did not ask what that time was, but had he in his own mind any particular time fixed, when a movement could be commenced. He replied, he had. 'Then,' rejoined the President, 'I will adjourn this meeting.'" This unfortunate episode aggravated the discord, and removed confidence and coöperation farther away than ever before.

The absence of the secretary of war from these meetings was due to the fact that a change in the War Department was in process contemporaneously with them. The President had been allowed to understand that Mr. Cameron did not find his duties agreeable, and might prefer a diplomatic post. Accordingly, with no show of reluctance, Mr. Lincoln, on January 11, 1862, offered to Mr. Cameron the post of minister to Russia. It was promptly accepted, and on January 13 Edwin M. Stanton was nominated and confirmed to fill the vacancy. [159] The selection was a striking instance of the utter absence of vindictiveness which so distinguished Mr. Lincoln, who, in fact, was simply insensible to personal feeling as an influence. In choosing incumbents for public trusts, he knew no foe, perhaps no friend; but as dispassionately as if he were manoeuvring pieces on a chessboard, he considered only which available piece would serve best in the square which he had to fill. In 1859 he and Stanton had met as associate counsel in perhaps the most important lawsuit in which Mr. Lincoln had ever been concerned, and Stanton had treated Lincoln with his habitual insolence. [160] Later, in the trying months which closed the year 1861, Stanton had abused the administration with violence, and had carried his revilings of the President even to the point of coarse personal insults. [161] No man, not being a rebel, had less right to expect an invitation to become an adviser of the President; and most men, who had felt or expressed the opinions held by Mr. Stanton, would have had scruples or delicacy about coming into the close relationship of confidential adviser with the object of their contempt; but neither scruples nor delicacy delayed him; his acceptance was prompt. [162]

So Mr. Lincoln had chosen his secretary solely upon the belief of the peculiar fitness of the individual for the special duties of the war office. Upon the whole the choice was wisely made, and was evidence of Mr. Lincoln's insight into the aptitudes and the uses of men. Stanton's abilities commanded some respect, though his character never excited either respect or liking; just now, however, all his good qualities and many of his faults seemed precisely adapted to the present requirements of his department. He had been a Democrat, but was now zealous to extremity in patriotism; in his dealings with men he was capable of much duplicity, yet in matters of business he was rigidly honest, and it was his pleasure to protect the treasury against the contractors; he loved work, and never wearied amid the driest and most exacting toil; he was prompt and decisive rather than judicial or correct in his judgments concerning men and things; he was arbitrary, harsh, bad-tempered, and impulsive; he often committed acts of injustice or cruelty, for which he rarely made amends, and still more rarely seemed disturbed by remorse or regret. These traits bore hard upon individuals; but ready and unscrupulous severity was supposed to have its usefulness in a civil war. Many a time he taxed the forbearance of the President to a degree that would have seemed to transcend the uttermost limit of human patience, if Mr. Lincoln had not taken these occasions to show to the world how forbearing and patient it is possible for man to be. But those who knew the relations of the two men are agreed that Stanton, however browbeating he was to others, recognized a master in the President, and, though often grumbling and insolent, always submitted if a crisis came. Undoubtedly Mr. Lincoln was the only ruler known to history who could have coöperated for years with such a minister. He succeeded in doing so because he believed it to be for the good of the cause, to which he could easily subordinate all personal considerations; and posterity, agreeing with him, concedes to Stanton credit for efficiency in the conduct of his department.

It is worth while here to pause long enough to read part of a letter which, on this same crowded thirteenth day of January, 1862, the President sent to General Halleck, in the West: "For my own views: I have not offered, and do not now offer, them as orders; and while I am glad to have them respectfully considered, I would blame you to follow them contrary to your own clear judgment, unless I should put them in the form of orders.... With this preliminary, I state my general idea of this war to be that we have the greater numbers and the enemy has the greater facility of concentrating forces upon points of collision; that we must fail unless we can find some way of making our advantage an overmatch for his; and that this can only be done by menacing him with superior forces at different points at the same time, so that we can safely attack one or both if he makes no change; and if he weakens one to strengthen the other, forbear to attack the strengthened one, but seize and hold the weakened one, gaining so much."

In a personal point of view this short letter is pregnant with interest and suggestion. The writer's sad face, eloquent of the charge and burden of one of the most awful destinies of human-kind, rises before us as we read the expression of his modest self-distrust amid the strange duties of military affairs. But closely following this comes the intimation that in due time *"orders"* will come. Such was the quiet, unflinching way in which Lincoln always faced every test, apparently with a tranquil and assured faith that, whatever might seem his lack of fitting preparation, his best would be adequate to the occasion. The habit has led many to fancy that he believed himself divinely chosen, and therefore sure of infallible guidance; but it is observable far back, almost from the beginning of his life; it was a trait of mind and character, nothing else. The letter closes with a broad general theory concerning the war, wrought out by that careful process of thinking whereby he was wont to make his way to the big, simple, and fundamental truth. The whole is worth holding in memory through the narrative of the coming weeks.

The conference of January 13 developed a serious difference of opinion as to the plan of campaign, whenever a campaign should be entered upon. The President's notion, already shadowed forth in his memorandum of December, was to move directly upon the rebel army at Centreville and Manassas and to press it back upon Richmond, with the purpose of capturing that city. But McClellan presented as his project a movement by Urbana and West Point, using the York River as a base of supplies. General McDowell and Secretary Chase favored the President's plan; General Franklin and Postmaster Blair thought better of McClellan's. The President had a strong fancy for his own scheme, because by it the Union army was kept between the enemy and Washington; and therefore the supreme point of importance, the safety of the national capital, was insured. The discussion, which was thus opened and which remained long unsettled, had, among other ill effects, that of sustaining the vexatious delay. While the anti-McClellan faction—for the matter was becoming one of factions [163] —grew louder in denunciation of his inaction, and fastened upon him the contemptuous nickname of "the Virginia creeper," the friends of the general retorted that the President, meddling in what he did not understand, would not let the military commander manage the war.

Nevertheless Mr. Lincoln, dispassionate and fair-minded as usual, allowed neither their personal difference of opinion nor this abusive outcry to inveigle into his mind any prejudice against McClellan. The Southerner who, in February, 1861, predicted that Lincoln "would do his own thinking," read character well. Lincoln was now doing precisely this thing, in his silent, thorough, independent way, neither provoked by McClellan's cavalier assumption of superior knowledge, nor alarmed by the danger of offending the politicians. In fact, he decided to go counter to both the disputants; for he resolved, on the one hand, to compel McClellan to act; on the other, to maintain him in his command. He did not, however, abandon his own plan of campaign. On January 27, as commander-in-chief of the army, he issued his "General War Order No. 1." In this he directed "that the 22d day of February, 1862, be the day for a general movement of the land and naval forces of the United States against the insurgent forces;" and said that heads of departments and military and naval commanders would "be held to their strict and full responsibilities for prompt execution of this order." By this he practically repudiated McClellan's scheme, because transportation and other preparations for pursuing the route by Urbana could not be made ready by the date named.

Critics of the President have pointed to this document as a fine instance of the follies to be expected from a civil ruler who conducts a war. To order an advance all along a line from the Mississippi to the Atlantic, upon a day certain, without regard to differing local conditions and exigencies, and to notify the enemy of the purpose nearly a month beforehand, were acts preposterous according to military science. But the criticism was not so fair as it was obvious. The order really bore in part the character of a manifesto; to the people of the North, whose confidence must be kept and their spirit sustained, it said that the administration meant action at once; to commanding officers it was a fillip, warning them to bestir themselves, obstacles to the contrary notwithstanding. It was a reveille. Further, in a general way it undoubtedly laid out a sound plan of campaign, substantially in accordance with that which McClellan also was evolving, viz.: to press the enemy all along the western and middle line, and thus to prevent his making too formidable a concentration in Virginia. In the end, however, practicable or impracticable, wise or foolish, the order was never fulfilled. The armies in Virginia did nothing till many weeks after the anniversary of Washington's birthday; whereas, in the West, Admiral Foote and General Grant did not conceive that they were enforced to rest in idleness until that historic date. Before it arrived they had performed the brilliant exploits of capturing Fort Henry and Fort Donelson.

On January 31 the President issued "Special War Order No. 1," directing the army of the Potomac to seize and occupy "a point upon the railroad southwestward of what is known as Manassas Junction;... the expedition to move before or on the 22d day of February next." This was the distinct, as the general order had been the indirect, adoption of his own plan of campaign, and the overruling of that of the general. McClellan at once remonstrated, and the two rival plans thus came face to face for immediate and definitive settlement. It must be assumed that the President's order had been really designed only to force exactly this issue; for on February 3, so soon as he received the remonstrance, he invited argument from the general by writing to him a letter which foreshadowed an open-minded reception for views opposed to his own:—

"If you will give satisfactory answers to the following questions, I shall gladly yield my plan to yours:—

"1st. Does not your plan involve a greatly larger expenditure of *time* and *money* than mine?

"2d. Wherein is a victory *more certain* by your plan than mine?

"3d. Wherein is a victory *more valuable* by your plan than mine?

"4th. In fact, would it not be *less* valuable in this: that it would break no great line of the enemy's communications, while mine would?

"5th. In case of disaster would not a retreat be more difficult by your plan than mine?"

To these queries McClellan replied by a long and elaborate exposition of his views. He said that, if the President's plan should be pursued successfully, the "results would be confined to the possession of the field of battle, the evacuation of the line of the upper Potomac by the enemy, and the moral effect of the victory." On the other hand, a movement in force by the route which he advocated "obliges the enemy to abandon his intrenched position at Manassas, in order to hasten to cover Richmond and Norfolk." That is to say, he expected to achieve by a manoeuvre what the President designed to effect by a battle, to be fought by inexperienced troops against an intrenched enemy. He continued: "This movement, if successful, gives us the capital, the communications, the supplies, of the rebels; Norfolk would fall; all the waters of the Chesapeake would be ours; all Virginia would be in our power, and the enemy forced to abandon Tennessee and North Carolina. The alternative presented to the enemy would be, to beat us in a position selected by ourselves, disperse, or pass beneath the Caudine forks." In case of defeat the Union army would have a "perfectly secure retreat down the Peninsula upon Fort Monroe." "This letter," he afterward wrote, "must have produced some effect upon the mind of the President!" The slur was unjust. The President now and always considered the views of the general with a liberality of mind rarely to be met with in any man, and certainly never in McClellan himself. In this instance the letter did in fact produce so much "effect upon the mind of the President" that he prepared to yield views which he held very strongly to views which he was charged with not being able to understand, and which he certainly could not bring himself actually to believe in.

Yet before quite taking this step he demanded that a council of the generals of division should be summoned to express their opinions. This was done, with the result that McDowell, Sumner, Heintzelman, and Barnard voted against McClellan's plan; Keyes voted for it, with the proviso "that no change should be made until the rebels were driven from their batteries on the Potomac." Fitz-John Porter, Franklin, W.F. Smith, McCall,

Blenker, Andrew Porter, and Naglee (of Hooker's division) voted for it. Stanton afterward said of this: "We saw ten generals afraid to fight." The insult, delivered in the snug personal safety which was suspected to be very dear to Stanton, was ridiculous as aimed at men who soon handled some of the most desperate battles of the war; but it is interesting as an expression of the unreasoning bitterness of the controversy then waging over the situation in Virginia, a controversy causing animosities vastly more fierce than any between Union soldiers and Confederates, animosities which have unfortunately lasted longer, and which can never be brought to the like final and conclusive arbitrament. The purely military question quickly became snarled up with politics and was reduced to very inferior proportions in the noxious competition. "Politics entered and strategy retired," says General Webb, too truly. McClellan himself conceived that the politicians were leagued to destroy him, and would rather see him discredited than the rebels whipped. In later days the strong partisan loves and hatreds of our historical writers have perpetuated and increased all this bad blood, confusion, and obscurity.

The action of the council of generals was conclusive. The President accepted McClellan's plan. Therein he did right; for undeniably it was his duty to allow his own inexperience to be controlled by the deliberate opinion of the best military experts in the country; and this fact is wholly independent of any opinion concerning the intrinsic or the comparative merits of the plans themselves. Indeed, Mr. Lincoln had never expressed positive disapproval of McClellan's plan *per se*, but only had been alarmed at what seemed to him its indirect result in exposing the capital. To cover this point, he now made an imperative preliminary condition that this safety should be placed beyond a question. He was emphatic and distinct in reiterating this proviso as fundamental. The preponderance of professional testimony, from that day to this, has been to the effect that McClellan's strategy was sound and able, and that Mr. Lincoln's anxiety for the capital was groundless. But in spite of all argument, and though military men may shed ink as if it were mere blood, in spite even of the contempt and almost ridicule which the President incurred at the pen of McClellan, [164] the civilian will retain a lurking sympathy with the President's preference. It is impossible not to reflect that precisely in proportion as the safety of the capital, for many weighty reasons, immeasurably outweighed any other possible consideration in the minds of the Northerners, so the desire to capture it would be equally overmastering in the estimation of the Southerners. Why might not the rebels permit McClellan to march into Richmond, provided that at the same time they were marching into Washington? Why might they not, in the language afterward used by General Lee, "swap Queens?"

They would have a thousand fold the better of the exchange. The Northern Queen was an incalculably more valuable piece on the board than was her Southern rival. With the Northern government in flight, Maryland would go to the Confederacy, and European recognition would be sure and immediate; and these two facts might, almost surely would, be conclusive against the Northern cause. Moreover, memory will obstinately bring up the fact that long afterward, when General Grant was pursuing a route to Richmond strategically not dissimilar to that proposed by McClellan, and when all the circumstances made the danger of a successful attack upon Washington much less than it was in the spring of 1862, the rebels actually all but captured the city; and it was saved not alone by a rapidity of movement which would have been impossible in the early stages of the war, but also by what must be called the aid of good luck. It is difficult to see why General Jackson in 1862 might not have played in fatal earnest a game which in 1864 General Early played merely for the chances. Pondering upon these things, it is probable that no array of military scientists will ever persuade the non-military world that Mr. Lincoln was so timid, or so dull-witted, or so unreasonable, as General McClellan declared him to be.

Another consideration is suggested by some remarks of Mr. Swinton. It is tolerably obvious that, whether McClellan's plan was or was not the better, the President's plan was entirely possible; all that could be said against it was that it promised somewhat poorer results at somewhat higher cost. This being the case, and in view of the fact that the President's disquietude concerning Washington was so profound and his distrust of McClellan's plan so ineradicable, it would have been much better to have had the yielding come from the general than from the President. A man of less stubborn temper and of broader intellect than belonged to McClellan would have appreciated this. In fact, it was in a certain sense even poor generalship to enter upon a campaign of such magnitude, when a thorough and hearty coöperation was really not to be expected. For after all might be ostensibly settled and agreed upon, and however honest might be Mr. Lincoln's intentions to support the commanding general, one thing still remained certain: that the safety of the capital was Mr. Lincoln's weightiest responsibility, that it was a matter concerning which he was sensitively anxious, and that he was perfectly sure in any moment of alarm concerning that safety to insure it by any means in his power and at any sacrifice whatsoever. In a word, that which soon did happen was precisely that which ought to have been foreseen as likely to happen. For it was entirely obvious that Mr. Lincoln did not abandon his own scheme because his own reason was convinced of the excellence of McClellan's; in fact, he never was and never pretended to be thus convinced. To his mind, McClellan's reasoning never overcame his own reasoning; he only gave way before professional authority; and, while he sincerely meant to give McClellan the most efficient aid and backing in his power, the anxiety about Washington rested immovable in his thought. If the two interests should ever, in his opinion, come into competition, no one could doubt which would be sacrificed. To push forward the Peninsula campaign under these conditions was a terrible mistake of judgment on McClellan's part. Far better would it have been to have taken the Manassas route; for even if its inherent demerits were really so great as McClellan had depicted, they would have been more than offset by preserving the undiminished coöperation of the administration. The personal elements in the problem ought to have been conclusive.

An indication of the error of forcing the President into a course not commended by his judgment, in a matter where his responsibility was so grave, was seen immediately. On March 8 he issued General War Order No. 3: That no change of base should be made "without leaving in and about Washington such a force as, in the opinion of the general-in-chief and the commanders of army corps, shall leave said city entirely secure;" that not more than two corps (about 50,000 men) should be moved en route for a new base until the Potomac, below Washington, should be freed from the Confederate batteries; that any movement of the army via Chesapeake Bay should begin as early as March 18, and that the general-in-chief should be "responsible that it moves as early as that day." This greatly aggravated McClellan's dissatisfaction; for it expressed the survival of the President's anxiety, it hampered the general, and by its last clause it placed upon him a responsibility not properly his own.

Yet at this very moment weighty evidence came to impeach the soundness of McClellan's opinion concerning the military situation. On February 27 Secretary Chase wrote that the time had come for dealing decisively with the "army in front of us," which he conceived to be already so weakened that "a victory over it is deprived of half its honor." Not many days after this writing, the civilian strategists, the President and his friends, seemed entitled to triumph. For on March 7, 8, and 9 the North was astonished by news of the evacuation of Manassas by Johnston. At once the cry of McClellan's assailants went up: If McClellan had only moved upon the place! What a cheap victory he would have won, and attended with what invaluable "moral effects"! Yet, forsooth, he had been afraid to move upon these very intrenched positions which it now appeared that the Confederates dared not hold even when unthreatened! But McClellan retorted that the rebels had taken this backward step precisely because they had got some hint of his designs for advancing by Urbana, and that it was the exact fulfillment, though inconveniently premature, of his predictions.

This explanation, however, wholly failed to prevent the civilian mind from believing that a great point had been scored on behalf of the President's plan. Further than this, there were many persons, including even a majority of the members of the Committee on the Conduct of the War, who did not content themselves with mere abuse of McClellan's military intelligence, but who actually charged him with being disaffected and nearly, if not quite, a traitor. None the less Mr. Lincoln generously and patiently adhered to his agreement to let McClellan have his own way.

Precisely at the same time that this evacuation of Manassas gave to McClellan's enemies an argument against him which they deemed fair and forcible and he deemed unfair and ignorant, two other occurrences added to the strain of the situation. McClellan immediately put his entire force in motion towards the lines abandoned by the Confederates, not with the design of pressing the retreating foe, which the "almost impassable roads" prevented, but to strip off redundancies and to train the troops in marching. On March 11, immediately after he had started, the President issued his Special War Order No. 3: "Major-General McClellan having personally taken the field at the head of the army of the Potomac,... he is relieved from the command of the other military departments, he retaining command of the Department of the Potomac." McClellan at once wrote that he should continue to "work just as cheerfully as before;" but he felt that the removal was very unhandsomely made just as he was entering upon active operations. Lincoln, on the other hand, undoubtedly looked upon it in precisely the opposite light, and conceived that the opportunity of the moment deprived of any apparent sting a change which he had determined to make. The duties which were thus taken from McClellan were assumed during several months by Mr. Stanton. He was utterly incompetent for them, and, whether or not it was wise to displace the general, it was certainly very unwise to let the secretary practically succeed him. [165] The way in which, both at the East and West, our forces were distributed into many independent commands, with no competent chief who could compel all to coöperate and to become subsidiary to one comprehensive scheme, was a serious mistake in general policy, which cost very dear before it was recognized. [166] McClellan had made some efforts to effect this combination or unity in purpose, but Stanton gave no indication even of understanding that it was desirable.

The other matter was the division of the army of the Potomac into four army corps, to be commanded respectively by the four senior generals of division, viz., McDowell, Sumner, Heintzelman, and Keyes. The propriety of this action had been for some time under consideration, and the step was now forced upon Mr. Lincoln by the strenuous insistence of the Committee on the Conduct of the War. That so large an army required organization by corps was admitted; but McClellan had desired to defer the arrangement until his generals of division should have had some actual experience in the field, whereby their comparative fitness for higher responsibilities could be measured. An incapable corps commander was a much more dangerous man than an incapable commander of a division or brigade. The commander naturally felt the action now taken by the President to be a slight, and he attributed it to pressure by the band of civilian advisers whose untiring hostility he returned with unutterable contempt. Not only was the taking of the step at this time contrary to his advice, but he was not even consulted in the selection of his own subordinates, who were set in these important positions by the blind rule of seniority, and not in accordance with his opinion of comparative merit. His irritation was perhaps not entirely unjustifiable.

[146] A reconnoissance or "slight demonstration" ordered for the day before by McClellan had been completed, and is not to be confounded with this movement, for which he was not responsible.

[147] For example, see his *Own Story*, 82; but, unfortunately, one may refer to that book *passim* for evidence of the statement.

[148] N. and H. iv. 469.

[149] *Ibid.* v. 140.

[150] Letter to Lincoln, February 3, 1862.

[151] *Army of Potomac*, 97. Swinton says: "He should have made the lightest possible draft on the indulgence of the people." *Ibid.* 69. General Webb says: "He drew too heavily upon the faith of the public." *The Peninsula*, 12.

[152] The Southern generals had a similar propensity to overestimate the opposing force; *e.g.*, Johnston's *Narrative*,

108, where he puts the Northern force at 140,000, when in fact it was 58,000; and on p. 112 his statement is even worse.

[153] The Southerners also had the same notion, hoping by one great victory to discourage and convince the North and make peace on the basis of independence; *e.g.*, see Johnston's *Narrative* 113, 115. Grant likewise had the notion of a decisive battle. *Memoirs*, i. 368.

[154] The position taken by Messrs. Nicolay and Hay, I think, fully warrants this language.

[155] General Palfrey says of this committee that "the worst spirit of the Inquisition characterized their doings." *The Antietam and Fredericksburg* (Campaigns of Civil War Series), 182.

[156] Through Stanton; McClellan, *Own Story*, 156.

[157] Only a few days before this time Lincoln had said that he had no "right" to insist upon knowing the general's plans. Julian, *Polit. Recoll.* 201.

[158] It appears that he feared that what he said would leak out, and ultimately reach the enemy.

[159] For an interesting account of these incidents, from Secretary Chase's Diary, see Warden, 401.

[160] Lamon, 332; Herndon, 353-356; N. and H. try to mitigate this story, v. 133.

[161] He did not always feel his tongue tied afterward by the obligations of office; *e.g.*, see Julian, *Polit. Recoll.* 210.

[162] For a singular tale, see McClellan, *Own Story*, 153.

[163] In fact, the feeling against McClellan was getting so strong that some of his enemies were wild enough about this time to accuse him of disloyalty. He himself narrates a dramatic tale, which would seem incredible if his veracity were not beyond question, of an interview, occurring March 8, 1862, in which the President told him, apparently with the air of expecting an explanation, that he was charged

with laying his plans with the traitorous intent of leaving Washington defenseless. McClellan's *Own Story*, 195. On the other hand, McClellan retaliated by believing that his detractors wished, for political and personal motives, to prevent the war from being brought to an early and successful close, and that they intentionally withheld from him the means of success; also that Stanton especially sought by underhand means to sow misunderstanding between him and the President. *Ibid.* 195.

[164] McClellan afterward wrote that the administration "had neither courage nor military insight to understand the effect of the plan I desired to carry out." *Own Story*, 194. This is perhaps a mild example of many remarks to the same purport which fell from the general at one time and another.

[165] See remarks of Mr. Blaine, *Twenty Years of Congress*, i. 368.

[166] *E.g.,* McClellan, *Rep.* (per Keyes), 82; Grant, *Mem.* i. 322; and indeed all writers agree upon this.

CHAPTER XI
MILITARY MATTERS OUTSIDE OF VIRGINIA

The man who first raised the cry "On to Richmond!" uttered the formula of the war. Richmond was the gage of victory. Thus it happened, as has been seen, that every one at the North, from the President down, had his attention fast bound to the melancholy procession of delays and miscarriages in Virginia. At the West there were important things to be done; the States of Kentucky, Tennessee, and Missouri, trembling in the balance, were to be lost or won for the Union; the passage down the Mississippi to the Gulf was at stake, and with it the prosperity and development of the boundless regions of the Northwest. Surely these were interests of some moment, and worthy of liberal expenditure of thought and energy, men and money; yet the swarm of politicians gave them only side glances, being unable for many minutes in any day to withdraw their eyes from the Old Dominion. The consequence was that at the East matters military and matters political, generals and "public men" of all varieties were mixed in a snarl of backbiting and quarreling, which presented a spectacle most melancholy and discouraging. On the other hand, the West throve surprisingly well in the absence of political nourishment, and certain local commanders achieved cheering successes without any aid from the military civilians of Washington. The contrast seems suggestive, yet perhaps it is incorrect to attach to these facts any sinister significance, or any connection of cause and effect. Other reasons than civilian assistance may account for the Virginia failures, while Western successes may have been won in spite of neglect rather than by reason of it. Still, simply as naked facts, these things were so.

Upon occurrences outside of Virginia Mr. Lincoln bestowed more thought than was fashionable in Washington, and maintained an oversight strongly in contrast to the indifference of those who seemed to recognize no other duty than to discuss the demerits of General McClellan. The President had at least the good sense to see the value of unity of plan and coöperation along the whole line, from the Atlantic seaboard to the extreme West. Also at the West as at the East he was bent upon advancing, pressing the enemy, and doing something positive. He had not occasion to use the spur at the West either so often or so severely as at the East; yet Halleck and Buell needed it and got it more than once. The Western commanders, like those at the East, and with better reason, were importunate for more men and more equipment. The President could not, by any effort, meet their requirements. He wrote to McClernand after the battle of Belmont: "Much, very much, goes undone; but it is because we have not the power to do it faster than we do." Some troops were without arms; but, he said, "the plain matter of fact is, our good people have rushed to the rescue of the government faster than the government can find arms to put in their hands." Yet, withal, it is true that Mr. Lincoln's actual interferences at the South and West were so occasional and incidental, that, since this writing is a biography of him and not a history of the war, there is need only for a list of the events which were befalling outside of that absorbing domain which lay around the rival capitals.

Along the southern Atlantic coast some rather easy successes were rapidly won. August 29, 1861, Hatteras Inlet was taken, with little fighting. November 7, Port Royal followed. Lying nearly midway between Charleston and Savannah, and being a very fine harbor, this was a prize of value. January 7, 1862, General Burnside was directed to take command of the Department of North Carolina. February 8, Roanoke Island was seized by the Federal forces. March 14, Newbern fell. April 11, Fort Pulaski, at the mouth of the Savannah River, was taken. April 26, Beaufort was occupied. The blockade of the other Atlantic ports having long since been made effective, the Eastern seaboard thus early became a prison wall for the Confederacy.

At the extreme West Missouri gave the President some trouble. The bushwhacking citizens of that frontier State, divided not unequally between the Union and Disunion sides, entered upon an irregular but energetic warfare with ready zeal if not actually with pleasure. Northerners in general hardly paused to read the newspaper accounts of these rough encounters, but the President was much concerned to save the State. As it lay over against Illinois along the banks of the Mississippi River, and for the most part above the important strategic point where Cairo controls the junction of that river with the Ohio, possession of it appeared to him exceedingly desirable. In the hope of helping matters forward, on July 3, 1861, he created the Department of the West, and placed it under command of General Fremont. But the choice proved unfortunate. Fremont soon showed himself inefficient and troublesome. At first the President endeavored to allay the local bickerings; on September 9, 1861, he wrote to General Hunter: "General Fremont needs assistance which it is difficult to give him. He is losing the confidence of men near him.... His cardinal mistake is that he isolates himself;... he does not know what is going on.... He needs to have by his side a man of large experience. Will you not, for me, take that place? Your rank is one grade too high;... but will you not serve the country, and oblige me, by taking it voluntarily?" Kindly consideration, however, was thrown away upon Fremont, whose self-esteem was so great that he could not see that he ought to be grateful, or that he must be subordinate. He owed his appointment largely to the friendly urgency of the Blair family; and now Postmaster-General Blair, puzzled at the disagreeable stories about him, went to St. Louis on an errand of investigation. Fremont promptly placed him under arrest. At the same time Mrs. Fremont was journeying to Washington, where she had an extraordinary interview with the President. "She sought an audience with me at midnight," wrote Lincoln, "and taxed me so violently with many things that I had to exercise all the awkward tact I have to avoid quarreling with her.... She more than once intimated that if General Fremont should decide to try conclusions with me, he could set up for himself." Naturally the angry lady's threats of treason, instead of seeming a palliation of her husband's shortcomings, tended to make his displacement more inevitable. Yet the necessity of being rid of him was unfortunate, because he was the pet hero of the Abolitionists, who stood by him without the slightest regard to reason. Lincoln was loath to offend them, but he felt that he had no choice, and therefore ordered the removal. He preserved, however, that habitual strange freedom from personal resentment which made his feelings, like his action, seem to be strictly official. After the matter was all over he uttered a fair judgment: "I thought well of Fremont. Even now I think well of his impulses. I only think he is the prey of wicked and designing men; and I think he has absolutely no military capacity." For a short while General Hunter filled Fremont's place, until, in November, General Henry W. Halleck was assigned to command the Department of Missouri. In February, 1862, General Curtis drove the only regular and considerable rebel force across the border into Arkansas; and soon afterward, March 7 and 8, within this latter State, he won the victory of Pea Ridge.

In Tennessee the vote upon secession had indicated that more than two thirds of the dwellers in the mountainous eastern region were Unionists. Mr. Lincoln had it much at heart to sustain these men, and aside from the personal feeling of loyalty to them it was also a point of great military consequence to hold this district. Near the boundary separating the northeastern corner of the State from Kentucky, the famous Cumberland Gap gave passage through the Cumberland Mountains for the East Tennessee and Virginia Railroad, "the artery that supplied the rebellion." The President saw, as many others did, and appreciated much more than others seemed to do, the desirability of gaining this place. To hold it would be to cut in halves, between east and west, the northern line of the Confederacy. In the early days a movement towards the Gap seemed imprudent in face of Kentucky's theory of "neutrality." But this foolish notion was in time effectually disposed of by the Confederates. Unable to resist the temptation offered by the important position of Columbus at the western end of the State on the Mississippi River, they seized that place in September, 1861. The state legislature, incensed at the intrusion, immediately embraced the Union cause and welcomed the Union forces within the state lines.

This action opened the way for the President to make strenuous efforts for the protection of the East Tennesseeans and the possession of the Gap. In his annual message he urged upon Congress the construction of a military railroad to the Gap, and afterward appeared in person to advocate this measure before a committee of the Senate. If the place had been in Virginia, he might have gained for his project an attention which, as matters stood, the politicians never accorded to it. He also endeavored to stir to action General Buell, who commanded in Kentucky. Buell, an appointee and personal friend of General McClellan, resembled his chief somewhat too closely both in character and history. Just as Mr. Lincoln had to prick McClellan in Virginia, he now had to prick Buell in Kentucky; and just as McClellan, failed to respond in Virginia, Buell also failed in Kentucky. Further, Buell, like McClellan, had with him a force very much greater than that before him; but Buell, like McClellan, would not admit that his troops were in condition to move. The result was that Jefferson Davis, more active to protect a crucial point than the North was to assail it, in December, 1861, sent into East Tennessee a force which imprisoned, deported, and hanged the loyal residents there, harried the country without mercy, and held it with the iron hand. The poor mountaineers, with good reason, concluded that the hostility of the South was a terribly serious evil, whereas the friendship of the North was a sadly useless good. The President was bitterly chagrined, although certainly the blame did not rest with him. Then the parallel between Buell and McClellan was continued even one step farther; for Buell at last intimated that he did not approve of the plan of campaign suggested for him, but thought it would be better tactics to move upon Nashville. It so happened, however, that when he expressed these views McClellan was commander-in-chief of all the armies, and that general, being little tolerant of criticism from subordinates when he himself was the superior, responded very tartly and imperiously. Lincoln, on the other hand, according to his wont, wrote modestly: "Your dispatch ... disappoints and distresses me.... I am not competent to criticise your views." Then, in the rest of the letter, he maintained with convincing clearness both the military and the political soundness of his own opinions.

In offset of this disappointment caused by Buell's inaction, the western end of Kentucky became the theatre of gratifying operations. So soon as policy ceased to compel recognition of the "neutrality" of the State, General

Grant, on September 6, 1861, entered Paducah at the confluence of the Ohio and Tennessee rivers. By this move he checked the water communication hitherto freely used by the rebels, and neutralized the advantage which they had expected to gain by their possession of Columbus. But this was only a first and easy step. Farther to the southward, just within the boundaries of Tennessee, lay Fort Henry on the Tennessee River and Fort Donelson on the Cumberland, presenting a kind of temptation which Grant was less able to resist than were most of the Union generals at this time. Accordingly he arranged with Admiral Foote, who commanded the new gunboats on the Mississippi, for a joint excursion against these places. On February 6, Fort Henry fell, chiefly through the work of the river navy. Ten days later, February 16, Fort Donelson was taken, the laurels on this occasion falling to the land forces. Floyd and Pillow were in the place when the Federals came to it, but when they saw that capture was inevitable they furtively slipped away, and thus shifted upon General Buckner the humiliation of the surrender. This mean behavior excited the bitter resentment of that general, which was not alleviated by what followed. For when he proposed to discuss terms of capitulation, General Grant made that famous reply which gave rise to his popular nickname: "No terms except unconditional and immediate surrender can be accepted. I propose to move immediately upon your works."

Halleck telegraphed the pleasant news that the capture of Fort Donelson carried with it "12,000 to 15,000 prisoners, including Generals Buckner and Bushrod R. Johnson, also about 20,000 stands of arms, 48 pieces of artillery, 17 heavy guns, from 2000 to 4000 horses, and large quantities of commissary stores." He also advised: "Make Buell, Grant, and Pope major-generals of volunteers, and give me command in the West. I ask this in return for Forts Henry and Donelson." Halleck was one of those who expect to reap where others sow. The achievements of Grant and Foote also led him, by some strange process of reasoning, to conclude that General C.W. Smith was the most able general in his department.

Congress, highly gratified at these cheering events, ordered a grand illumination at Washington for February 22; but the death of the President's little son, at the White House, a day or two before that date, checked a rejoicing which in other respects also would not have been altogether timely.

The Federal possession of these two forts rendered Columbus untenable for the Confederates, and on March 2 they evacuated it. This was followed by the fall of New Madrid on March 13, and of Island No. 10 on April 7. At the latter place between 6000 and 7000 Confederates surrendered. Thus was the Federal wedge being driven steadily deeper down the channel of the Mississippi.

Soon after this good service of the gunboats on the Western rivers, the salt-water navy came in for its share of glory. On March 8 the ram Virginia, late Merrimac, which had been taking on her mysterious iron raiment at the Norfolk navy yard, issued from her concealment, an ugly and clumsy, but also a novel and terrible monster. Straight she steamed against the frigate Cumberland, and with one fell rush cut the poor wooden vessel in halves and sent her, with all on board, to the bottom of the sea. Turning then, she mercilessly battered the frigate Congress, drove her ashore, and burned her. All this while the shot which had rained upon her iron sides had rolled off harmless, and she returned to her anchorage, having her prow broken by impact with the Cumberland, but otherwise unhurt. Her armor had stood the test, and now the Federal government contemplated with grave anxiety the further possible achievements of this strange and potent destroyer.

But the death of the Merrimac was to follow close upon her birth; she was the portent of a few weeks only. For, during a short time past, there had been also rapidly building in a Connecticut yard the Northern marvel, the famous Monitor. When the ingenious Swede, John Ericsson, proposed his scheme for an impregnable floating battery, his hearers were divided between distrust and hope; but fortunately the President's favorable opinion secured the trial of the experiment. The work was zealously pushed, and the artisans actually went to sea with the craft in order to finish her as she made her voyage southward. It was well that such haste was made, for she came into Hampton Roads actually by the light of the burning Congress. On the next day, being Sunday, March 9, the Southern monster again steamed forth, intending this time to make the Minnesota her prey; but a little boat, that looked like a "cheese-box" afloat, pushed forward to interfere with this plan. Then occurred a duel which, in the annals of naval science, ranks as the most important engagement which ever took place. It did not actually result in the destruction of the Merrimac then and there, for, though much battered, she was able to make her way back to the friendly shelter of the Norfolk yard. But she was more than neutralized; it was evident that the Monitor was the better craft of the two, and that in a combat à outrance she would win. The significance of this day's work on the waters of Virginia cannot be exaggerated. By the armor-clad Merrimac and the Monitor there was accomplished in the course of an hour a revolution which differentiated the naval warfare of the past from that of the future by a chasm as great as that which separated the ancient Greek trireme from the flagship of Lord Nelson.

As early as the middle of November, 1861, Mr. Lincoln was discussing the feasibility of capturing New Orleans. Already Ship Island, off the Mississippi coast, with its uncompleted equipment, had been seized as a

Gulf station, and could be used as a base. The naval force was prepared as rapidly as possible, but it was not until February 3 that Captain Farragut, the commander of the expedition, steamed out of Hampton Roads in his flagship, the screw steam sloop Hartford. On April 18 he began to bombard forts St. Philip and Jackson, which lie on the river banks seventy-five miles below New Orleans, guarding the approach. Soon, becoming impatient of this tardy process, he resolved upon the bold and original enterprise of running by the forts. This he achieved in the night of April 24; and on April 27 the stars and stripes floated over the Mint in New Orleans. Still two days of shilly-shallying on the part of the mayor ensued, delaying a formal surrender, until Farragut, who had no fancy for nonsense, sharply put a stop to it, and New Orleans, in form and substance, passed under Northern control. On April 28 the two forts, isolated by what had taken place, surrendered. On May 1 General Butler began in the city that efficient régime which so exasperated the men of the South. On May 7 Baton Rouge, the state capital, was occupied, without resistance; and Natchez followed in the procession on May 12.

With one Union fleet at the mouth of the Mississippi and another at Island No. 10, and the Union army not far from the riverside in Kentucky and Tennessee, the opening and repossession of the whole stream by the Federals became a thing which ought soon to be achieved. On June 5 the gunboat fleet from up the river came down to within two miles of Memphis, engaged in a hard fight and won a complete victory, and on the next day Memphis was held by the Union troops. Farragut also, working in his usual style, forced his way up to Vicksburg, and exchanged shots with the Confederate batteries on the bluffs. He found, however, that without the coöperation of a land force he could do nothing, and had to drop back again to New Orleans, arriving there on June 1. In a few weeks he returned in stronger force, and on June 27 he was bombarding the rebel works. On June 28, repeating the operation which had been so successful below New Orleans, he ran some of his vessels by the batteries and got above the city. But there was still no army on the land, and so the vessels which had run by, up stream, had to make the dangerous gauntlet again, down stream, and a second time the fleet descended to New Orleans.

General Halleck had arrived at St. Louis on November 18, 1861, to take command of the Western Department. Perhaps a more energetic commander would have been found ready to coöperate with Farragut at Vicksburg by the end of June, 1862; for matters had been going excellently with the Unionists northeast of that place, and it would seem that a powerful and victorious army might have been moving thither during that month. Early in March, however, General Halleck reported that Grant's army was as much demoralized by victory as the army at Bull Run had been by defeat. He said that Grant "richly deserved" censure, and that he himself was worn out by Grant's neglect and inefficiency. By such charges he obtained from McClellan orders relieving General Grant from duty, ordering an investigation, and even authorizing his arrest. But a few days later, March 13, more correct information caused the reversal of these orders, and March 17 found Grant again in command. He at once began to busy himself with arrangements for moving upon Corinth. General Buell meanwhile, after sustaining McClellan's rebuke and being taught his place, had afterward been successful in obtaining for his own plan preference over that of the administration, had easily possessed himself of Nashville toward the end of February, and was now ready to march westward and coöperate with General Grant in this enterprise. Corinth, lying just across the Mississippi border, was "the great strategic position" at this part of the West. The Mobile and Ohio Railroad ran through it north and south; the Memphis and Charleston Railroad passed through east and west. If it could be taken and held, it would leave, as the only connection open through the Confederacy from the Mississippi River to the Atlantic coast, the railroad line which started from Vicksburg. The Confederates also had shown their estimation of Corinth by fortifying it strongly, and manifesting plainly their determination to fight a great battle to hold it. Grant, aiming towards it, had his army at Pittsburg Landing, on the west bank of the Tennessee, and there awaited Buell, who was moving thither from Nashville with 40,000 men. Such being the status, Grant expected General A.S. Johnston to await in his intrenchments the assault of the Union army. But Johnston, in an aggressive mood, laid well and boldly his plan to whip Grant before Buell could join him, then to whip Buell, and, having thus disposed of the Northern forces in detail, to carry the war up to, or even across, the Ohio. So he came suddenly out from Corinth and marched straight upon Pittsburg Landing, and precipitated that famous battle which has been named after the church of Shiloh, because about that church the most desperate and bloody fighting was done.

The conflict began on Sunday, April 6, and lasted all day. There was not much plan about it; the troops went at each other somewhat indiscriminately and did simple stubborn fighting. The Federals lost much ground all along their line, and were crowded back towards the river. Some say that the Confederates closed that day on the way to victory; but General Grant says that he felt assured of winning on Monday, and that he instructed all his division commanders to open with an assault in the morning. The doubt, if doubt there was, was settled by the arrival of General Buell, whose fresh forces, coming in as good an hour as the Prussians came at Waterloo, were put in during the evening upon the Federal left. On Sunday the Confederates had greatly outnumbered the Federals, but this reinforcement reversed the proportions, so that on Monday the Federals were in the greater force. Again the conflict was fierce and obstinate, but again the greater numbers whipped the smaller, and by afternoon the Confederates were in full retreat. Shiloh, says General Grant, "was the severest battle fought at the West during the war, and but few in the East equaled it for hard, determined fighting." It ended in a complete Union victory. General A.S. Johnston was killed and Beauregard retreated to Corinth, while the North first exulted because he was compelled to do so, and then grumbled because he was allowed to do so. It was soon said that Grant had been surprised, that he was entitled to no credit for winning clumsily a battle which he had not expected to fight, and that he was blameworthy for not following up the retreating foe more sharply. The discussion survives among those quarrels of the war in which the disputants have fought over again the contested field, with harmless fierceness, and without any especial result. Congress took up the dispute, and did a vast deal of talking, in the course of which there occurred one sensible remark. This was made by Mr. Richardson of Illinois, who said that the armies would get along much better if the Riot Act could be read, and the members of Congress dispersed and sent home.

General Grant found that General Halleck was even more obstinately in the way of his winning any success than were the Confederates themselves. As commander of the department, Halleck now conceived that it was his fair privilege to do the visible taking of that conspicuous prize which his lieutenant had brought within sure reach. Accordingly, on April 11, he arrived and assumed command for the purpose of moving on Corinth. Still he was sedulous in his endeavors to neglect, suppress, and even insult General Grant, whom he put nominally second in command, but practically reduced to insignificance, until Grant, finding his position "unendurable," asked to be relieved. This conduct on the part of Halleck has of course been attributed to jealousy; but more probably it was due chiefly to the personal prejudice of a dull man, perhaps a little stimulated by a natural desire for reputation. Having taken charge of the advance, he conducted it slowly and cautiously, intrenching as he went, and moving with pick and shovel, in the phrase of General Sherman, who commanded a division in the army. "The movement," says General Grant, "was a siege from the start to the close." Such tactics had not hitherto been tried at the West, and apparently did not meet approval. There were only about twenty-two miles to be traversed, yet four weeks elapsed in the process. The army started on April 30; twice

Pope got near the enemy, first on May 4, and again on May 8, and each time he was ordered back. It was actually May 28, according to General Grant, when "the investment of Corinth was complete, or as complete as it was ever made." But already, on May 26, Beauregard had issued orders for evacuating the place, which was accomplished with much skill. On May 30 Halleck drew up his army in battle array and "announced in orders that there was every indication that our left was to be attacked that morning." A few hours later his troops marched unopposed into empty works.

Halleck now commanded in Corinth a powerful army,—the forces of Grant, Buell, and Pope, combined,—not far from 100,000 strong, and he was threatened by no Southern force at all able to face him. According to the views of General Grant, he had great opportunities; and among these certainly was the advance of a strong column upon Vicksburg. If he could be induced to do this, it seemed reasonable to expect that he and Farragut together would be able to open the whole Mississippi River, and to cut the last remaining east-and-west line of railroad communication. But he did nothing, and ultimately the disposition made of this splendid collection of troops was to distribute and dissipate it in such a manner that the loss of the points already gained became much more probable than the acquisition of others.

Early in July, as has been elsewhere said, Halleck was called to Washington to take the place of general-in-chief of all the armies of the North; and at this point perhaps it is worth while to devote a paragraph to comparing the retirement of McClellan with the promotion of Halleck. Some similarities and dissimilarities in their careers are striking. The dissimilarities were: that McClellan had organized the finest army which the country had yet seen, or was to see; also that he had at least made a plan for a great campaign; and he had not suppressed any one abler than himself; that Halleck on the other hand had done little to organize an army or to plan a campaign, had failed to find out the qualities of General W.T. Sherman, who was in his department, and had done all in his power to drive General Grant into retirement. The similarities are more worthy of observation. Each general had wearied the administration with demands for reinforcements when each already outnumbered his opponent so much that it was almost disgraceful to desire to increase the odds. If McClellan had been reprehensibly slow in moving upon Yorktown, and had blundered by besieging instead of trying an assault, certainly the snail-like approach upon Corinth had been equally deliberate and wasteful of time and opportunity; and if McClellan had marched into deserted intrenchments, so also had Halleck. If McClellan had captured "Quaker guns" at Manassas, Halleck had found the like peaceful weapons frowning from the ramparts of Corinth. If McClellan had held inactive a powerful force when it ought to have been marching to Manassas, Halleck had also held inactive another powerful force, a part of which might have helped to take Vicksburg. If the records of these two men were stated in parallel columns, it would be difficult to see why one should have been taken and the other left. But the explanation exists and is instructive, and it is wholly for the sake of the explanation that the comparison has been made. McClellan was "in politics," and Halleck was not; McClellan, therefore, had a host of active, unsparing enemies in Washington, which Halleck had not; the Virginia field of operations was ceaselessly and microscopically inspected; the Western field attracted occasional glances not conducive to a full knowledge. Halleck, as commander in a department where victories were won, seemed to have won the victories, and no politicians cared to deny his right to the glory; whereas the politicians, whose hatred of McClellan had, by the admission of one of themselves, become a mania, [167] were entirely happy to have any one set over his head, and would not imperil their pleasure by too close an inspection of the new aspirant's merits. These remarks are not designed to have any significance upon the merits or demerits of McClellan, which have been elsewhere discussed, nor upon the merits or demerits of Halleck, which are not worth discussing; but they are made simply because they afford so forcible an illustration of certain important conditions at Washington at this time. The truth is that the ensnarlment of the Eastern military affairs with politics made success in that field impossible for the North. The condition made it practically inevitable that a Union commander in Virginia should have his thoughts at least as much occupied with the members of Congress in the capital behind him as with the Confederate soldiers in camp before him. Such division of his attention was ruinous. At and before the outbreak of the rebellion the South had expected to be aided efficiently by a great body of sympathizers at the North. As yet they had been disappointed in this; but almost simultaneously with this disappointment they were surprised by a valuable and unexpected assistance, growing out of the open feuds, the covert malice, the bad blood, the partisanship, and the wire-pulling introduced by the loyal political fraternity into campaigning business. The quarreling politicians were doing, very efficiently, the work which Southern sympathizers had been expected to do.

[167] George W. Julian, *Polit. Recoll.* 204.

CHAPTER XII
FOREIGN AFFAIRS

To the people who had been engaged in changing Illinois from a wilderness into a civilized State, Europe had been an abstraction, a mere colored spot upon a map, which in their lives meant nothing. Though England had been the home of their ancestors, it was really less interesting than the west coast of Africa, which was the home of the negroes; for the negroes were just now of vastly more consequence than the ancestors. So even Dahomey had some claim to be regarded as a more important place than Great Britain, and the early settlers wasted little thought on the affairs of Queen Victoria. Amid these conditions, absorbed even more than his neighbors in the exciting questions of domestic politics, and having no tastes or pursuits which guided his thoughts abroad, Mr. Lincoln had never had occasion to consider the foreign relations of the United States, up to the time when he was suddenly obliged to take an active part in managing them.

At an early stage of the civil dissensions each side hoped for the good-will of England. For obvious reasons, that island counted to the United States for more than the whole continent of Europe; indeed, the continental nations were likely to await and to follow her lead. Southern orators, advocating secession, assured their hearers that "King Cotton" would be the supreme power, and would compel that realm of spinners and weavers to friendship if not to alliance with the Confederacy. Northern men, on the other hand, expressed confidence that a people with the record of Englishmen against slavery would not countenance a war conducted in behalf of that institution; nor did they allow their hopes to be at all impaired by the consideration that, in order to found them upon this support, they had to overlook the fact that they were at the same time distinctly declaring that slavery really had nothing to do with the war, in which only and strictly the question of the Union, the integrity of the nation, was at stake. When the issue was pressing for actual decision, each side was disappointed; and each found that it had counted upon a motive which fell far short of exerting the anticipated influence. It was, of course, the case that England suffered much from the short supply of cotton; but she made shift to procure it elsewhere, while the working people, sympathizing with the North, were surprisingly patient. Thus the political pressure arising from commercial distress was much less than had been expected, and the South learned that cotton was only a spurious monarch. Not less did the North find itself deceived; for the upper and middle classes of Great Britain appeared absolutely indifferent to the humanitarian element which, as they were assured, underlay the struggle. Perhaps they were not to be blamed for setting aside these assurances, and accepting in place thereof the belief that the American leaders spoke the truth when they solemnly told the North that the question at issue was purely and simply of "the Union." The unfortunate fact was that it was necessary to say one thing to Englishmen and a different thing to Americans.

That which really did inspire the feelings and the wishes, and which did influence, though it could not be permitted fully to control, the action of England, had not been counted upon by either section of the country; perhaps its existence had not been appreciated. This was the intense dislike felt for the American republic by nearly all Englishmen who were above the social grade of mechanics and mill operatives. The extent and force of this antipathy and even contempt were for the first time given free expression under the irresistible provocation which arose out of the delightful likelihood of the destruction of the United States. The situation at least gave to the people of that imperiled country a chance to find out in what estimation they were held across the water. The behavior of the English government and the attitude of the English press during the early part of the civil war have been ascribed by different historians to one or another dignified political or commercial motive. But while these influences were certainly not absent, yet the English newspapers poured an inundating flood of evidence to show that genuine and deep-seated dislike, not to say downright hatred, was by very much the principal motive. This truth is so painful and unfortunate that many have thought best to suppress or deny it; but no historian is entitled to use such discretion. From an early period, therefore, in the administration of Mr. Lincoln, he and Mr. Seward had to endeavor to preserve friendly relations with a power which, if she could only make entirely sure of the worldly wisdom of yielding to her wishes, would instantly recognize the independence of the South. This being the case, it was matter for regret that the rules of international law concerning blockades, contraband of war, and rights of neutrals were perilously vague and unsettled.

Earl [168] Russell was at this time in charge of her majesty's foreign affairs. Because in matters domestic he was liberal-minded, Americans had been inclined to expect his good-will; but he now disappointed them by appearing to share the prejudices of his class against the republic. A series of events soon revealed his temper. So soon as there purported to be a Confederacy, an understanding had been reached betwixt him and the French emperor that both powers should take the same course as to recognizing it. About May 1 he admitted three Southern commissioners to an audience with him, though not "officially." May 13 there was published a proclamation, whereby Queen Victoria charged and commanded all her "loving subjects to observe a strict neutrality" in and during the hostilities which had "unhappily commenced between the government of the United States and certain States styling themselves 'the Confederate States of America.'" This action— this assumption of a position of "neutrality," as between enemies—taken while the "hostilities" had extended only to the single incident of Fort Sumter, gave surprise and some offense to the North. It was a recognition of belligerency; that is to say, while not in any other respect recognizing the revolting States as an independent power, it accorded to them the rights of a belligerent. The magnitude very quickly reached by the struggle would have made this step necessary and proper, so that, if England had only gone a trifle more slowly, she would soon have reached the same point without exciting any anger; but now the North felt that the queen's government had been altogether too forward in assuming this position at a time when the question of a real war was still in embryo. Moreover, the unfriendliness was aggravated by the fact that the proclamation was issued almost at the very hour of the arrival in London of Mr. Charles Francis Adams, the new minister sent by Mr. Lincoln to the court of St. James. It seemed, therefore, not open to reasonable doubt that Earl Russell had purposely hastened to take his position before he could hear from the Lincoln administration.

When Mr. Seward got news of this, his temper gave way; so that, being still new to diplomacy, he wrote a dispatch to Mr. Adams wherein occurred words and phrases not so carefully selected as they should have been. He carried it to Mr. Lincoln, and soon received it back revised and corrected, instructively. *A priori*, one would have anticipated the converse of this.

The essential points of the paper were:—

That Mr. Adams would "desist from all intercourse whatever, unofficial as well as official, with the British government, so long as it shall continue intercourse of either kind with the domestic enemies of this country."

That the United States had a "right to expect a more independent if not a more friendly course" than was indicated by the understanding between England and France; but that Mr. Adams would "take no notice of that or any other alliance."

He was to pass by the question as to whether the blockade must be respected in case it should not be maintained by a competent force, and was to state that the "blockade is now, and will continue to be, so maintained, and therefore we expect it to be respected."

As to recognition of the Confederacy, either by publishing an acknowledgment of its sovereignty, or officially receiving its representatives, he was to inform the earl that "no one of these proceedings will pass unquestioned." Also, he might suggest that "a concession of belligerent rights is liable to be construed as a recognition" of the Confederate States. Recognition, he was to say, could be based only on the assumption that these States were a self-sustaining power. But now, after long forbearance, the United States having set their forces in motion to suppress the insurrection, "the true character of the pretended new state is at once revealed. It is seen to be a power existing in pronunciamento only. It has never won a field. It has obtained no forts that were not virtually betrayed into its hands or seized in breach of trust. It commands not a single port on the coast, nor any highway out from its pretended capital by land. Under these circumstances, Great Britain is called upon to intervene, and give it body and independence by resisting our measures of suppression. British recognition would be British intervention to create within our own territory a hostile state by overthrowing this republic itself." In Mr. Seward's draft a menacing sentence followed these words, but Mr. Lincoln drew his pen through it.

Mr. Adams was to say that the treatment of insurgent privateers was "a question exclusively our own," and that we intended to treat them as pirates. [169] If Great Britain should recognize them as lawful belligerents and give them shelter, "the laws of nations afford an adequate and proper remedy;" —"and we shall avail ourselves of it," added Mr. Seward; but again Mr. Lincoln's prudent pen went through these words of provocation.

Finally Mr. Adams was instructed to offer the adhesion of the United States to the famous Declaration of the Congress of Paris, of 1856, which concerned sundry matters of neutrality.

The letter ended with two paragraphs of that patriotic rodomontade which seems eminently adapted to domestic consumption in the United States, but which, if it ever came beneath the eye of the British minister, probably produced an effect very different from that which was aimed at. Mr. Lincoln had the good taste to write on the margin: "Drop all from this line to the end;" but later he was induced to permit the nonsense to stand, since it was really harmless.

The amendments made by the President in point of quantity were trifling, but in respect of importance were very great. All that he did was here and there to change or to omit a phrase, which established no position, but which in the strained state of feeling might have had serious results.

The condition calls to mind the description of the summit of the Alleghany Ridge, where the impulses given by almost imperceptible inequalities in the surface of the rock have for their ultimate result the dispatching of mighty rivers either through the Atlantic slope to the ocean, or down the Mississippi valley to the Gulf of Mexico. A few adjectives, two or three ever so little sentences, in this dispatch, might have led to peace or to war; and peace or war with England almost surely meant, respectively, Union or Disunion in the United States. In fact, no more important state paper was issued by Mr. Seward. It established our relations with Great Britain, and by consequence also with France and with the rest of Europe, during the whole period of the civil war. Its positions, moderate in themselves, and resolutely laid down, were never materially departed from. The English minister did not afterward give either official or unofficial audiences to accredited rebel emissaries; the blockade was maintained by a force so competent that the British government acquiesced in it; no recognition of the Confederacy was ever made, either in the ways prohibited or in any way whatsoever; it is true that bitter controversies arose concerning Confederate privateers, and to some extent England failed to meet our position in this matter; but it was rather the application of our rule than the rule itself which was in dispute; and she afterward, under the Geneva award, made full payment for her derelictions. The behavior and the proposal of terms, which constituted a practical exclusion of the United States from the benefits of the Treaty of Paris, certainly involved something of indignity; but in this the country had no actual *rights*; and to speak frankly, since she had refused to come in when invited, she could hardly complain of an inhospitable reception when, under the influence of immediate and stringent self-interest, her diplomatists saw fit to change their course. So, on the whole, it is not to be denied that delicate and novel business in the untried department of foreign diplomacy was managed with great skill, under trying circumstances. A few months later, in his message to Congress, at the beginning of December, 1861, the President referred to our foreign relations in the following paragraphs:—

"The disloyal citizens of the United States, who have offered the ruin of our country in return for the aid and comfort which they have invoked abroad, have received less patronage and encouragement than they probably expected. If it were just to suppose, as the insurgents have seemed to assume, that foreign nations, in this case, discarding all moral, social, and treaty obligations, would act solely and selfishly for the speedy restoration of commerce, including especially the acquisition of cotton, those nations appear as yet not to have seen their way to their object more directly or clearly through the destruction than through the preservation of the Union. If we could dare to believe that foreign nations are actuated by no higher principle than this, I am quite sure a sound argument could be made to show them that they can reach their aim more readily and easily by aiding to crush this rebellion than by giving encouragement to it.

"The principal lever relied on by these insurgents for exciting foreign nations to hostility against us, as already intimated, is the embarrassment of commerce. Those nations, however, not improbably saw from the first that it was the Union which made as well our foreign as our domestic commerce. They can scarcely have failed to perceive that the effort for disunion produces the existing difficulty; and that one strong nation promises more durable peace and a more extensive, valuable, and reliable commerce than can the same nation broken into hostile fragments.

"It is not my purpose to review our discussions with foreign states; because, whatever might be their wishes or dispositions, the integrity of our country and the stability of our government mainly depend not upon them but on the loyalty, virtue, patriotism, and intelligence of the American people. The correspondence itself with the usual reservations is herewith submitted. I venture to hope it will appear that we have practiced prudence and liberality toward foreign powers, averting causes of irritation, and with firmness maintaining our own rights and honor."

While this carefully measured language certainly fell far short of expressing indifference concerning European action, it was equally far from betraying any sense of awe or dependence as towards the great nations across the Atlantic. Yet in fact beneath its self-contained moderation there unquestionably was politic concealment of very profound anxiety. Since the war did in fact maintain to the end an entirely domestic character, it is now difficult fully to appreciate the apprehensions which were felt, especially in its earlier stages, lest England or France or both might interfere with conclusive effect in favor of the Confederacy. It was very well for Mr. Lincoln to state the matter in such a way that it would seem an unworthy act upon their part to encourage a rebellion, especially a pro-slavery rebellion; and very well for him also to suggest that their commerce could be better conducted with one nation than with two. In plain fact, they were considering nothing more lofty than their own material interests, and upon this point their distinguished statesmen did not feel the need of seeking information or advice from the Western lawyer who had just been so freakishly picked out of a frontier town to take charge of the destinies of the United States. The only matter which they contemplated with some interest, and upon which they could gather enlightenment from his words, related to the greater or less degree of firmness and confidence with which he was likely to meet them; for even in their eyes this must be admitted to constitute one of the elements in the situation. It was, therefore, fortunate that Mr. Lincoln successfully avoided an appearance either of alarm or of defiance.

But, difficult as it may have been skillfully to compose the sentences of the message so far as it concerned foreign relationships, some occurrences were taking place, at this very time of the composition, which reduced verbal manoeuvring to insignificance. A sudden and unexpected menace was happily turned into a substantial aid and advantage; and the administration, not long after it had firmly declared its resolution to maintain its clear and lawful rights, was given the opportunity greatly to strengthen its position by an event which, at first, seemed untoward enough. In the face of very severe temptation to do otherwise, it had the good sense to seize this opportunity, and to show that it had upon its own part the will not only to respect, but to construe liberally as against itself, the rights of neutrals; also that it had the power to enforce its will, upon the instant, even at the cost of bitterly disappointing the whole body of loyal citizens in the very hour of their rejoicing.

The story of Mason and Slidell is familiar: accredited as envoys of the Confederacy to England and France, in the autumn of 1861, they ran the blockade at Charleston and came to Havana. There they did not conceal their purpose to sail for England, by the British royal mail steamship Trent, on November 7. Captain Wilkes of the United States steam sloop of war San Jacinto, hearing all this, lay in wait in the Bahama Channel, sighted the Trent on November 8, fired a shot across her bows, and brought her to. He then sent on board a force of marines to search her and fetch off the rebels. This was done against the angry protests of the Englishman, and with such slight force as constituted technical compulsion, but without violence. The Trent was then left to proceed on her voyage. The envoys, or "missionaries," as they were called by way of avoiding the recognition of an official character, were soon in confinement in Fort Warren, in Boston Harbor. Everywhere at the North the news produced an outburst of joy and triumph. Captain Wilkes was the hero of the hour, and received every kind of honor and compliment. The secretary of the navy wrote to him a letter of congratulation, declaring that his conduct was "marked by intelligence, ability, decision, and firmness, and has the emphatic approval of this department." Secretary Stanton was outspoken in his praise. When Congress convened, on December 1, almost the first thing done by the House of Representatives was to hurry through a vote of thanks to the captain for his "brave, adroit, and patriotic conduct." The newspaper press, public meetings, private conversation throughout the country, all reechoed these joyous sentiments. The people were in a fever of pleasurable excitement. It called for some nerve on the part of Mr. Lincoln and Mr. Seward suddenly to plunge them into a chilling bath of disappointment.

Statements differ as to what was Mr. Seward's earliest opinion in the matter. [170] But all writers agree that Mr. Lincoln did not move with the current of triumph. He was scarcely even non-committal. On the contrary, he is said at once to have remarked that it did not look right to stop the vessel of a friendly power on the high seas and take passengers out of her; that he did not understand whence Captain Wilkes derived authority to turn his quarter-deck into a court of admiralty; that he was afraid the captives might prove to be white elephants on our hands; that we had fought Great Britain on the ground of like doings upon her part, and that now we must stick to American principles; that, if England insisted upon our surrendering the prisoners, we must do so, and must apologize, and so bind her over to keep the peace in relation to neutrals, and to admit that she had been wrong for sixty years.

The English demand came quickly, forcibly, and almost offensively. The news brought to England by the Trent set the whole nation in a blaze of fury,—and naturally enough, it must be admitted. The government sent out to the navy yards orders to make immediate preparations for war; the newspapers were filled with abuse and menace against the United States; the extravagance of their language will not be imagined without actual reference to their pages. Lord Palmerston hastily sketched a dispatch to Lord Lyons, the British minister at Washington, demanding instant reparation, but couched in language so threatening and insolent as to make compliance scarcely possible. Fortunately, in like manner as Mr. Seward had taken to Mr. Lincoln his letter of instructions to Mr. Adams, so Lord Palmerston also felt obliged to lay his missive before the queen, and the results in both cases were alike; for once at least royalty did a good turn to the American republic. Prince Albert, ill with the disease which only a few days later carried him to his grave, labored hard over that important document, with the result that the royal desire to eliminate passion sufficiently to make a peaceable settlement possible was made unmistakably plain, and therefore the letter, as ultimately revised by Earl Russell, though still disagreeably peremptory in tone, left room for the United States to set itself right without loss of self-respect. The most annoying feature was that Great Britain insisted upon instant action; if Lord Lyons did not receive a favorable reply within seven days after formally preferring his demand for reparation, he was to call for his passports. In other words, delay by diplomatic correspondence and such ordinary shilly-shallying meant war. As the London "Times" expressed it,

America was not to be allowed "to retain what she had taken from us, at the cheap price of an interminable correspondence."

December 19 this dispatch reached Lord Lyons; he talked its contents over with Mr. Seward informally, and deferred the formal communication until the 23d. Mr. Lincoln drew up a proposal for submission to arbitration. But it could not be considered; the instructions to Lord Lyons gave no time and no discretion. It was aggravating to concede what was demanded under such pressure; but the President, as has been said, had already expressed his opinion upon the cardinal point,—that England had the strength of the case. Moreover he remarked, with good common sense, "One war at a time." So it was settled that the emissaries must be surrendered. The "prime minister of the *Northern States of America*," as the London "Times" insultingly called Mr. Seward, was wise enough to agree; for, under the circumstances, to allow discourtesy to induce war was unjustifiable. On December 25 a long cabinet council was held, and the draft of Seward's reply was accepted, though with sore reluctance. The necessity was cruel, but fortunately it was not humiliating; for the President had pointed to the road of honorable exit in those words which Mr. Lossing heard uttered by him on the very day that the news arrived. In 1812 the United States had fought with England because she had insisted, and they had denied, that she had the right to stop their vessels on the high seas, to search them, and to take from them British subjects found on board them. Mr. Seward now said that the country still adhered to the ancient principle for which it had once fought, and was glad to find England renouncing her old-time error. Captain Wilkes, not acting under instructions, had made a mistake. If he had captured the Trent and brought her in for adjudication as prize in our admiralty courts, a case might have been maintained and the prisoners held. He had refrained from this course out of kindly consideration for the many innocent persons to whom it would have caused serious inconvenience; and, since England elected to stand upon the strict rights which his humane conduct gave to her, the United States must be bound by their own principles at any cost to themselves. Accordingly the "envoys" were handed over to the commander of the English gunboat Rinaldo, at Provincetown, on January 1, 1862.

The decision of the President and the secretary of state was thoroughly wise. Much hung upon it; "no one," says Arnold, "can calculate the results which would have followed upon a refusal to surrender these men." An almost certain result would have been a war with England; and a highly probable result would have been that erelong France also would find pretext for hostilities, since she was committed to friendship with England in this matter, and moreover the emperor seemed to have a restless desire to interfere against the North. What then would have been the likelihood of ultimate success in that domestic struggle, which, by itself, though it did not exhaust, yet very severely taxed both Northern endurance and Northern resources? It is fair also to these two men to say that, in reaching their decision, instead of receiving aid or encouragement from outside, they had the reverse. Popular feeling may be estimated from the utterances which, even after there had been time for reflection, were made by men whose positions curbed them with the grave responsibilities of leadership. In the House of Representatives Owen Lovejoy pledged himself to "inextinguishable hatred" of Great Britain, and promised to bequeath it as a legacy to his children; and, while he was not engaging in the war for the integrity of his own country, he vowed that if a war with England should come, he would "carry a musket" in it. Senator Hale, in thunderous oratory, notified the members of the administration that if they would "not listen to the voice of the people, they would find themselves engulfed in a fire that would consume them like stubble; they would be helpless before a power that would hurl them from their places." The great majority at the North, though perhaps incapable of such felicity of expression, was undoubtedly not very much misrepresented by the vindictive representative and the exuberant senator. Yet a brief period, in which to consider the logic of the position, sufficed to bring nearly all to intelligent conclusions; and then it was seen that what had been done had been rightly and wisely done. There was even a sense of pride in doing fairly and honestly, without the shuffling evasions of diplomacy, an act of strict right; and the harder the act the greater was the honor. The behavior of the people was generous and intelligent, and greatly strengthened the government in the eyes of foreigners. By the fullness and readiness of this reparation England was put under a moral obligation to treat the United States as honorably as the United States treated her. She did not do so, it is true; but in more ways than one she ultimately paid for not doing so. At any rate, for the time being, after this action it would have been nothing less than indecent for her to recognise the Confederacy at once; and a little later prudence had the like restraining effect. Yet though recognition and war were avoided they never entirely ceased to threaten, and Mr. Chittenden is perfectly correct in saying that "every act of our government was performed under the impending danger of a recognition of the Confederacy, a disregard of the blockade, and the actual intervention of Great Britain in our attempt to suppress an insurrection upon our own territory."

[168] Lord John Russell was raised to the peerage, as Earl Russell, just after this time, *i.e.*, in July, 1861.

[169] An effort was made to carry out this theory in the case of the crew of the privateer Savannah; but the jury failed to agree, and the attempt was not afterward renewed, privateersmen being exchanged like other prisoners of war.

[170] Mr. Welles declares that Seward at first opposed the surrender; but Mr. Chittenden asserts that he knows that Mr. Seward's first opinion coincided with his later action; see Mr. Welles's *Lincoln and Seward*, and Chittenden's *Recollections*, 148.

INDEX

Abolitionists

Adams, Charles Francis

Adams, Charles F., Jr.

Adams, John Quincy

Alabama

Alabama

describes drilling of Army of Potomac

on importance of Lincoln's action in Trent case

introduces bill abolishing slavery under federal jurisdiction

on composition of Gettysburg address

dreads danger in election of 1864

Lincoln's only supporter in Congress

refusal of Lincoln to help in campaign

on Lincoln's attempt to push thirteenth amendment through Congress

on second vote on thirteenth amendment

Arnold, Samuel

accomplice of Booth, tried and condemned

Ashley, James M.

in House in 1861

moves to reconsider thirteenth amendment

Ashmun, George

presides over Republican Convention of 1860

Assassination of Lincoln

plot of 1861-

threats during term of office

successful plot of 1865

death of Booth

trial and punishment of other persons concerned

Atlanta

battle of

Atzerodt, Geo. A.

accomplice of Booth, tried and condemned

Baker, Edward D.

in Illinois campaign of 1838

at Illinois bar

candidate for Congress

elected

his agreement with Lincoln and others

introduces Lincoln at inauguration

killed at Ball's Bluff

responsible for disaster

Ball's Bluff

battle of

Banks, Nathaniel P.

in Federal army

his corps in 1862

defeated by Jackson

takes Port Hudson

Barnard, General John G.

opposes McClellan's plan of campaign

on impossibility of taking Yorktown

Bates, Edward

candidate for Republican nomination

favored by Greeley

his chances as a moderate candidate

vote for

attorney-general

opposes reinforcing Sumter

Bayard, James A.

in Senate in 1861

Beauregard, General P.G.T.

commands at Charleston

notified by Lincoln of purpose to reinforce Sumter

requests surrender of Sumter

commands bombardment

commands Confederate army at Manassas

at battle of Bull Run

at battle of Shiloh

evacuates Corinth

Bell, John

candidate of Constitutional Union party

vote for

Benjamin, Judah P.

denounces Buchanan

in Confederate cabinet

Bentonsville

battle of

Berry, Wm. F.

his partnership with Lincoln, and failure

Big Bethel

battle of

Black, Jeremiah S.

in Buchanan's cabinet

succeeds Cass in State Department

after vacillation turns toward coercion

forces Buchanan to alter reply to South Carolina commissioners

Black Hawk war ,

Blaine, James G.

on purpose of war

on Lincoln's order to McDowell to pursue Jackson

on crisis in congressional elections of 1862

on admission of West Virginia

on Vallandigham case

Blair, F.P., Jr.

tries to keep Lee in Union army

leads Unionist party in Missouri

in House in 1861

confers with Davis

Blair, Montgomery

in Lincoln's cabinet

wishes to relieve Sumter

at council of war

favors McClellan's plan of war

visits Missouri to investigate Fremont

arrested by Fremont

warns Lincoln that emancipation proclamation will lose fall elections

hated by radicals

his dismissal urged

upheld by Lincoln

resigns at Lincoln's request

wishes chief-justiceship

Blenker, General Louis

favors McClellan's plan of campaign

sent to strengthen Fremont

Booth, John Wilkes

murders Lincoln

his character

his end

Border States

necessity of retaining in Union

dealings of Lincoln with, in 1861, -

their neutrality policy explained in annual message

both pro-slavery and Unionist

desire to conciliate controls Lincoln's policy

with their slave property guaranteed by North

oppose bill freeing slaves used in war

oppose other anti-slavery bills

irritated by congressional policy

urged by Lincoln to agree to emancipation

refuse to approve

Lincoln's policy toward, denounced by Abolitionists

their support in 1862 saves Lincoln

Boutwell, George S.

urges emancipation upon Lincoln

Bragg, General Braxton

invades Kentucky

outmarched by Buell

at battle of Stone's River

retreats

reinforced

at battle of Chickamauga

besieges Chattanooga

defeated by Grant

Breckenridge, John C.

elected Vice-President

nominated by South for President

carries Southern States

announces election of Lincoln

expelled from Senate

Bright, Jesse D.

expelled from Senate

Brooks, Preston S.

assaults Sumner

praised at the South

Brough, John

nominated for governor in Ohio and elected

Brown, Aaron V.

in Buchanan's cabinet

Brown, B. Gratz

supports Fremont against Lincoln in 1864

Brown, Mayor Geo. W.

thinks Maryland will secede

burns bridges and cuts wires north of Baltimore

Browning, O.H.

at Illinois bar

Bryant, William Cullen

introduces Lincoln in New York

favors postponement of Republican convention in 1864

Buchanan, James

nominated by Democrats

elected President, his character

refers to Dred Scott decision in inaugural address

his recognition of Lecompton Constitution in Kansas

despised by Douglas

accused by Lincoln of plotting to make slavery national

his hard situation in 1860

distracted in body and mind

receives secession commissioners of South Carolina

a Unionist in feeling

his message on secession

wishes to shirk responsibility

declares coercion unconstitutional

ridiculed by Republicans

excuse for his position

declines to receive Southern commissioners

virtually abdicates power to cabinet

denounced by South

forced to appoint Dix to Treasury Department

calls extra session of Senate to aid Lincoln

his futile policy towards Fort Sumter

Buckner, General Simon B.

surrenders Fort Donelson

Buell, General D.C.

his resemblance in character to McClellan

refuses to seize East Tennessee

snubbed by McClellan

recommended by Halleck for promotion

takes Nashville

saves battle of Shiloh

allows slave-owners to reclaim fugitives

seizes Louisville before Bragg

opposes Halleck's plan to invade Tennessee

resigns

Bull Run

first battle of-

second battle of

Burlingame, Anson D.

hopes that Douglas will join Republicans

Burns, Anthony

seized as a slave in Boston

Burnside, General Ambrose E.

commands in North Carolina

given command of Army of Potomac

at Fredericksburg

loses confidence of army

ordered by Lincoln to do nothing without informing him

offers to resign

wishes to dismiss several generals

resigns

his campaign in East Tennessee

relieved by Sherman

alarmed at Copperheads

commands in Ohio

issues order threatening traitors

tries and condemns Vallandigham

comment of Lincoln on

offers resignation

instructs Butler not to return slaves

authorizes Sherman to use negroes

suggests arming slaves in annual report

his report suppressed by Lincoln

supports Lincoln for reëlection

Campbell, Judge John A.

acts as intermediary between Seward and Confederate commissioners

on Confederate Peace Commission

Cartwright, Peter

defeated by Lincoln for Congress

his character as itinerant preacher

Cass, Lewis

attacked by Lincoln in Congress

in Buchanan's cabinet

wishes to coerce South

resigns when Buchanan refuses to garrison Southern forts

Caucus

denounced by Whigs in Illinois

Cedar Mountain

battle of

Chambrun, Comte de

on Lincoln's magnanimity

Chancellorsville

battle of

Chandler, Zachariah

in Senate in 1861

denounces conservatives

threatens Lincoln

Chase, Salmon P.

in debate on Compromise

candidate for Republican nomination in 1860,

secretary of treasury

objected to by Pennsylvania protectionists

wishes to reinforce Sumter

dislikes subordination to Lincoln

wishes McClellan to advance

asks him his plans and is snubbed

favors Lincoln's plan of campaign

on ease of a victory

considers Lincoln inefficient

leader of discontented Republicans

on Lincoln's responsibility for emancipation proclamation

suggests an addition to it

wishes to present bankers to Lincoln

left undisturbed in control of Treasury

his resignation taken by Lincoln

letter of Lincoln to

hesitates to withdraw resignation

finally does so

irritated by Lincoln's independence

becomes candidate for Republican nomination

not feared by Lincoln

his offer to resign declined

fails to obtain support

withdraws name

continues to dislike Lincoln

frequently offers resignation

finally leaves office

on bad terms with Blair

appointed chief justice

Chestnut, James

defies North in 1860

Chickamauga

battle of

favored by Lincoln

Compromise of 1850

history of-

Confederate States

formed by convention

organization of

sends commissioners to United States

its envoys rejected by Lincoln, -

prepares to seize Fort Sumter

amused at Lincoln's call for volunteers

receives Virginia

belligerency of, recognized by England and France

refusal of Lincoln to receive Stephens embassy from

sells bonds in England

dealings of supposed emissaries from, with Greeley

refusal of Lincoln to negotiate with

dealings of Blair with

sends commissioners

conference of Lincoln and Seward with commissioners of

government of, collapses

Congress

proposes amendment to Constitution to protect slavery

counts electoral votes

extra session called

votes to support Lincoln

creates Committee on Conduct of War

discusses battle of Shiloh

passes Crittenden resolution disavowing slavery as cause of war

passes bill freeing slaves used in war

refuses to reaffirm Crittenden resolution

passes bill for emancipation in District

prohibits officers to return fugitive slaves

Constitutional Union party

Corbett, Boston

kills Booth

Covode, John

in House in 1861

Cox, Samuel S.

in House in 1861

Crittenden, John J.

offers compromise in 1861

in House in 1861

offers resolution that war is not against slavery

opposes Lincoln's plan of emancipation in Kentucky

Curtin, Governor Andrew G.

invites governors to meet at Altoona

on connection of conference with emancipation proclamation

reflected

Curtis, Benjamin R.

his opinion in Dred Scott case

Curtis, General Samuel R.

his campaign in Missouri and Arkansas

Cushing, Lieutenant William B.

destroys the Albemarle

Davis, David

at Illinois bar

disgusted at election of Trumbull in 1855

Lincoln's manager in convention of 1860

Davis, Garrett

succeeds Breckenridge in Senate

his plea against arming negroes

Davis, Henry Winter

introduces reconstruction bill

issues address denouncing Lincoln for vetoing bill

obliged to support Lincoln rather than McClellan

Davis, Jefferson

advocates extension of Missouri Compromise in 1850

sneers at attempted compromise in 1861

elected President of Confederate States

defies North

hopes to entrap Seward into debate with commissioners

urged by South to do something

prefers to make North aggressor

tries to win over Kentucky

offers to issue "letters of marque and reprisal,"

when secretary of war, sent McClellan to Europe

sends troops to seize East Tennessee

wishes to free Kentucky

his escape wished by Lincoln

replaces Johnston by Hood

proposition of Blair to

expresses willingness to treat for peace

nominates commissioners to treat for peace with independence

notified by Lee of approaching fall of Richmond

escapes from city

makes himself ridiculous and escapes punishment

suspected of complicity in Booth's plot

Dawson, — —

leads Lincoln in vote for legislature in 1834

Dayton, William L.

nominated by Republicans in 1856

candidate for nomination in 1860,

Democratic party

controls Illinois, -

wins in 1852

Seward's proposed foreign wars to prevent disunion-

recognition of Southern belligerency by England and France

instructions of Seward to Adams, -

difficulties over English privateers

message of Lincoln on foreign relations

the Trent affair, -

the Oreto affair

the Alabama affair

District of Columbia

bill to emancipate slaves in, advocated by Lincoln

slave trade in, abolished

abolition in, favored by Lincoln

emancipation in, carried

Dix, John A.

on possible secession of New York

appointed to Treasury Department

his order to protect American flag

Dixon, Archibald

offers amendment repealing Missouri Compromise

Donelson, Andrew J.

nominated for presidency by Whigs and Know-Nothings

Donelson, Fort

battle of

Doolittle, James R.

in Senate in 1861

Doubleday, General Abner

on Hooker's plan in Chancellorsville campaign

Douglas, Stephen A.

meets Lincoln in 1835

encounters him in campaign of 1840

Lincoln's rival in love affair

his position at Illinois bar

charges Lincoln with lacking patriotism in opposing Mexican war

introduces Kansas-Nebraska Bill

mobbed in Chicago

debates with Lincoln in campaign of 1854

proposes a truce

candidate for Democratic nomination in 1856

opposes Lecompton Constitution

leading figure in public life

his character and ability

his doctrine of "popular sovereignty,"

avoids consequences of Dred Scott decision

defies Buchanan

his conduct in Lecompton case dictated by desire to secure rëlection
to Senate

attacks "English Bill" as unfair

his candidacy for reëlection gives Lincoln opportunity

renominated by Democrats

denounced by South

opposed by administration

accepts Lincoln's challenge to joint debates

his attacks upon Lincoln

accused by Lincoln of a plot to make slavery national

denies any plot

on status of negro under Declaration of Independence

sneered at by Lincoln

keeps temper with difficulty

attempts to reconcile Dred Scott decision with popular sovereignty

fails to satisfy South

cornered by Lincoln

gains reëlection

on difficulty of debating with Lincoln

speaks in Ohio

in debate ignores secession

nominated by Democrats in 1860

reasons why repudiated by South

his vigorous canvass in 1860

vote for

offers to aid Lincoln after fall of Sumter

value of his assistance

Dred Scott case

decision in

equivocal attitude of Douglas toward

discussed by Lincoln, , , -, -

Duane, Captain

escorts Lincoln at inauguration

Early, General Jubal A.

tries to capture Washington

repulsed

retreats

defeated by Sheridan

East

ignorant of Lincoln

led to respect Lincoln by his speeches

Edwards, Ninian W.

in frontier political debates

member of Illinois bar

Emancipation

Lincoln's plan for, in 1849

compensation for, wished by Lincoln

again proposed by Lincoln with compensation and colonization, , -

discussion of Lincoln's proposal

demanded instantly by Abolitionists

question of its constitutionality

opposition to, in North

demanded by clergymen

does not tell McClellan

favors McClellan's plan of attack

his division sent to McClellan, but not used

his force occupies West Point

Fremont, Mrs. Jessie Benton

her interview with Lincoln

Fremont, John C.

nominated for presidency by Republicans

appointed to command in Missouri

his quarrelsomeness and inefficiency

arrests Blair

the idol of Abolitionists

removed

declares slaves of rebels free in Missouri

asked by Lincoln to modify order

refuses, and becomes enemy of Lincoln

reinforced by Lincoln under political pressure

commands force in West Virginia

ordered to catch Jackson

fails

resigns

upheld by Lincoln's enemies in Missouri, as rival for presidency

nominated for presidency

failure of his candidacy

withdraws

his followers hate Blair

France

recognizes belligerency of South

would have joined England in case of war

proposes mediation

Fredericksburg

battle of

Free Soil party

origin of

Fugitive Slave Law

passed

Lincoln's opinion of

Garrison, William Lloyd

disapproves of Republican party

supports Lincoln in 1864

Georgia

not ready for secession

wishes a Southern convention

how led to secede,

Union minority in

Gettysburg

battle of

Lincoln's address at

Giddings, Joshua R.

favors Lincoln's emancipation bill in 1849

member of Republican Convention of 1860

Gilmer, John A.

refuses to enter Lincoln's cabinet

Gist

governor of South Carolina, sends circular letter asking about secession

feeling in South

Grant, Ulysses S.

his operations in 1862

captures Forts Henry and Donelson

recommended by Halleck for promotion

condemned by Halleck and relieved from command

reinstated

advances to Pittsburg Landing

attacked by Johnston

does not admit defeat at Shiloh

on severity of battle

his conduct of battle criticised

harassed by Halleck, asks to be relieved

on Halleck's mistakes

on Copperheads

forms plan to take Vicksburg

tries to approach city from south

besieges and takes Vicksburg

his credit for campaign

his relations with Lincoln

accused of drunkenness

congratulated by Lincoln

given command of the West

orders Thomas to hold Chattanooga

relieves siege

wins battle of Chattanooga

sends Sherman to relieve Burnside

on reconstruction

his conference with Lincoln

movement to nominate for President in 1864

appointed lieutenant-general

given free control

prepares plan of campaign

correspondence with Lincoln

his campaigns in Virginia

sends force to hold Washington against Early

sends Sheridan against Early

character of his military methods

reports proposal of Lee for a conference

ordered by Lincoln to refuse

on desertions from Lee's army

his plan to entrap Lee's army

wishes to capture Lee without Sherman's aid

enters Petersburg

pursues Lee

urges Lee to surrender

his liberal terms to Lee

praised by Lincoln

unable to accept Lincoln's invitation to theatre the evening of his assassination

Greeley, Horace

prefers Douglas to Lincoln in 1858

in convention of 1860, works against Seward

his influence used against Lincoln

willing to admit peaceable secession, -

on comparative strength of North and South

suddenly denounces compromise

a secessionist in 1861

publishes address to President

his influence

answered by Lincoln

his abusive retort

suggests French mediation

condemns Lincoln in 1864

on movement to delay nomination

his political creed

claims to be a Republican while denouncing Lincoln

favors Fremont

wishes peace at any price

wishes to treat with Confederates

authorized to do so by Lincoln

conditions named by Lincoln

abuses Lincoln for causing failure of negotiations

Green, Duff

tries to induce Lincoln to support Buchanan

Hayti

recognized, 18

Heintzelman, General Samuel P.

opposes McClellan's plan of campaign

appointed corps commander

on force necessary to protect Washington

Henderson, John B.

approves Lincoln's emancipation scheme

Henry, Fort

captured

Herndon, William H.

law partner of Lincoln

prevents Lincoln from association with Abolitionists

aids Lincoln in organizing Republican party

visits East to counteract Greeley's influence against Lincoln

Herold, David E.

tried for assassination of Lincoln

hanged

Hickman, John

calls Lincoln's emancipation scheme unmanly

Hicks, Governor Thomas H.

opposed to secession

suggests referring troubles to Lord Lyons as arbitrator

"Higher Law,"

Seward's doctrine of

Hitchcock, General Ethan A.

considers Washington insufficiently protected

Holt, Joseph

succeeds Floyd in Buchanan's cabinet

joins Black and Stanton in coercing Buchanan

fears attempt of South to seize Washington

Hood, General John Bell

succeeds Johnston

defeated by Sherman

Hooker, General Joseph

allows slave owners to reclaim fugitives

replaces Burnside in command

letter of Lincoln to

his abilities

in Chancellorsville campaign

throws away chance of success

fails to use all of troops

orders retreat

wishes to resume attack

first prevented, then urged by Lincoln

wishes to capture Richmond

follows Lee to North

instructed by Lincoln to obey Halleck

irritated by Halleck, resigns

sent to aid Rosecrans

storms Lookout Mountain

House of Representatives

election of Lincoln to, and career in-

members of

debates Mexican war

struggles in, over Wilmot proviso

refuses to pass Lincoln's emancipation bill of 1849, -

settles question of admission of Kansas

proposes Constitutional amendment in 1861

rejects plan of Peace Congress

leaders of, in 1861

thanks Captain Wilkes

approves emancipation proclamation

fails to pass thirteenth amendment

later passes amendment

Houston, Samuel

opposes secession in Texas

Hunter, General David

asked by Lincoln to aid Fremont

succeeds Fremont

proclaims martial law and abolishes slavery in Georgia, Florida, and South Carolina

his order revoked

organizes a negro regiment

Hunter, R.M.T.

on Confederate peace commission

retort of Lincoln to

Hyer, Tom

hired by Seward's supporters in Republican Convention

Illinois

early settlers and society of-

in Black Hawk war

early politics in, -,

land speculation in,

career of Lincoln in legislature of, -

the career of "Long Nine" in, -

internal improvement craze in

adopts resolutions condemning Abolitionists and emancipation in the District

suffers from financial collapse

carried by Van Buren against Harrison

legal profession in

carried by Democrats in 1844

upholds Mexican war

denounces Kansas-Nebraska Act

breaks Federal right at Chancellorsville

accidentally shot by his own soldiers

Johnson, Andrew

in Congress with Lincoln

in Senate in 1861

instructed by Lincoln to reorganize government in Tennessee

stern opinion of treason

repudiates Sherman's terms with Johnston

his nomination for vice-presidency aided by Lincoln

protested against, by Tennesseeans

his accession to presidency welcomed by radicals

refuses to commute Mrs. Surratt's sentence

Johnson, Bushrod R.

captured at Fort Donelson

Johnson, Herschel V.

nominated for Vice-President in 1860

votes against secession in 1860

Johnson, Oliver

supports Lincoln in 1864

Johnston, General A.S.

plans to crush Grant and Buell in detail

commands at battle of Shiloh

killed

Johnston, Joseph

succeeds Jackson at Harper's Ferry

aids Beauregard at Bull Run

on condition of Confederate army

evacuates Manassas

fears that McClellan will storm Yorktown

begins attack on McClellan

retreats from Sherman after Vicksburg

terms of Sherman with, in 1865

campaign against Sherman in 1864

removed by Davis

campaign against Sherman in Carolinas

plan of Lee to join

surrenders

Johnston, Sally

marries Thomas Lincoln

her character

Jones, Abraham

ancestor of Lincoln

Judd, N.B.

asked by Lincoln to help his canvass in 1860

urges Lincoln to avoid danger of assassination

Julian, George W.

in House in 1861

on Republican dissatisfaction with Lincoln

Kane, Marshal Geo. P.

telegraphs for Southern aid to oppose passage of troops through Baltimore

Kansas

struggle in, between free and slave-state men

rival constitutions of

admission of, under Lecompton Constitution, urged by Buchanan

opposed by Douglas

attempt of Congress to bribe into acceptance of Lecompton Constitution

rejects offer

speeches of Lincoln in

Kansas-Nebraska bill

introduced

repeals Missouri Compromise

Keitt, Lawrence M.

his fight with Grow

Kellogg, Win. Pitt

Kentucky

Keyes, General Erasmus D.

Know-Nothings

Lamon, Colonel Ward H.

Lane, James H.

Lane, Joseph

Lee, Robert E.

opposes secession

resigns from army and accepts command of State troops

becomes Confederate general

commands against Pope

prepares to invade Maryland

his contempt for McClellan

at Antietam

at Fredericksburg

outmanoeuvred by Hooker

at Chancellorsville

hopes to conquer a peace

enters Pennsylvania

retreats after Gettysburg

sends reinforcements to Bragg

campaign in Virginia against Meade

his campaign against Grant

suggests a conference with Grant

notifies Davis that Richmond must fall

his chance of escape

attacks Federal lines

tries to escape

surrenders at Appomattox

asks for food

Liberia

recognized

Lincoln, Abraham

his ignorance concerning his ancestry

sensitive regarding it

his own statements

anxious to appear of respectable stock

his genealogy as established later, -

his reputed illegitimacy

his birth

his references to his mother

his childhood

befriended by his step-mother

his education

early reading

early attempts at humorous writing

storytelling

youthful exploits

let out by his father

helps his father settle in Sangamon County, Ill.

works for himself

his trip to New Orleans for Offut

impressed with slavery

in Offut's store

fights Armstrong

later friendship with Armstrong

borrows a grammar

his honesty

loses situation

involved in border quarrels

his temperance considered eccentric

careless habits of dress

in the country groceries

coarseness of speech

his sympathetic understanding of the people, -

his standards dependent on surroundings

enlists in Black Hawk war

chosen captain

his services

Frontier Politician

Announces himself a candidate for the legislature

a "Clay man,"

his campaign and defeat

enters grocery store, fails

pays off debt

studies law

postmaster at New Salem

settles account with government

surveyor

elected to legislature

borrows money to ride to capital

his career in legislature

love affair with Ann Rutledge

his gloom, -

its inexplicable character

affair with Mary Owens, and n

again a candidate, his platform

calms excitement in campaign

his fairness

his retort to Forquer

elected as one of "Long Nine,"

favors unlimited internal improvements

acknowledges his blunder

his skill as log-roller

gains popularity in county

protests against anti-abolition resolutions

admitted to bar, settles in Springfield

partnership with Stuart

studies debating

political ambitions

shows evidences of high ideals

incidents of his canvass in 1838

opposes repudiation, in legislature

reflected in 1840, unsuccessful candidate for speaker

jumps out of window to break a quorum

in campaign of 1840

his courtship of Mary Todd

fails to appear on wedding day

married

character of his married life

quarrels with Shields

later ashamed of it

improves prospects by a partnership with Logan

later joins with Herndon

his competitors at the bar

considers law secondary to politics

his legal ability, -

a "case lawyer,"

his ability as jury lawyer

refuses to conduct a bad case

on Whig electoral ticket in 1844

later disillusioned with Clay

fails to get nomination to Congress

alleged understanding with Baker and others

renews candidacy in 1846

nominated

elected, his vote

In Congress

Agrees with Whig programme on Mexican war

introduces "Spot Resolutions" against Polk

his speech

his doctrine of right of revolution

votes for Ashmun's amendment condemning war

defends himself from charge of lack of patriotism

his honesty

damages Whigs in Illinois

favors candidacy of Taylor

his speech in House for Taylor against Cass

votes for Wilmot Proviso

his bill to prohibit slave trade in District of Columbia

enters field in 1859

nominated as candidate by Illinois Republican Convention

his managers at National Convention

yelled for by hired shouters

supposed to be more moderate than Seward

his own statement of principles

votes secured for, by bargains

nominated on third ballot

accepts nomination in dejection

his nomination a result of "availability,"

little known in country at large

anxious to avoid discussion of side issues

opposed by Abolitionists

supported by Giddings

elected

the choice of a minority

President-elect

His trying position during interregnum

his election the signal for secession

damaged by persistent opposition of New York "Tribune,"

his opinion of the proposed constitutional amendment to guarantee slavery

declared elected by electoral count

alleged plot to assassinate

maintains silence during winter

privately expresses dislike of compromise

declares against interfering with slavery

pronounces for coercing seceded States

his journey to Washington, -

warned of plot against

speeches in Pennsylvania

induced to avoid danger

accused of cowardice

in message suggests compensated emancipation and colonization

approves bill abolishing slavery, with compensation, in District

signs bill prohibiting return of fugitive slaves

signs bill abolishing slavery in United States Territories

signs bill to emancipate slaves of rebels

slow to execute bill to enlist slaves

finally recognizes value of black troops

his conciliatory policy not followed by Congress

his reasons for advocating compensated emancipation

hopes to induce Border States to emancipate voluntarily

sends special message urging gradual emancipation

practically warns Border State men

denounced by both sides

tries in vain to persuade Border State representatives

his plans repudiated

repeats appeal in proclamation

his scheme impracticable, but magnanimous

sees future better than others

refrains from filling vacancies on Supreme Bench with Northern men

agrees to McClellan's peninsular campaign

still worried over safety of capital

neglects to demand any specific force to protect it

forced to detach troops from McClellan to reinforce Fremont

nearly orders McClellan to attack

his plan better than McClellan's

orders McDowell to return to Washington

alarmed at condition of defenses of capital

question of his error in retaining McDowell

shows apparent vacillation

explains situation in letter to McClellan

urges him to strike

annoyed by politicians

tries to forward troops

orders McDowell to join McClellan without uncovering capital criticised by McClellan

refuses to let McDowell move in time

sends McDowell to rescue Banks

loses his head

insists on McDowell's movement

his blunder a fatal one

not a quick thinker

ruins McClellan's campaign

begins to lose patience with McClellan's inaction

appoints Halleck commander-in-chief

his constancy in support of McClellan

does not sacrifice McClellan as scapegoat

visits Harrison's Landing

avoids any partisanship in whole affair

appears better than McClellan in campaign

yet makes bad blunders

stands alone in failure

remains silent

allows Halleck a free hand

his reasons for appointing Halleck and Pope

decides to reappoint McClellan

shows sound judgment

places everything in McClellan's hands

indignant at slight results from Antietam

urges McClellan to pursue

his order ignored by McClellan

writes McClellan a blunt letter insinuating sluggishness or cowardice

replaces McClellan by Burnside

his extreme reticence as to his motives

attacked by Copperheads

criticised by defenders of the Constitution

harassed by extreme Abolitionists

denounced for not issuing a proclamation of emancipation

his reasons for refusing

explains his attitude as President toward slavery

struggles to hold Border States

general dissatisfaction with, in

held inefficient by Chase

and by Congressmen

but believed in by people

addressed by Greeley with "Prayer of 20,000,000,"

his reply to Greeley

his reply to Abolitionist clergymen

points out folly of a mere proclamation

thinks silently for himself under floods of advice

writes draft of Emancipation Proclamation

questions expediency of issuing

reads proclamation to cabinet

adopts Seward's suggestion to postpone until a victory

issues preliminary proclamation after Antietam

takes entire responsibility

not influenced by meeting of governors

fails to appease extremists

supported by party

thinks an earlier proclamation would not have been sustained

warned that he will cause loss of fall elections

always willing to trust people on a moral question

supported by Border States in election

renews proposals for compensated emancipation

favors it as a peaceful measure

his argument

fails to persuade Missouri to accept plan

issues definite proclamation

his remark on signing

tries to stimulate enlistment of blacks

threatens retaliation for Southern excesses

shows signs of care and fatigue

never asks for sympathy

slow to displace McClellan until sure of a better man

doubtful as to Burnside's plan of attack

refuses to accept Burnside's resignation after Fredericksburg

declines to ratify Burnside's dismissals

his letter to Hooker

suggestions to Hooker after Chancellorsville

opposes plan to dash at Richmond

directs Hooker to obey Halleck

appoints Meade to succeed Hooker

urges Meade to attack Lee after Gettysburg

angry at Meade's failure

his letter to Meade

annoyed by Democratic proposals for peace

refuses to receive Stephens.

annoyed by inaction of Rosecrans

urged to remove Grant

refuses to disturb him

his letter to Grant after Vicksburg

wishes Rosecrans to unite with Burnside

tries to encourage Rosecrans after Chickamauga

sends aid to Rosecrans

replaces him by Thomas and puts Grant in command in West

wishes Meade to attack in Virginia

refuses to interfere in finances

his attitude in Alabama affair

refuses foreign arbitration

asked by radicals to dismiss Seward

secures resignations of Chase and Seward, and then urges them to resume duties

his wisdom in avoiding a rupture

asks opinion of cabinet on admission of West Virginia

his reasons for signing bill

not alarmed by Copperhead societies

his relation to Vallandigham case

supports Burnside

sends Vallandigham within Confederate lines

replies to addresses condemning martial law

obliged to begin draft

insists upon its execution

his letter to Illinois Union Convention

shows necessity of war

impossibility of compromise

justifies emancipation

points to successes

really controls government autocratically

able to, because supported by people

gains military experience

has measure of generals

henceforward supervises rather than specifically orders

begged by Chandler to disregard conservatives

prepares address for Gettysburg

the address

his theory of "reconstruction,"

recognizes a state government of Virginia

appoints military governors for conquered States

urges them to organize state governments

wishes only Union men to act

wishes bona fide elections

instructs new State organizers to recognize emancipation

fails to prevent quarrels

issues amnesty proclamation

proposes reconstruction by one tenth of voters

at first generally applauded

later opposed by Congress

on negro suffrage

doubts power of Congress over slavery in States

refuses to sign reconstruction bill

denounced by radicals

defends his course

his conference with Sherman, Grant, and Porter

wishes to let Davis escape

his authority appealed to by Sherman later

question of practicability of his plan

its generosity and humanity

Reëlection

Opposition to his reëlection in Republican party

exasperates Congressmen by his independence

not disquieted by Chase's candidacy

desires reëlection

trusts in popular support

letter of Pomeroy against

refuses Chase's resignation

renominated by Ohio and Rhode Island Republicans

opposition to, collapses

relations with Chase strained

accepts Chase's resignation

nominates as successor, Tod, who declines

forces Fessenden to accept Treasury

angers Missourians by refusing to remove Schofield

denounced by them and by Phillips

gradually wins support of Abolitionists

witty remark on Fremont's nomination

remark on Grant's candidacy

generally supported by local party organizations

the "people's candidate,"

refuses to interfere actively to secure renomination

desires admission of delegates from South

nominated

question of his having dictated nomination of Johnson

accepts nomination

feels need of some military success

assailed by Greeley

embarrassed by Greeley's dealings with Confederate emissaries

authorizes Greeley to confer

charged by Greeley with failure

asked if he intends to insist on abolition

for political reasons, does not reply

renews call for soldiers

waits for military success

appoints Grant lieutenant-general

agrees not to interfere with Grant

wishes Grant success

astonished by a civil reply

under fire during Early's attack on Washington

discredited by fact of Washington's being still in danger

thanks Sherman for victory of Atlanta

rewards Sheridan for defeating Early

his election secured by these successes

urged by radicals to remove Blair

refuses at first, later does so

refuses to interfere in campaign

refuses to postpone call for more troops

refutes campaign slanders

prepares for defeat

re-elected easily

his remarks on election

refuses to intervene to secure counting of electoral

votes of Border States

signs bill rejecting elections in Southern States,

his reasons

shows magnanimity in appointing Chase chief justice

refuses to try to hasten matters

refuses to negotiate with Davis

permits Blair to see Davis

sends Seward to confer with Southern peace commissioners

later himself confers with them

insists on complete submission

other positions

recognizes decline of Confederacy

wishes to hasten peace by offer of money compensation and an amnesty proclamation

his scheme disapproved by cabinet

his second inaugural address

Second Term

Possibly thinks Emancipation Proclamation unconstitutional

on its practical results

unable to touch institution of slavery

wishes a constitutional amendment

wishes it mentioned in Republican platform

on impossibility of renewing slavery

led to make war on slavery by situation

sees necessity of its abolition to secure results of war

unable to treat with seceded States

renews appeal for Constitutional amendment in 1864

exerts influence with Congressmen

congratulates crowd on passage of amendment

his responsibility in last weeks of war

forbids Grant to treat with Lee on political matters

conference with Grant, Sherman, and Porter

enters Petersburg

visits Richmond

speech on returning to White House

his disgust with office-seekers

superstitious concerning assassination

receives threats, but ignores them

persuaded to accept a guard

his remarks

refuses to consider Americans as his enemies

war, purpose of, , -, , ,
Wilmot Proviso

Lincoln, Abraham

grandfather of Lincoln, emigrates to Kentucky

his marriage

shot by Indians

Lincoln, John

son of Mordecai, inherits property in New Jersey

moves to Virginia

his descendants

Lincoln, Mordecai

son of Samuel, lives in Scituate, Mass.

his descendants

Lincoln, Mordecai

son of Mordecai, moves to Pennsylvania

his property

Lincoln, Mordecai

son of Abraham, saves life of Thomas Lincoln

Lincoln, Samuel

ancestor of Lincoln, emigrates to New England

Lincoln, Solomon

establishes Lincoln's pedigree

Lincoln, Thomas

father of Abraham

life saved from Indians

denies Puritan or Quaker ancestry

his parentage of Abraham denied

marries Nancy Hanks

his children

moves from Kentucky to Indiana

marries again

moves to Illinois

later relations with Abraham

his manner of fighting

Logan, Stephen T.

partnership with, and influence upon, Lincoln

leader of Illinois bar

agrees with Lincoln to receive election to House in turn

defeated for Congress

manages Lincoln's candidacy in Republican Convention of

Longstreet, General James

sent to reinforce Jackson

enters Pennsylvania

sent to reinforce Bragg

at battle of Chickamauga

sent to crush Burnside

retreats from Sherman

Louisiana

not ready for secession

but prepared to resist coercion

plan of Lincoln to reconstruct

Lovejoy, Elijah P.

killed at Alton

Lovejoy, Owen

tries to commit Lincoln to joining Abolitionists

prevents Lincoln's election as senator

in House in 1861

his rage after Trent affair

supports Lincoln in 1864

Lyons, Lord

suggested by Hicks as arbitrator between North and South

instructed to insist on instant reply in Trent affair

confers with Seward

McCall, General George A.

favors McClellan's plan of campaign

his division sent to aid McClellan

McClellan, George B.

given command of Army of Potomac

his record prior to 1861

his organizing ability

promoted to succeed Scott

his arrogance and contempt for civilians

causes discontent by inactivity

considers army unfit to move

unwilling from temperament to take any risks

fails to appreciate political situation

overestimates preparations of Confederates

overestimates Confederate numbers

wishes to end war by a crushing campaign

ignores Lincoln's suggestion to move

falls ill

hearing of conferences, becomes well and makes appearance

snubs McDowell and Chase

objects to a direct attack on Confederates

his plan

his opponents become a recognized faction

his scheme repudiated by Lincoln

protests and explains views, -

liberality of Lincoln towards

thinks politicians plot to destroy him

his plan accepted by Lincoln

discussion of its merit, -

makes mistake in insisting on his plan against Lincoln's wish, -

hampered by Lincoln's detaching men to protect Washington

discredited by Johnston's evacuation of Manassas

denounced Committee on Conduct of War

begins advance

annoyed at being relieved from general command

exasperated at action of Lincoln in forming corps and appointing commanders

authorizes Halleck to arrest Grant

approves Buell's plan

his career compared with Halleck's

promises to put down any slave insurrection

in spite of evacuation of Manassas, insists on Peninsular campaign

approved by corps commanders

estimate of forces needed to defend Washington

fears no danger from Manassas

protests against removal of Blenker's brigade

begins campaign at Fortress Monroe

besieges Yorktown

sneers at Lincoln's suggestion of storming it

his excuses always good

exasperated at retention of McDowell before Washington

question of his responsibility

not really trusted by Lincoln

still outnumbers enemy

letter of Lincoln to, answering his complaints

takes Yorktown

advances slowly

predicts Confederate evacuation of Norfolk

continues advance

forbidden to use McDowell so as to uncover Washington

protests

follows Lincoln's plan and extends right wing to meet McDowell

informed by Lincoln of withdrawal of McDowell to pursue Jackson

attacked by Johnston and Jackson

refuses to move for two weeks

wears out Lincoln's patience by delay

retorts sharply to suggestions

retreats to James River

writes bitter letter to Stanton

proves his incapacity to attack

wishes to resume offensive by James River

his prestige ruined at Washington

his recall demanded by Pope and Halleck

supported by Lincoln in spite of attacks

finally ordered to retreat

discussion of his conduct

beloved by army

predicts defeat of Pope

accused of failing to support Pope

exchanges telegrams with Halleck

his aid asked by Halleck after Pope's defeat

kept inactive during Pope's campaign

appointed by Lincoln, in spite of protests, to command in Washington

his fitness to reorganize army

describes steps taken to put him in command

cautious attitude toward Lee

at Antietam

welcomed by troops

fails to use advantages

urged by Lincoln to pursue

disappoints country by inaction

ordered by Lincoln to advance

letter of Lincoln to

fails to move

relieved from command

conduct of Lincoln towards, -

praised by conservative Democrats

endangers of emancipation

nominated for President

repudiates peace plank

his election hoped for by South

McClernand, General John A.

letter of Lincoln to, on difficulties of equipping armies

McClure, A.K.

on influence of New York "Tribune,"

McDougall, James A.

in Congress in 1861

McDowell, General Irwin

commands Federal army

obliged to attack

at battle of Bull Run

summoned by Lincoln to consultation

does not tell McClellan

describes McClellan's appearance at conference

favors Lincoln's plan of campaign

appointed to command a corps

on force necessary to defend Washington

his corps retained at Washington

reasons of Lincoln for retaining

again ordered to support McClellan

ordered not to uncover Washington

prevented from advancing by Lincoln's superstition

ordered to turn and pursue Jackson

protests vigorously

obliged to abandon McClellan

foretells that Jackson will escape

McLean, John

candidate for Republican nomination in 1860

Magruder, General J.B.

confronts McClellan at Yorktown

evacuates Yorktown

Maine

Democratic gains in, during 1862

Mallory, S.R.

in Confederate cabinet

Malvern Hill

battle of

Maryland

passage of troops through

effect of Baltimore conflict upon

danger of its secession

determines to stand neutral

importance of its action

furnishes South with troops

military arrests in, to prevent secession

Lee's invasion of

Mason, James M.

captured by Wilkes

imprisoned in Port Warren

surrendered

Massachusetts

prepared for war by Governor Andrew

sends troops to front

Matteson, Governor Joel A.

Democratic candidate for Senator in Illinois

Maynard, Horace

in House in 1861

approves Lincoln's emancipation scheme

Meade, General George G.

on McClellan's organizing ability

replaces Burnside in command

question of his powers

at Gettysburg

Mississippi

not ready to secede

secedes

sends commissioner to persuade North Carolina

Missouri

refuses to furnish Lincoln with troops

Unionist and Southern elements in

civil war in

refuses to secede

Fremont's career in, -

saved from South by General Curtis

refuses compensated emancipation

factional quarrels in

declares for Fremont against Lincoln

delegates from, in Republican Convention

Missouri Compromise

its sacred character

its extension demanded in 1850

questioned by South

repealed

Morgan, Edwin D.

urged by Lincoln to put emancipation plank in Republican platform

Morton, Governor Oliver P.

harassed by Copperheads

tries to alarm Lincoln

Mudd, Samuel

accomplice of Booth, tried and condemned

Naglee, General Henry M.

favors McClellan's plan of campaign

Napoleon

Lincoln contrasted with

Napoleon I

agrees with Earl Russell to recognize belligerency of South

offers mediation

his course suggested by Greeley

Negroes

equality of, Lincoln's feeling toward-

Nesmith, James W.

in Senate in 1861

New England

speeches of Lincoln in

New Jersey

carried by Democrats in 1862

New Mexico

plan of South to occupy as slave territory

urged by Taylor to ask for admission as a State

organized as a Territory

New York

Lincoln's speech in-

secession threatened in

carried by Democrats in 1862

tries to evade draft

draft riots in

North

surpasses South in development

begins to oppose spread of slavery

denounces Kansas-Nebraska Act

anti-Southern feeling in

enraged at Dred Scott decision

annoyed at both Secessionists and Abolitionists

effect of Lincoln's "House divided" speech upon

effect of Lincoln's speeches in

its attitude toward slavery the real cause of secession

carried by Republicans in 1860

its condition between Lincoln's election and his inauguration

panic in, during 1860, -

urged to let South secede in peace

proposals in, to compromise with South

led by Lincoln to oppose South on grounds of union, not slavery, -

irritated at inaction of Lincoln

effect of capture of Fort Sumter upon

rushes to arms

compared with South infighting qualities

responds to Lincoln's call for troops

military enthusiasm

doubtful as to Lincoln's ability, -

wishes to crush South without delay

forces McDowell to advance

enlightened by Bull Run

impatient with slowness of McClellan to advance, -

expects sympathy of England

annoyed at recognition of Southern belligerency by England

rejoices at capture of Mason and Slidell

its hatred of England

unity of, in 1861

inevitably led to break on slavery question

depressed by Peninsular campaign

opponents of the war in

public men of, condemn Lincoln

popular opinion supports him

effect of Emancipation Proclamation upon

forced by Lincoln to choose between emancipation and failure of war

depressed after Chancellorsville

discouraged by European offers of mediation

adjusts itself to war

waning patriotism in

tries to evade draft

draft riots in

bounty-jumping in

Republican gains in

really under Lincoln's dictatorship

relieved from gloom by successes of 1864

rejoicings in 1865

North Carolina

not at first in favor of secession

ready to oppose coercion

urged by Mississippi to secede

refuses to furnish Lincoln troops

finally secedes

Offut, Denton, sends Lincoln to New Orleans with a cargo

makes Lincoln manager of a store

brags of Lincoln's abilities

fails and moves away

Oglesby, Governor R.J.

presides over Illinois Republican Convention

Ohio

campaign of 1858 in

carried by Democrats in 1862

career of Vallandigham in

reply of Lincoln to Democrats of

election of 1863 in

renominates Lincoln in 1864

O'Laughlin, Michael

accomplice of Booth, tried and condemned

Ordinance of 1787

its adoption and effect

Owens, Mary

rejects Lincoln

Pain, John

Lincoln's only hearer at "mass meeting" to organize Republican party

Palmerston, Lord

drafts British ultimatum in Mason and Slidell case

shows it to Queen

Paris, Comte de

on condition of Union army in 1861

on McDowell's advance from Washington to aid McClellan

Patterson, General Robert

commands force in Pennsylvania

fails to watch Johnston

Payne, Lewis

accomplice of Booth, tried and hanged

Peace Congress

its composition and action

repudiated by South

Pea Ridge

battle of

Pemberton, General John C.

surrenders Vicksburg

Pendleton, George H.

in House in 1861

Pennsylvania

carried by Democrats in 1862

regained by Republicans

renominates Lincoln

Penrose, Captain — —

on Lincoln's rashness in entering Richmond

Perryville

battle of

Peters, — —

refuses to trust a Republican

Phillips, Wendell

remark on nomination of Lincoln

denounces Lincoln

welcomes secession

upholds right of South to secede

opposes Lincoln's renomination

Pickens, Fort

relief of, in 1861

Pickens, Governor F.W.

sends commissioners to Buchanan regarding dissolution of Union by South Carolina

Pierce, Franklin

elected President

defeated for renomination

Pierpoint, Francis H.

recognized as governor of Virginia

Pillow, Fort

massacre at

Pillow, General Gideon J.

runs away from Fort Donelson

Pinkerton, Allan

discovers plot to assassinate Lincoln

Plug Uglies

feared in 1861

mob Massachusetts troops

Polk, James K.

carries Illinois in 1844

brings on Mexican war

his policy attacked by Lincoln's "Spot Resolutions,"

asks for two millions to buy territory

Pomeroy, Samuel C.

senator from Kansas

an enemy of Lincoln

urges Chase's friends to organize to oppose Lincoln's renomination

Pope, General John

recommended by Halleck for promotion

prevented by Halleck from fighting

urges recall of McClellan from Peninsula

his military abilities

commands Army of Virginia

shows arrogance and lack of tact

fails to cut off Jackson from Lee

insists on fighting

beaten at Bull Run

discredited

Popular sovereignty

doctrine of, in Compromise of 1850

used by Douglas to justify repeal of Missouri Compromise

theory of, destroyed by Dred Scott decision

attempt of Douglas to reconcile, with Dred Scott case

Porter, General Andrew

favors McClellan's

plan of campaign

Porter, David D.

takes Powhatan under Lincoln's orders

refuses to obey Seward's order

aids Grant at Vicksburg

confers with Lincoln

upholds Sherman in referring to Lincoln as authorizing Johnston's terms of surrender

Porter, General Fitz-John

favors McClellan's plan of campaign

sent to meet McDowell

Powell, L.W.

denounces Lincoln's emancipation scheme

Rathbone, Major Henry R.

at Lincoln's assassination

Raymond, Henry J.

warns Lincoln of danger done to Republican party by emancipation policy

reply of Lincoln to

Reagan, J.H.

in Confederate cabinet

Reconstruction

constitutional theory of

begun by appointment of military governors

Lincoln's plan for

blocked by refusal of Congress to receive representatives

usually associated with new constitutions

method laid down in amnesty proclamation

difficulties in way of

extremist proposals concerning

Reconstruction bill passed

bill for, vetoed by Lincoln

later statements of Lincoln concerning

involved in Sherman's terms of surrender given to Johnston

Lincoln's scheme discussed

problem of, in 1865

intention of Lincoln to keep, in his own control

Republican party

nominates Lincoln

nominates Johnson for Vice-President

receives reluctant support of radicals

damaged by Greeley's denunciations of Lincoln

dreads defeat in summer of 1864

damaged by draft

radical element of, forces dismissal of Blair

conduct of campaign by

gains election in 1864

makes thirteenth amendment a plank in platform

radical members of, rejoice at accession of Johnson after murder of Lincoln

Reynolds, Governor

calls for volunteers in Black Hawk war

Rhode Island

renominates Lincoln

Richardson, W.A.

remark on congressional interference with armies

Rives, W.C.

remark of Lincoln to, on coercion

Rosecrans, General William S.

succeeds Buell

disapproves Halleck's plan to invade East Tennessee

fights battle of Stone's River

reluctant to advance

drives Bragg out of Tennessee

refuses to move

finally advances to Chattanooga

defeated at Chickamauga

unnerved after Chickamauga

cheered by Lincoln

besieged in Chattanooga

relieved by Grant

Russell, Earl

Rutledge, Ann

Saulsbury, Willard

Saxton, General Rufus

Schofield, General John M.

Schurz, General Carl

Scott, Winfield

instructed to watch Maryland legislature

authorized to suspend writ of habeas corpus

has difficulties with McClellan

retires

Seaton, William W.

promises to help Lincoln's emancipation bill

Secession

mention of, avoided by Douglas and Lincoln

question of its justification in 1860, -

process of, in 1860-, -

discussed by Buchanan, -

admitted by Northern leaders,

threatened by New York Democrats

Lincoln's view of,

Southern theory of

its success makes union, not slavery, the issue at stake, -

renewed by Border States, -

recognized as not the ultimate cause of war

again asserted by Lincoln to be cause of war

Sedgwick, General John

beaten at Chancellorsville

Semmes, Captain Raphael

his career with the Alabama

Senate of United States

proposes "Union-saving devices,"

defeats Crittenden compromise

rejects plan of Peace Congress

leaders of, in 1861

passes thirteenth amendment

Seward, Frederick

warns Lincoln of plot in 1861

Seward, W.H.

appeals to higher law

candidate for Republican nomination to presidency

opposed by Greeley

methods of his supporters

considered too radical

defeated by a combination, -

deserves the nomination

adopts conciliatory attitude in 1860

sends son to warn Lincoln

meets Lincoln at Washington

his theory of irrepressible conflict

wishes to submit to South

secretary of state

tries to withdraw consent

attempt of Davis to involve, in discussion with Confederate commissioners

refuses to receive them

announces that Sumter will be evacuated

reproached by commissioners

opposes reinforcing Sumter

authorized to inform Confederates that Lincoln will not act without warning

makes mistake in order concerning Powhatan

said to have led Lincoln to sign papers without understanding contents

made to feel subordination by Lincoln

submits thoughts for President's consideration, -

wishes foreign war

offers to direct the government

reasons for his actions

repressed by Lincoln

advises against a paper blockade

wishes to maintain friendly relations with England

angered at Russell's conduct

remark of Lincoln to

paper duel of Lincoln with

loses reëlection to Senate

his force joined to McDowell's

Shipley, Mary

ancestor of Lincoln

Short, James

lends Lincoln money

Sickles, Daniel E.

threatens secession of New York city

Sigel, General Franz

replaces Fremont

Slavery

its entrance into politics described-

compromises concerning, in Constitution

settled by Missouri Compromise

attitude of South toward

necessity of extending area of, in order to preserve

Lincoln's description of struggle over, -

attitude of Lincoln toward,

moral condemnation of, by North, the real cause of secession, -

wisdom of Lincoln in passing over, as cause of war, -

forced to front as real cause of war

comes into question through action of Federal generals

attempts of Fremont and Hunter to abolish, revoked by Lincoln

acts of Congress affecting

Emancipation Proclamation against, -

regard for, hinders War Democrats from supporting Lincoln

not touched as an institution by Emancipation Proclamation

necessity of a constitutional amendment to abolish

desire of Copperheads to reëstablish

Slaves

during Civil War, called "contraband" by Butler

escape to Northern armies

declared free by Fremont

this declaration revoked by Lincoln

declared free by Hunter

inconsistent attitude of generals toward

proposal of Cameron to arm, cancelled by Lincoln

protected from return to owners by Congress

armed, -

not paid equally with whites until 1864

armed in 1863

threatened with death by South

Slidell, John

seized by Wilkes

imprisoned in Fort Warren

released

Smith, Caleb B.

delivers votes to Lincoln in convention of 1860

secretary of interior

opposes relieving Sumter

Smith, General C.W.

praised by Halleck

Smith, General W.F.

favors McClellan's plan of campaign

Smoot, Coleman

lends Lincoln money

South

its early sectionalism

demands political equality with North

its inferior development

gains by annexation of Texas

enraged at organization of California as a free State

threatens disunion

expects aid from Northern sympathizers

hopes of aid from England disappointed

after Chancellorsville, wishes to invade North and conquer a peace

welcomes Vallandigham

economically exhausted in 1863

reconstruction in

applauds McClellan

evidently exhausted in 1864

hopes of Lincoln to make its surrender easy

South Carolina

desires secession

suggests it to other States

secedes

sends commissioners to treat for division of property with United States

refusal of Buchanan to receive

refuses to participate in Peace Congress

besieges Fort Sumter

Spangler, Edward

aids Booth to escape

tried by court martial

condemned

Speed, Joshua

letter of Lincoln to, on slavery

goes with Lincoln to Kentucky

Spottsylvania

battle of

Sprague, Governor William

of Rhode Island

Stanton, Edwin M.

attorney-general under Buchanan

joins Black in forcing Buchanan to alter reply to South Carolina

Stevens, Thaddeus

> leader of House in 1861
> denounces Lincoln's emancipation scheme
> considers Constitution destroyed
> on admission of West Virginia
> on unpopularity of Lincoln in Congress
> admits Lincoln to be better than McClellan

Stone, General Charles P.

> commands at Ball's Bluff
> his punishment

Stuart, John T.

> law partnership of Lincoln with

Stuart, General J.E.B.

> rides around Federal army
> repeats feat after Antietam

Sumner, Charles

> assaulted by Brooks
> in Senate in 1861

Sumner, General Edwin V.

> objects to Lincoln's trying
> to avoid murder plot, on ground of cowardice
> opposes plan of Peninsular campaign
> appointed corps commander
> on force necessary to protect Washington

Sumter, Fort

> question of its retention in 1861, , -

Supreme Court

> left to determine status of slavery in Territories
> in Dred Scott case
> in Merryman case, -
> reluctance of Lincoln to fill, exclusively with Northern men

Chase appointed chief justice of

Surratt, John H.

escapes punishment for complicity in assassination plot

Surratt, Mary E.

accomplice of Booth, tried and executed

Swinton, William

on McClellan's self-sufficiency

on campaign of 1862

on extraordinary powers given Meade

Tanet, Roger B.

his opinion in Dred Scott case discussed-

administers inaugural oath to Lincoln

attempts to liberate Merryman by habeas corpus

denounces Lincoln's action as unconstitutional

succeeded by Chase

Tatnall, Captain Josiah

destroys Merrimac

Taylor, Dick

amusingly tricked by Lincoln

Taylor, General Zachary

his victories in Mexican war

supported by Lincoln for President

urges New Mexico to apply for admission as a State

Tennessee

refuses to furnish Lincoln with troops

at first opposed to secession

eastern counties of, Unionist

forced to secede

desire of Lincoln to save eastern counties of

prevented from Northern interference by Kentucky's "neutrality,"

seized by South

her married life with Lincoln

involves Lincoln in quarrel with Shields

Toombs, Robert

in Congress with Lincoln

works for secession in 1860

declares himself a rebel in the Senate

secretary of state under Jefferson Davis

Toucey, Isaac

in Buchanan's cabinet

"Tribune," New York

See Greeley, Horace

Trumbull, Lyman

leader of Illinois bar

elected senator from Illinois through Lincoln's influence, -

said to have bargained with Lincoln

in Senate in 1861

introduces bill to confiscate slaves of rebels

Tucker, John

prepares for transportation of Army of Potomac to Fortress Monroe

Utah

organized as a Territory

Vallandigham, Clement L.

in House in 1861

his speeches in 1863

tried and condemned for treason

imprisoned in Fort Warren

sent by Lincoln to Confederate lines

goes to Canada, nominated for governor in Ohio

opinion of Lincoln on

defeated

forces peace plank into National Democratic platform

transportation to Fortress Monroe

Yorktown

retention of McDowell before Washington

advance of McClellan

Jackson's raid on Harper's Ferry

McDowell ordered to pursue Jackson

criticism of Lincoln's orders

Seven Pines and Fair Oaks

halt and retreat of McClellan

Malvern Hill

retreat continued

discussion of campaign

Halleck commander-in-chief

abandonment of campaign

Army of Virginia formed under Pope

Pope's campaign in Virginia

Cedar Mountain

second battle of Bull Run

quarrels between officers

reinstatement of McClellan

reorganization of army

Lee's campaign in Maryland

Antietam

McClellan fails to pursue Lee

Lincoln's proposals

McClellan superseded by Burnside

Fredericksburg campaign

quarrels in army

Burnside succeeded by Hooker

Chancellorsville campaign

failure of Hooker to fight Lee in detail

Lee's invasion of Pennsylvania

Hooker replaced by Meade

battle of Gettysburg

failure of Meade to pursue Lee

Bragg's invasion of Kentucky

battle of Perryville

Buell replaced by Rosecrans

battle of Stone's River

Rosecrans drives Bragg out of Tennessee

siege and capture of Vicksburg

fall of Port Hudson

Rosecrans' Chattanooga campaign

battle of Chickamauga

siege of Chattanooga

Rosecrans replaced by Thomas, Grant given command of West

battle of Chattanooga

liberation of East Tennessee

Meade's campaign in mud

steps leading to draft

diminishing influence of politicians in

Grant made lieutenant-general

new plan of campaign

Grant's Virginia campaign

battle of Wilderness

battle at Spottsylvania

battle of Cold Harbor

Butler "bottled up,"

Early's raid against Washington

Sherman's Atlanta campaign

capture of Mobile

Sheridan's Valley campaign

Sherman's march to the sea

Thomas's destruction of Hood's army

sinking of the Alabama and of the Albemarle

decay of Confederate army in

siege of Petersburg

march of Sherman through Carolinas

disapproves of Lincoln's scheme of amnesty

West

social characteristics of frontier life in-
democracy in
vagrants in
violence and barbarity of
manners and customs, -
grows in civilization
economic conditions of
frontier law and politics, -
popular eloquence in
its ignorance of foreign countries

West Virginia

origin of; campaign of McClellan in
forms a state Constitution
question of its admission
its vote counted in 1864

Whigs

character of, in Illinois
support Lincoln for speaker
fail to carry Illinois in 1840
and in 1844
elect Lincoln to Congress
oppose Mexican war
elect Taylor
defeated in 1852
join Know-Nothings in 1856

White, Hugh L.

supported by Lincoln in 1836

Whiteside, General Samuel

in Black Hawk war

Wigfall, Lewis T.

jeers at North in 1860

Wilderness

battle of

Wilkes, Captain Charles

seizes Mason and Slidell

applauded in North

condemned by Lincoln

Wilmot, David

in Congress with Lincoln

in Senate in 1861

Wilson, Henry

hopes that Douglas will become Republican in 1858

in Senate in 1861

introduces bill to emancipate slaves in District

on negro troops

admits small number of radical emancipationists

denounces Blair to Lincoln

Winthrop, Robert C.

chosen speaker of House

Wisconsin

admitted as free State to balance Texas

Democratic gains in

Wood, Fernando

advocates secession of New York City

wishes Lincoln to compromise

Wool, General John E.

commands at Fortress Monroe

Yorktown

siege of

Yulee, David L.

remains in Senate in 1861 to embarrass government